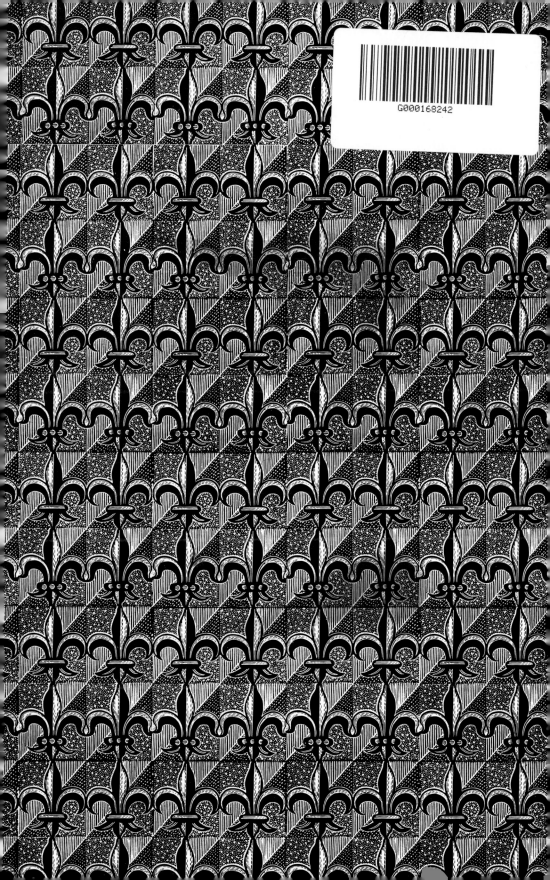

The Sadler's Wells Royal Ballet

THE SADLER'S WELLS ROYAL BALLET

NOW THE BIRMINGHAM ROYAL BALLET

BY

SARAH C. WOODCOCK

SINCLAIR-STEVENSON

Frontisepiece
Margaret Barbieri as Odette in *Swan Lake*, 1985.
Photograph by Graham Brandon. From the collections of the Theatre Museum. Reproduced by courtesy of the Trustees of the Victoria and Albert Museum.

First published in Great Britain by
Sinclair-Stevenson Limited
7/8 Kendrick Mews
London SW7 3HG, England

British Library Cataloguing in Publication Data
A CIP catalogue record for this book is available from the British Library.
ISBN: 1 85619 034 X

Typeset, printed and bound in Great Britain by
Butler & Tanner Ltd, Frome and London

Foreword

Circumstance and timing sometimes combine to make a story particularly worth telling. This is just such a moment for The Sadler's Wells Royal Ballet, which has just undergone a metamorphosis to emerge with a new lease of life as The Birmingham Royal Ballet. As the company prepares to explore new artistic horizons, with a new home in a new host city, one chapter has closed and another has begun.

PowerGen's own story has a number of parallels. We too have recently faced up to the challenge of being launched as a new company with strong links – including our operational centre – in the Midlands. We have already forged a strong relationship with The Birmingham Royal Ballet by backing a new production of *The Nutcracker*, premiered in Birmingham, our first major arts sponsorship.

We consider it a privilege to support a company with such a heritage of excellence and commitment to professionalism. It is equally fitting that we should consolidate our link by supporting the publication of this book which puts on the record the company's distinguished history.

Ed Wallis
Chief Executive
PowerGen

Contents

⟨◦ᵂᵂ◦⟩

Introduction and Acknowledgements

The Birmingham Royal Ballet is the name by which we must now learn to call the Sadler's Wells Royal Ballet, formerly the Royal Ballet on Tour, formerly the New Group, formerly the Royal Ballet Touring Company, formerly the Sadler's Wells Theatre Ballet, originally the Sadler's Wells Opera Ballet. Not for the first time in its history, the company stands on the brink of major change that will affect its whole being – from its Director, Peter Wright, to the newest member of the *corps de ballet*. In moving its base from London to Birmingham the company faces the biggest adventure in its forty-four year existence.

The company is part of the Royal Ballet organisation, that remarkable feature of British theatrical life founded nearly sixty years ago by an extraordinary Irish-born idealist, Ninette de Valois, who believed in a native British ballet in the 1920s, at a time when dance was perceived to be the province of the glamorous Russians of the Diaghilev Ballets Russes, of which company de Valois herself had been a soloist. Undaunted, she began in 1926 by founding a school, whose pupils she then offered to another exceptional woman, Lilian Baylis, Manager of the Old Vic, to appear there in plays and operas until such time as a second theatre, Sadler's Wells, was ready for the foundation of a permanent British ballet company. In 1931 the company, consisting of six dancers and de Valois as Principal Dancer, was born. By the time this chronicle begins, fifteen years later, it had become the Sadler's Wells Ballet, led by Margot Fonteyn and Robert Helpmann, whose wartime tours had helped introduce a generation of audiences to ballet and established the company as the national ballet in all but name.

With apologies to Oscar Wilde, to found one ballet company may be considered foolhardy, to found two looks like carelessness, but circumstances dictated that this is exactly what de Valois would do. From her original six dancers has grown something very special – two permanent companies, both from the same stem, but each with its own personality and part to play in the cultural life of the nation. The elder of the two, the former Sadler's Wells Ballet, now The Royal Ballet and resident company at the Royal Opera House, is the elder by some fifteen years, the younger, now the Birmingham Royal Ballet, is the subject of this chronicle. Like the senior company, for much of its life the junior company bore the name of its home theatre – the 'dancing' branch of Sadler's Wells' activities.

This record of the company could not have happened without the generous sponsorship of PowerGen, and I am grateful to Ed Wallis for providing the Foreword. My thanks, too, to Sandy Robertson, Sponsorship Manager of The Birmingham Royal Ballet, for his help in seeking the sponsorship for the book.

This history would have been impossible without the help and encouragement of a number of very busy people who gave generously of their time and shared their memories. My thanks first and foremost to Peter Wright for making time in his extraordinarily hectic schedule, for his constant encouragement, enthusiasm and practical help in seeking sponsorship and his perceptive comments on the manuscript; to Sir Kenneth MacMillan and Christopher Nourse, Administrative Director of the Birmingham Royal Ballet, for reading the manuscript and for their helpful suggestions; to Dame Ninette de Valois, for finding time to talk to me in her still busy schedule; and to Kathrine Sorley Walker for her practical suggestions and constant support.

My thanks go, too, to present and past dancers and administrators whose memories and experiences made the company live anew for me: Margaret Barbieri, Alexander Bennett, Meryl Chapell, Karen Donovan, Barbara Fewster, John Field, Anne Heaton, Stephen Jefferies, Desmond Kelly, Leo Kersley, Maryon Lane, Brenda Last, Henry Legerton, David Morse, Michael O'Hare, Ronald Plaisted, David Poole, Marion Tait, Mrs Doris Thellusson and Pirmin Trecu.

I am grateful to the Royal Opera House for allowing me access to the records of meetings of the Royal Opera House Board of Directors and the Ballet Sub Committee. Thanks also to Francesca Franchi, Archivist of the Royal Opera House, for her patience, tolerance and hospitality, and to the staff of the Sadler's Wells Royal Ballet Press Office. The resources of the Theatre Museum proved invaluable. David Withey of the Finsbury Public Library arranged access for me to papers relating to the Sadler's Wells Theatre Ballet.

Lack of space has precluded a complete statistical survey of the Company. However, full production, casting and company details, compiled by Sarah C. Woodcock, can be found in *The Royal Ballet: The First Fifty Years* by Alexander Bland, and concise statistics (up to 1985) in *The Royal Ballet: A Picture History* by Kathrine Sorley Walker and Sarah C. Woodcock.

Sarah C. Woodcock,
August 1990.

NOTE

The performing year runs from September to July and the tours are therefore referred to as autumn (roughly October to December), winter (January to April), spring (April to June) and summer (June to July).

Part I

The Sadler's Wells Theatre Ballet

Chapter I

There was nothing at first to show that it was not an ordinary day in the life of the Sadler's Wells Royal Ballet. The company was on a high, having just celebrated its fortieth anniversary with an extremely successful London season; Birmingham had now been reached in the course of the 1987 winter tour without more than the usual number of headaches for the ballet staff caused by injury and illness, and subsequent recasting, and three new ballets, all by Royal Ballet dancers, were in rehearsal. The Birmingham Hippodrome was one of the most pleasant dates on their touring schedule, a haven of luxury compared with many regional theatres, having been lovingly restored and modernized, and giving the company plenty of space in which to work.

The responsibility for running the company lay with its Director, Peter Wright, who had wrought upon it a transformation that might have been envied by any of the good fairies who graced his current successful production of *The Sleeping Beauty*. In twenty years he had nurtured, bullied and driven it from being a failing small experimental group into the best loved and most successful touring ballet company in the country, and one that was challenging the reputation of its elder sister, The Royal Ballet, at Covent Garden.

Thus there seemed nothing untoward when Richard Johnston, Director of the Birmingham Hippodrome, asked for a word with Wright and his Company Manager, Christopher Nourse. What he proposed, however, left them reeling. He suggested nothing less than the Sadler's Wells Royal Ballet moving its base to Birmingham, to become the Midlands' own ballet company; in return the Hippodrome would build them facilities that would rival anything enjoyed by the London based

3

Royal Ballet at Covent Garden, which would allow them to work and develop in a way impossible in the unstable world of constant touring. The implications of the suggestion left Wright stunned. The question was could the company refuse the challenge?

The Sadler's Wells Royal Ballet had been used to change and uncertainty in the course of its forty year existence. Indeed, it had been born into a world of uncertainty, deprivation and hardship and had triumphantly survived all that fate and Boards of Directors could devise for it. It had all begun in the Age of Austerity, that drab, depressed period that followed the Second World War, when the relief at the end of a long war was tempered by the reality of shortages of food, resources and manpower. In such an atmosphere of euphoria, exhaustion and anxiety, few, apart from the balletomane, would have noted a statement issued to the *Dancing Times* on 17 October 1945 by the authorities of the Royal Opera House, Covent Garden. This read 'The Governors of Sadler's Wells and the Covent Garden Committee have arranged that after January 1st, 1946, the Sadler's Wells Ballet Company will operate under the management of the Covent Garden Committee for an initial period of four years. Later in the year the Ballet will appear at the Royal Opera House, Covent Garden'.[1]

The move of the Sadler's Wells Ballet from its eponymous theatre was inevitable. Six years of war had destroyed much, but it had seen the company accepted as the national ballet in all but name by its constant touring and wildly successful London seasons. Its wartime success was partly because it was a survivor, a link to pre-war normality as everything was being destroyed around it. Ballet had evolved from an esoteric art into part of the theatrical mainstream, with a huge, if not totally discriminating, audience. The company's development had been restricted over the previous six years; it was now ripe for expansion and needed the challenge of a larger theatre. Negotiations therefore began in 1945 for control of the company to pass to the new Covent Garden management. The Sadler's Wells Ballet would thus become the resident ballet company at the Royal Opera House where it was planned to establish year-round native opera and ballet, replacing the pre-war system of short international seasons. The theatre was hallowed to ballet-goers as home of the pre-war De Basil Ballets Russes, whose reputation the Sadler's Wells Ballet would be challenging in taking up residence. But at this stage in its development, the Sadler's Wells Ballet needed the Royal Opera House as much as the Opera House needed it.

The Sadler's Wells Ballet was not its own master, and could not move without the agreement of the Governors of Sadler's Wells. Generously, they recognised its needs above their own and agreed to the transfer. In return the company, out of the profits of its wartime tours, paid a half-share of the building debt which was crippling Sadler's Wells Theatre. The company obligation to provide not only evenings of ballet but also dancers for the Sadler's Wells Opera, however, remained, and Ninette de Valois agreed to set up a second company at Sadler's Wells.

In agreeing de Valois was being characteristically far-sighted. Running a company and school in wartime had not fogged her vision, and as early as October 1940, when it was doubtful if civilisation, let alone a ballet company, would survive, she had written to Arnold Haskell that 'she had three plans that she wished to implement at the earliest possible moment. The first was to engage a distinguished Russian choreographer as a guest; then to have a nursery where young cho-reographers would have a chance; and finally, most ambitious of all, to enlarge the Sadler's Wells Ballet School so that it could give a secondary at the same time as a vocational education'.[2] Conditions at Covent Garden might be conducive to the first plan (indeed Massine was engaged in 1947), but not to the second. The larger theatre meant a larger company and productions; most of the repertory had been created for Sadler's Wells, and only the classics were capable of immediate expansion, until a new repertory could be built up, initially using the established choreographers, Frederick Ashton and Robert Helpmann (de Valois herself had virtually given up choreography by this time). But the size and prestige of Covent Garden would not be helpful in nurturing young choreographic talent, nor for producing quickly a new generation of soloists and principals. Thus de Valois welcomed the idea of a second company where young choreographers and dancers could be developed to feed the parent company at Covent Garden.

Dancers for the new company would be drawn from the senior students at the School, reinforced by more mature artists. The senior students were not without theatre experience. Ballets had been dropped from the operas in the early years of the war, but in 1943 *The Bartered Bride* had been revived with choreography by the Czech ballet master Sasha Machov. Students from the school had appeared as Clowns and Dancers, among them Brian Earnshaw (now Shaw), Philip Chatfield, Barbara Fewster, Romayne Austin (now Grigorova) and Pauline Wads-worth. A small group of students was then formed to perform on tour with the opera company, receiving the munificent sum of 10s 0d a week, and staying in workers' hostels. It was all valuable experience.

It may be well to take a look at the state of the school from which the new company was to be drawn. Throughout the war, except for three months in the summer of 1944 at the height of the V-1 bombing, students worked from 9 a.m. to 2 p.m. in the rehearsal room at the top of Sadler's Wells, though the rest of the theatre was crowded with bombed-out Islingtonians. De Valois ran the school until 1941 with Nicolai Sergeyev, when she transferred all her energies to the company. Her old friends and colleagues Ursula Moreton and then Ailne Phillips took over, and eventually Sergeyev was replaced by Vera Volkova.

De Valois in *Come Dance With Me* paid tribute to the students' parents who allowed their children to stay in wartime London, and yet never complained or harried her. But understandably there were those who would not allow their children to remain under such dangerous conditions, and it is impossible to estimate how much talent was so lost. There were no educational classes, nor residential facilities, only full time dance training. The official school leaving age was fourteen, and it was imperative that boys were taken into the company as quickly as possible, to give them the maximum stage experience before their call up at eighteen.

Rationing was another problem. The Government made claims for the high nourishment of children, but rations were only just enough for developing children and hardly enough for those using up their energy on dancing instead of growing. De Valois noted in 1946 that although there was no shortage of children at auditions for the school, most were undersized and of poor physique. But a flow of talent was vital now that there were to be two Sadler's Wells companies, one of which could admit nothing but the highest possible standards at Covent Garden.

De Valois had two choices, to strengthen her company with an intake of foreign artists, and provide a repertory of novel ballets, or to opt for a slower rate of development using native talent, and risk being called parochial. She chose the latter, and her choice was rewarded by an influx of dancers from a perhaps to be expected source.

Hardly had hostilities ceased than a steady trickle of dancers arrived in London on the first boats from the Commonwealth – mainly South Africans, but also Australians, New Zealanders and Canadians – with one aim, to study at the Sadler's Wells Ballet School and join the famous company. They mostly came from countries which had teaching and performances on a high amateur level but few regular professional companies, and the magic of London and the Sadler's Wells Ballet exercised a pull that was irresistible. They needed to work and learn from fully professional dancers working in the atmosphere of a professional theatre (de Valois' organisations were nothing if not professional) and they provided competition for the English students. Like them, they were little more than children, but in comparison they were well nourished, with consequent strength and stamina, and their anxious parents sent them food parcels, which were gratefully received by them and their English colleagues. They were all prepared for the competition – at home they were the cream of the available talent, but, as Maryon Lane recalled, it had been drummed into all of them that they would have to be sixteen times better if they were to hold their own in London.[3] One by one they arrived, Nadine Judd (later Nadia Moore, then Nadia Nerina), Elaine Fifield, Pat Mills (Maryon Lane), Rowena Jackson, David Poole, John Cranko and Patricia Miller, to spend a period in the school along with their English colleagues – Annette Page, Rosemary Scott Giles (Lindsay), Pirmin Trecu, David Butterfield (Blair), 'a thin, tall boy of great talent'[4] called Kenneth MacMillan, and Anya Elenton (Linden). By the time the company established itself at the Wells, there were so many of them that it became known in the theatre as Home and Colonial (the name of a grocery chain). In retaliation the dancers called the opera company Sadler's Wails.

With the return of the Sadler's Wells Opera to Sadler's Wells in 1945, the school moved to a temporary home at St Mary's Church Hall in Chalk Farm where conditions were 'pretty horrendous, but we were so excited and thrilled that we had actually got there and that made up for it'.[5] Once Covent Garden reopened in February 1946 there were standing passes available for students and the new company, the queue usually being headed by Pirmin Trecu, David Poole and Kenneth MacMillan.

Students were as young as eight, but those of school age went to Sadler's Wells to take lessons after school in the afternoons. At fourteen they 'graduated' to the Chalk Farm site, where there were 'day continuation' classes in the morning and then dancing. The fees were 21s 0d to 25s 0d a week. Throughout this period de Valois never lost sight of her dream – a school offering full education and dance training, and eventually full boarding facilities. The first she achieved in 1947 when it moved to Colet Gardens where in 1949 educational was added to the vocational training, the second when the Junior School moved to White Lodge in 1955.

The school was obviously vital to both Sadler's Wells companies. As throughout the 1930s and wartime, the Sadler's Wells Governors assumed full financial responsibility because it was essential to the Sadler's Wells Ballet. With the move to Covent Garden, however, a paradox arose – the Sadler's Wells Governors had supported the company over the difficult years and seen it transformed into a profitable concern. They now handed it over to another organisation, but were left with the expense of setting up a new company, whose success would be uncertain, and of maintaining the school – both of which also had the function of supplying the Opera House company; thus Covent Garden would be a beneficiary without actually contributing to the running of the second company or the school. This was to remain a bone of contention for several years, especially when the Governors of the Wells had to assume responsibility for the conversion and upkeep of the Colet Gardens site when the school moved there in 1947. It was several years before the Covent Garden Committee, which itself had formidable expenses to face in maintaining not only the Sadler's Wells Ballet but also in establishing a completely new opera company, was in a position to accept the school as integral to its organisation as well as to Sadler's Wells and take on some financial responsibility. De Valois, in charge of both companies and school, could see the overall pattern, but the Governors of Sadler's Wells could be forgiven some resentment and misgivings. It is a lasting tribute to them, and their chairman Lord Lytton, that they too were able to take the long term view and embark upon an uncertain future with faith if not total enthusiasm.

De Valois' 'second' company was born into a world of severe restrictions. The war had ended, but the battle against bureaucracy and hardship continued. It was, for most people, hardly the brave new world that they had expected. There was no immediate return to peace and plenty – restrictions continued for several years, and even, in some cases, worsened. But, as at the end of all wars, youth was at a premium, and it was youth that the new company had in abundance. For the dancers it was an exciting world where anything was possible. Finding the resources to put on the ballets was not their concern but the Administration, with an opera company as well as a ballet company to support, was hard pressed in mounting an almost entirely new repertory. The *Evening News* reported that 'it takes as many clothing coupons to dress a full opera production with ballet as it would take to clothe a woman, on the present allocation, for 500 years'.[6] Ballet shoes were also on coupons – the *corps de ballet* was rationed to one pair a week for eight shows, and Principals got two pairs a week. These were provided by the company, but dancers had to provide tights from their personal clothing

coupons, costing in 1947 three coupons and 21s od for cotton or up to
11 guineas for pure silk – if you could find them. Equity minimum
salary was £4 10s a week.

De Valois was to be Director of the new company, and as her Assistant
Director she turned to one of her oldest friends and colleagues, Ursula
Moreton. From the beginning, de Valois re-absorbed and re-used talent
in different ways as people and the company developed – a characteristic
of a long-established state company rather than one that had been in
existence for only fifteen years. The loyalty of her dancers and staff was
already exceptional, and 'the contentment of her staff is an unspectacular
but deeply impressive testimony to the moral as well as creative and
organisational qualities of her leadership'.[7]

Responsibility for the daily classes and rehearsals fell to the Ballet
Master, Claude Newman, another company member from the 1930s,
and Ballet Mistress, Peggy van Praagh. Van Praagh's experiences had
given her exactly the right qualities for the position she was to hold.
She had danced with Marie Rambert's Ballet Club, where she created
roles in ballets by Ashton, Andrée Howard and Antony Tudor, including
the Woman in His Past in *Jardin aux Lilas*. She then joined Tudor's
London Ballet, and had the invaluable experience of running the
company from 1939, and also of inaugurating the Lunch Hour Ballet at
the Arts Theatre, which had developed into three hourly shows every
day. The following year she joined the Sadler's Wells Ballet, mostly to
take company class and coach the younger dancers, but also scoring a
success as Swanilda in *Coppélia*.

What particularly struck van Praagh about the Sadler's Wells Ballet
was its discipline and professionalism, and she saw and understood de
Valois' way of running a company – 'it is often necessary for the director
to be ruthless. He or she must have a policy and stick to it, and cannot
consider individual dancers who have to be sacrificed to the whole. It is
hard, almost impossible, for the dancers to see this, and so they feel
unhappy and frustrated'.[8] She was admirably suited to work in a
company established to encourage young talent, both dance and
especially choreographic; her own career had made her believe that 'to
work with a choreographer at the height of his creative powers is, I
think, the most wonderful experience for a dancer and the quickest way
to develop her potentialities, to learn her emotional range'.[9]

The young company was strengthened by an intake of more experienced dancers, headed by June Brae, Leo Kersley, Alan Carter and Joan
Harris. Brae had been with the Sadler's Wells organisation since 1935;

she was not a strong technician, but her warmth and maturity were to be invaluable qualities in the early seasons. Kersley had danced with several companies, including the Sadler's Wells Ballet, with whom he had created the Gravedigger in Helpmann's ballet *Hamlet*. Short, with a bright, bouncy, open style, he had a strong technique and dramatic flair, and he set a style of male dancing for which the company was to become notable.

The excitement among the embryo company was intense. 'We were all such children really', remembers Anne Heaton. 'Our particular group were the luckiest group of dancers ever. No question ... getting on with what is a short career in any case at such an early age and such a wonderfully productive time'.[10] They could hardly believe their luck. Here they were, with a company built around them – a company that shared a famous name with their elder sister at the Opera House, where they too might go one day. Until then, this was to be *their* company, and their pride and anticipation can be imagined.

The repertory was to consist of ballets created for the Sadler's Wells Ballet which would not be suited to Covent Garden, and works specially created on the new company. The existing repertory was at once a blessing and a curse. It meant a repertory of tried and tested works, but these were often associated in the public mind with their creators. It was at once challenging and intimidating for a young company aged mainly between fifteen and seventeen.

The Sadler's Wells Opera Ballet made its début, as its name implies, in the operas produced when the Sadler's Wells Opera returned to its home theatre in June 1945. The opening night on 7 June was memorable, for it was the world première of Benjamin Britten's *Peter Grimes*. Milling among 'The People of the Borough' was one who was to play an important part in the future of the organisation, the company's future Ballet Mistress, and then Principal of the School – Barbara Fewster.

The main body of the company had to wait for its début until Boxing Day when *The Bartered Bride* was revived, with Anne Heaton (then known as Patsy Ann) and Eric Hyrst as the leading dancers and, among the Clowns and Dancers, Donald Britton, Barbara Fewster, Sheila Nelson, Sheilah O'Reilly, Michael Hogan, Kenneth MacMillan and Peter Skinner (later Peter Darrell). *The Times* singled out 'Miss Patsy Ann Heaton, who will one day do something on the ballet stage'.[11]

Over the next few months the company appeared in *Hansel and Gretel* and *Rigoletto* with dances arranged by their Assistant Ballet Mistress, Nancy McNaught. The operas were to prove invaluable for young choreographers as well as dancers, for there, out of the spotlight, they could learn the rudiments of stagecraft and presentation. However, the main energies of what the *Ballet Annual* ringingly described as 'de Valois' Second Front', were devoted to the first full evening of ballet on 8 April 1946.

Its importance was seen from the outset – 'quite apart from the pleasure it will give at Sadler's Wells on Monday nights and in the provinces. It provides the machinery for a continuous chain of development: school to second company; second company to first company. Such machinery does not exist outside State-supported institutions'.[12]

The first programme was a judicious mix of old and new. De Valois' *Promenade*, created for the Sadler's Wells Ballet in 1943, was a light, charming suite of dances, centered around a Lepidopterist in a park. Although much of the original subtlety was beyond most of the young dancers, they, nonetheless, were praised for their understanding of the folk dance in the Danse des Paysannes which brought the ballet to a rousing end. Claude Newman was the Lepidopterist, with Joan Harris and George Gerhardt in the *rendezvous pas de deux*.

Then came the first created work, *Assembly Ball*, choreographed by Andrée Howard to Bizet's Symphony in C, for which she designed her own scenery and costumes. Set in a ballroom, it was inventive, witty and full of elegant grace, with touches of dreamy magic in the slow movement, though lacking the emotional depth that might have made it more than a charming *divertissement*. It was, however, perfectly tailored to the young company, with a demanding role for Kersley as the Master of Ceremonies, jumping for twenty-eight of the ballet's thirty-eight minutes, beautifully contrasted with Brae as the Lady, in a role that perfectly displayed her 'languorous beauty and effortless charm'.[13] Claude Newman provided one of his invaluable character studies as An Elderly Gentleman.

The programme ended with Act III of *Casse-Noisette*, for which Margaret Dale and Norman Thompson were seconded from Covent Garden to appear as a sparkling Sugar Plum Fairy and the Nutcracker Prince. Some classical ballets were obviously necessary to provide experience and discipline. The dancers did not lack enthusiasm and confidence, indeed some reviewers felt they had too much, but these qualities were to prove one of the most endearing characteristics of the company. As Scott Goddard wrote, 'there was such infectious vitality, the dancers were manifestly so eager and enthusiastic, that they persuaded us to forget minor shortcomings and simply enjoy the occasion with them'.[14]

Assembly Ball. June Brae as the Lady and Leo Kersley as the Master of Ceremonies with George Gerhardt and Eric Hyrst as Cavaliers.

Photograph by Edward Mandinian. From the collections of the Theatre Museum. Reproduced by courtesy of the Board of Trustees of the Victoria and Albert Museum.

De Valois had always been a great admirer of Howard's work and for the first two seasons she was designated Resident Choreographer. Like many choreographers of the 1930s, she had developed under Marie Rambert at the Ballet Club, where her creations included *Death and the Maiden* and *Lady into Fox*, and later for the London Ballet she created her masterpiece *La Fête étrange*. Her fey vagueness, gentleness and need for constant support made it difficult for her to function within a rigid organisation, but at the Wells, as opposed to later at Covent Garden, she found a sympathy and patience that was conducive to her work. She was essentially a small scale choreographer, with a strong imagination and sense of understated atmosphere that gave her best work a dreamlike sense of mystery.

The company settled down to its routine of performances on Monday nights and occasional Saturday matinées. De Valois considered this the right number of performances, in view of the number of works the young dancers had to learn, but it was important to increase the number of performances as gently as possible from one a week to two.

Les Sylphides was an ambitious, if inevitable, choice for them. It was as yet beyond their capabilities, and at first several dancers came up from Covent Garden to dance the leads, but it demanded the discipline which would create a *corps de ballet* and was a challenge for the soloists. However, the size of the company meant that there were relatively few *corps de ballet* works; thus there was more opportunity for solo work and for individuals to develop, and indeed, the company was to be famous for the wide range of different personalities that it came to encompass.

Frederick Ashton came back to the Wells to revive and appear as the Dago in his ballet *Façade*, which has never lost its popularity with audiences, although it was a work that the company had to grow into, and learn to resist the temptation to turn Ashton's wit into crude humour by overplaying. The dancers also experienced the excitement of their first television appearances, in the dances from *The Bartered Bride*, and then, on 8 May, the transmission of *Assembly Ball* with Joan Harris as the Lady.

Alongside *Assembly Ball* the company had been rehearsing Celia Franca's *Khadra*, 'an attempt to depict in stylised classical dancing the mood evoked by Persian miniatures'.[15] She found the company very eager, and very deferential to her age and experience (she was all of twenty-four). As designer she chose Honor Frost, a Curator at the Tate Gallery, whose first stage work this was, and for the music she made the unlikely, but in the event very happy, selection of Sibelius' *Belschazzar's Feast*. The child Khadra, her mood of wonder magically evoked by Sheilah O'Reilly, observed the life around her, the young lovers, the revellers, the old and young; as night fell and the ballet ended, she had shed her childhood and stood on the brink of adolescence. Franca used her young artists sensitively, revealing in them an unexpected emotional depth. On the opening night, 27 May, there was a gasp of pleasure from the audience as the curtain went up on Frost's brilliantly coloured décor, its pink background split by a bright blue balustrade, and the dark green dado covered with bright stylised flowers. The costumes and choreography enhanced each other in the most subtle way, especially

Jane Shore as the Debutante and Anthony Burke as the Dago in *Façade*.

Photograph by Roger Wood.

emphasizing the effective use of hands and fingers. The *pas de deux* for Anne Heaton (who had now dropped the 'Patsy') and Kersley as the lovers, using intertwined arms instead of hands for support, was particularly praised.

The *Ballet Annual* summed up the season with a word of caution:

The Sadler's Wells audience is touching in its enthusiasm and its utter lack of reticence, but the atmosphere provided is a heady one for young dancers and they would be well advised to take praise and applause in Rosebery Avenue with more than one grain of salt. In spite of its youthful shortcomings, there can be no doubt that this company is more advanced than was the original one at the same period. One can see the influence of a school that has trained the majority of the members. The company has a personality from the very start. Moreover, the original company was largely a background

Khadra.

Photograph by Roger Wood.

for the brilliant Markova, while here all have an equal chance of development.[16]

Heartened by the response to their first season, the company set out on a six-week tour in the charge of van Praagh. It was planned that both Sadler's Wells companies would tour, the Covent Garden company visiting the main cities, the Opera Ballet taking in the smaller theatres in venues like Exeter, Bath and Cambridge. One much appreciated feature was that the company toured its own orchestra, twenty-four players under Ivan Clayton, instead of the two pianos which were usual with most small ballet groups. The provincial press waxed lyrical over the Sadler's Wells Opera Ballet, praising its overall standard and discipline in terms that are a sad reflection on some of the other companies that audiences saw. What the company lacked in technical and theatrical maturity it made up for with a youthful enthusiasm that captivated audiences. Cambridge, well used to ballet through the regular visits of the Sadler's Wells Ballet, felt that though 'longstanding balletomanes may quibble at certain aspects, the general result is a polished competence born of an artistic eagerness that makes comparison with the older company nothing near so disadvantageous as one might expect'.[17] It was a very successful first tour, and showed a small, welcome profit of £600 to offset against the mounting costs of establishing the company.

Having discovered ballet, the nation, for a time, could not get enough. In the past ballet had been confined to the major opera houses, which meant very few cities indeed. The 1930s had seen the rise of a genuine interest in ballet, although among a very limited audience. Now there were myriad smaller companies, the most distinguished being Ballet Rambert, by a whisker Britain's oldest company. Ballet had become part of the artistic life of the nation, helped in the post-war period by films and then the spread of television. In London the British companies were augmented by an influx of foreign companies, some challenging accepted standards, others confirming the already high level reached by British ballet. In the same week as the Sadler's Wells Opera Ballet was launched, the Ballets des Champs-Elysées arrived, an equally young company with a very French mixture of youth and sophistication. The youth was provided by the dancers, led by Roland Petit and the sensational Jean Babilée, and the sophistication by the mature and individual vision of Boris Kochno, Jean Cocteau and Christian Bérard. The combination of strong thematic ballets and brilliant design was to influence at least one student in the Sadler's Wells School – Kenneth MacMillan.

By the end of the summer, Ballet Theatre had swept into Covent Garden, bringing its well-nourished American energy, attack and vigour, a breeziness and healthy vitality that made the English dancers, debilitated by five years of rationing, constant touring, chronic overwork and lack of sleep, seem drab and cold. Van Praagh brought the Opera Ballet back to London off tour to see the Americans, and her boys tried to dance *Fancy Free* all the way back on the train. The remnants of the De Basil Ballet (the Original Ballets Russes), the Grand Ballet du Marquis de Cuevas, the Nouveau Ballet de Monte Carlo, the Ballets de Paris and the young New York City Ballet all visited London within the next few years, along with many national and ethnic groups, with Spanish predominating. The time was not yet ripe for British ballet's counter-invasion.

Chapter II

The Opera Ballet's first full season opened at Sadler's Wells in October 1946, and ran until the following May. The company first appeared in the opera *The Snow Maiden*, which included de Valois' Dance of the Tumblers in which the male dancers, led by Donald Britton, stopped the show with their virile attack and joy of movement. There were now two performances a week – alternate Tuesday and Saturday evenings one week and Monday evenings and Saturday matinées the next, so that the same programme could be given on Saturday night and Monday night without having to change the scenery.

If some of the audience was enthusiastic to a degree so were many of the critics. Caryl Brahms welcomed them back:

> This junior Wells is a high-spirited, inexorably energetic, most professional company whose hopefulness I find quite irresistible. ... it lacks the accomplishment, tradition and glamour of the parent company. But then it has none of the rather raddled radiance of the matriarch either; nor has its native vigour been groomed out of it.[1]

In fact it was surprising that the senior company had any vigour left at all, after its wartime touring and continuous performances at Covent Garden.

Balletomanes had already realized the importance of the company for that most popular of balletomane games – talent spotting. Indeed, the accent during the season was to be on the search for new talent – not only choreographers, but also young designers and composers. Four new works were planned, together with two major revivals in the New Year – de Valois' strongly melodramatic *The Haunted Ballroom* and

17

Howard's delicate *La Fête étrange*. The first of the new works was short, lively, a choreographic debut and a smash hit. Alan Carter's *The Catch* given on the first full ballet evening of the season on 19 October, was a three hander for himself, Joan Harris and Frank Ward. Built around a simple theme of two boys out fishing and the flirtations with the elder's girl friend, it was well timed, amusing, and thoroughly enjoyable.

In stark contrast was Anthony Burke's *The Vagabonds*, premièred on 29 October. Based upon Thomas Hardy's poem, 'A Trampwoman's Tragedy', the plot turned on the rivalry between two gypsy men for the same girl. Her lover kills his rival, but the gypsies exact their own justice, and hang him. The girl, insane with remorse, dies and the lovers are reunited in death. Not surprisingly for such a strong theme, Burke used the most experienced dancers, Brae, Carter and Kersley dancing and acting with 'strength, courage and command'.[2] The group movement was often inspired, and the sultry gypsy passion was admirably reflected in the sullen earthy colours of Vivienne Kernot's lowering set. Some found that the power of the work lay in John Ireland's music rather than its choreography, but it was a narrative ballet of the kind needed in the building of a varied repertory and was especially enjoyed on tour where audiences have always liked their ballets full-blooded.

The company's first commissioned score was by Leonard Salzedo for Howard's new work, *Mardi Gras* seen on 26 November. Hugh Stevenson provided a suitably menacing set and grotesque costumes as well as the theme 'My grief lies onward and my joy behind', a quotation from a Shakespeare sonnet. If *La Fête étrange* was one side of Howard, the delicate whimsical side, then *Mardi Gras* was another – a nightmare fantasy world of soulless carnival figures, in which a young girl is lost, the atmosphere of sorrow and foreboding all the more effective for being left without explanation. Reviews invoked the names of Dostoievsky, 'Monk' Lewis and Freud, as well as the witches' sabbath in their attempts to define its qualities. Although the work was praised for its homogeneity and was to attract many admirers, it was not a generally popular work. Its main importance was in bringing to the fore the remarkable dramatic talents of sixteen-year-old Heation, as the Girl, confronted by her terrors and fears, culminating in the sight of herself in her own coffin; as her foil, was the brilliant Circus Dancer, designed to show off the sparkling technique of Nadia Nerina.

Celia Franca's *Bailemos* followed on 4 February 1947, a precursor of the craze for Spanish dancing that hit London in the late 1940s, although the music, from Massenet's *Le Cid*, dictated that it was a Spain seen

The Vagabonds. Leo Kersley as The Other Man, Pamela Chrimes as His Woman, June Brae as The Vagabond Girl and Alan Carter as Her Lover.

Photograph by Edward Mandinian. From the collections of the Theatre Museum. Reproduced by courtesy of the Board of Trustees of the Victoria and Albert Museum.

through French eyes. Its title, the Spanish for 'Let us dance', summed up its theme of contrasted noble and peasant dances, although Franca had not absorbed the Spanish idiom well enough to give it full expression. The ballet's main failing lay in Honor Frost's designs; she made the fatal mistake of not overseeing their making up, and the sombre black costumes threw a pall over the essentially light-hearted choreography.

Meanwhile the opera ballets continued to give aspiring choreographers the chance to flex their talents. On Boxing Day 1946 *Hansel and Gretel* was revived with dances by John Cranko. Cranko had produced works for the Cape Town Ballet Club and the University of Cape Town Ballet, and almost as soon as he joined the Sadler's Wells School he had approached de Valois about doing choreography. She suggested that he get as much experience as possible of working with other dancers and choreographers and he had been taken into the Opera Ballet, mainly because he was strong enough to manage some of the overhead lifts in *Khadra*. There were not many opportunities while a number of people were being tried out and resources were so limited, but the operas were an invaluable training ground although there was not much scope for world shaking effects.

What Cranko did find was the sympathetic ear of van Praagh. She had a great respect for the individual, and his right to express himself in his own way, and her own experience with choreographers had made her particularly suited to nurse embryo talent. She offered Cranko, as she did so many of the young dancers cut off from their families, the warmth and understanding they needed to develop as both artists and individuals, at once parent and friend, but never at the expense of her authority or company discipline.

7 January 1947 brought *The Haunted Ballroom*, the first of the 1930s revivals that really challenged memories of the past. It was carefully mounted by de Valois, and had the Sadler's Wells chorus to heighten the mystery of the ballroom scene, but most people could not stifle their memories of Helpmann as the Master of Treginnis or Markova as Alicia. Carter was the first to undertake the thankless task of attempting to challenge Helpmann but it was not until David Poole took over with a strong and individual reading that the role regained something of its old effect. Poole, a South African, was a few years older than the average Opera Ballet dancer. An outstanding dance-actor, he had a magnetic stage presence and excellent sense of character, and was to prove a sensitive and invaluable performer and partner.

La Fête étrange had been created for the small stage of the Arts Theatre and the slender resources of the London Ballet, so for the revival on 25 March Howard and its designer, Sophie Fedorovitch, filled out the original choreography and designs for the larger spaces of the Wells. The ballet's elusive quality was not easy for young artists to capture, but they succeeded well, and Brae and Burke had the maturity of the Bride and Bridegroom and Britton the rough edge for the Country Boy. However, the young Basque dancer Pirmin Trecu was to be the ideal interpreter of the Country Boy, who wanders into the wedding celebration and, in his fixation with the Bride, unintentionally causes a rift between her and the Bridegroom. In Trecu's interpretation was a bewildered wonderment that captured the pleasure and confusion of adolescent love for an unattainable object.

As if to match the national mood of grey misery, caused by the fuel crisis and the worst winter in living memory, the Sadler's Wells Opera Ballet was undergoing its own crisis. Expenses were inevitably high while a repertory was being built up, and by January 1947 there was already a deficit of £6,150. By March it was suggested that the ballet company should make economies of £150 a week. The Governors of Sadler's Wells also had to face the expense of setting up the school on a fully educational and vocational training basis, having acquired for £12,000 the old Froebel Institute in Colet Gardens, they now had to pay for essential repairs and equipment. Lord Lytton, Chairman of the Sadler's Wells Governors, approached Sir John Anderson, Chairman of the Covent Garden Trust, to ask if the Opera House could not see its way to contributing to the running of the company and school, as Covent Garden benefited from both.

David Webster, General Administrator of Covent Garden, acknowledged the use of the company and school to Covent Garden, but felt that they should not be continued at such a loss. It was, however, pointed out that Covent Garden owed a great debt to the Wells, as the original transfer arrangement had been very advantageous to them. It had indeed. By May 1946 the Sadler's Wells Ballet had brought the Opera House £74,618 profit.

There was here a nice ethical problem of the sort beloved by committees. Should a theatre subsidized by the Arts Council use some of that subsidy to subsidize another theatre also receiving Arts Council subsidy? Some felt that it was really an accounting matter, and that the sums should be adjusted at Treasury level. But it was not just a matter of money, for the Wells also provided unseen subsidy in the form of the dancers trained to feed the Covent Garden company. By October 1947 the Treasury and Arts Council had agreed that it was proper for the Covent Garden Opera Trust to assist the school and the company, and Covent Garden agreed to accept liability up to £2,500 if Sadler's Wells would make an equal contribution for that year.

It was almost impossible not to make a loss on the ballet at the Wells with only two performances a week. Not only production costs, but running costs were high. Though tours might show a small profit, it was little to off-set against total costs, and by May 1947, as the company embarked upon a spring tour the losses had reached £12,439. To add to the company's problems Brae, Carter and Harris left at the end of the London season, and a number of others transferred to the *corps de ballet* at Covent Garden. Among the replacements taken from the school for the tour were a promising young Australian, Elaine Fifield, and David Poole. National Service was also to claim three male dancers in the near future – National Service was to play havoc with the young men's artistic development until conscription was abolished in 1960, although it did them nothing but good to get away from the hothouse atmosphere of the ballet for a while, and helped foster a rugged individualism.

In May 1947, despite appalling conditions (snow and ice had been followed by severe floods), the company embarked upon a successful twelve week tour with a new name – the Sadler's Wells Opera Ballet had become the Sadler's Wells Theatre Ballet, in recognition of its individual status. With a name still so close to the Sadler's Wells Ballet, publicity always stressed that, though it might be a junior company in years, it had its own particular personality and part to play in the organisation. The question of the company status was always a difficult one. The dancers always, naturally and without thinking, referred to the companies as 'first' and 'second' on the grounds that one was in existence before the other – a statement of fact with no qualitative judgement involved. As the years went by the always over-sensitive powers-that-be made so much of *not* calling the company 'the second company' that the public began to feel that they protested too much and must have something to hide. There would always be some of the audience who felt cheated that the Sadler's Wells Theatre Ballet was not the Sadler's Wells Ballet, even if it never pretended to be.

Audiences were good and reactions enthusiastic. Again it was the youth of the company that caught the imagination, and their eager vitality won many converts. Many towns and cities did not have much chance of seeing ballet, and even fewer chances of seeing ballet of such calibre. The *Sussex Daily News* admitted to some trepidation on their previous visit, knowing that it was 'only the junior company',[3] but had been amazed by their standards. This year it noted how much progress the company had made. It was the teamwork that always impressed, and the overall quality – not only of the dancing, but design ('to our austerity-wearied eyes a delight'[4]), production and music. The repertory, which included *Les Sylphides*, *The Vagabonds*, *Bailemos*, *Khadra*, *La Fête étrange*, *Façade* and *The Catch*, was well balanced and gave plenty of opportunities to the dancers – Nerina, Heaton and O'Reilly and Kersley, the 'older member' of the company, were much admired. It also helped audiences to develop their appreciation and understanding, while offering to the more knowledgeable known works by which they could assess progress.

On the first night of the tour, at the Theatre Royal in Brighton on 19 May, Cranko mounted his first ballet for the company. *Adieu* had originally been given at the Vic-Wells Ball the previous January, where de Valois had seen it. It was a brief and elaborately dressed, if cheaply set,[5] romantic interlude concerning the farewells of a nymph (Heaton) and her warrior lover (Poole). Any choreographic invention was swamped by Hugh Stevenson's ornate dresses and feathered head-dresses, but *The Stage* thought the 'liquid movement' admirably served by the Scarlatti score.[6]

Also at Brighton, the company added to its repertory the formidable challenge of Michel Fokine's *Carnaval*. It emerged with honour and immense promise and it was to develop into one of the best revivals by an English company, perhaps not surprisingly, for the mime was taught to them by Tamara Karsavina,[7] for whom Fokine had created the role of Columbine. The strong character roles suited a company of dancers who were nothing if not individuals, and among early notable interpreters were MacMillan as Florestan, Jane Shore as Estrella and Pauline Wadsworth as Chiarina. Heaton and Britton were the first Columbine and Harlequin, with Kersley as Pierrot, and Kersley was later to be a technically brilliant, if not particularly sly, Harlequin. The glory of the production, however, came when Poole took over as Pierrot, playing the character as an innocent soul seeking companionship in the midst of dejection and loneliness, tossed between joy and disappointment. 'His face is a mirror' wrote Richard Buckle, 'in which the joys and sorrows of his companions are reflected; and he can make his body no less expressive than his face'.[8] The production later won a tribute from Lydia Lopokova, who despaired of most revivals, '*Carnaval* has been a nightmare, but this young company has a kind of verve ... I came away with a feeling that trees do grow in every country'.[9]

Despite the critical and public success of the company, drastic measures were called for if it was to survive at all. The summer break saw more dancers leave, and it was known that Heaton, Nerina and Britton would be transferred to Covent Garden by the New Year. Cranko was also to spend some time with the senior company to allow him to observe the work of more experienced choreographers. Senior students, including Patricia Miller and Maryon Lane, were drafted in to fill the gaps, but the company was temporarily seriously weakened among the female principals. It was therefore decided that performances should be limited to Saturday matinées, except for premières, and the opera ballets. This showed some lack of foresight, for Saturday matinées were well established at Covent Garden and a clash could only work to the detriment of the smaller company. It would, however, mean that the new dancers and inexperienced principals could be carefully nursed. There would also be two short tours using two pianos to towns with theatres too small to accommodate a full orchestra. This would broaden the company's touring schedule while saving the costs of the orchestra, which at that time would, anyway, be required for opera performances at the Wells. The plan was encouraged by the Arts Council, who were trying to bring a higher standard of entertainment to theatres off the regular touring map.

Over the summer the company had benefited from classes given by Harijs Plucis, Ballet Master of the Covent Garden company, and Fifield had taken advantage of her summer break to take lessons in Paris from Preobrajenska. Fifield was an astonishingly gifted dancer, with a beautifully proportioned and expressive body which more than compensated for her inexpressive, though pretty, face. She was technically strong with an easy virtuosity, well-coordinated and with a clear lyricism that illuminated every movement. There was an inner reserve, sometimes degenerating into coldness, that could be attributed to her youth, but she could also display a delightful humour. Her promise was immense, and some saw in her a likeness to Fonteyn at the same age, but her emotional development came late, and she was to need careful guidance over the years.

Cranko's *Tritsch-Tratsch*, introduced on 20 September at the first matinée of the 1947–48 season, had been first given by the University of Cape Town Ballet Club in 1946. Set to the well-known polka by

Johann Strauss, and with new costumes designed by Hedley Briggs, it was an engaging piece, using the music well to show the flirtations between two sailors and a girl. As Mary Clarke pointed out, it could hardly fail with young dancers, pretty costumes and the music which kept them on the move, but tartly added that 'if the standard of dancing in British musicals was not so pitifully low, we should not get so much of this kind of thing on the ballet stage'.[10] Audiences, however, loved it. Michael Boulton and Poole were the Sailors and Fifield the Girl, all dancing with gusto and humour.

On the same programme was the *pas de trois* from *Le Lac des Cygnes*, danced by Heaton, Nerina and Kersley. It was known that both Heaton and Nerina would soon be lost to Covent Garden, and the promising dramatic intelligence of the former, and the sparkling technical verve of the latter would be much missed in Islington. The classical excerpts (the Peasant *pas de deux* from *Giselle* was added the following year and the Bluebird *pas de deux* in 1949) were performed with more attack than finesse, but it was important to give the young dancers some experience of classical choreography, especially those who might be taken to Covent Garden, and full-scale classical ballets were obviously out of the question. Too many short ballets and *divertissements*, however, made the programmes look scrappy and lightweight.

Heaton had one last role to create before her transfer. The major excitement of the season was Ashton's first ballet created for the company. It was felt, rightly, that the young dancers should not always be left in the hands of equally young and undeveloped choreographers, and the experience of creating a ballet with England's leading cho-reographer could only help them and strengthen the repertory. Van Praagh had suggested that he revive *Valentine's Eve*, which had been created for the Ballet Club in 1933, but he felt it would now prove too sentimental, so he produced a new ballet using the same Ravel music, and also annexing its title, *Valses Nobles et Sentimentales*.

As for *Valentine's Eve* his designer was Sophie Fedorovitch. The setting was the ante-room to a ballroom, the backcloth cast with shadows of palm trees and with folding screens at the back, behind which the dancers were silhouetted. The predominant colour of set and costumes was a raspberry pink with deep claret tunics for the men, colours that 'evoke a mood, hot-house and Proustian, that catches the very essence of the waltz'.[11] Ashton was a master at producing ballets for young dancers and now he created a ballet of youth. The five couples changed from waltz to waltz, suggesting but never emphasizing, shifting relation-

25

ships. As Richard Buckle, editor of the prestigious magazine *Ballet*, saw it:

> Two (boys) were both attracted by the same girl, at least she was always present in their thoughts, even when they were dancing with other girls. At the end she returned to them after an absence, and I was left in doubt as to which of them, if either, she would eventually choose.[12]

The ballet had all the Ashton hallmarks, exceptional response to the music, beauty of line and sensitivity to the particular qualities of his dancers. Like many of his works, it did not give up everything at first viewing, and the 'charm' that many felt to be its main virtue, was soon replaced by respect for its subtle richness and evocation of mood. There was an air of ethereal unreality that could so easily have been destroyed by 'interpretation', but his young cast responded sensitively. They also responded to the increasing demands Ashton made upon their technique, and Heaton, Britton and Boulton as the leading trio received high praise.

New opera productions included *Faust*. Pauline Grant was the choreographer, mixing academic steps and a freer modern style to create effects both macabre and realistic. Some movements rather shocked the young dancers, though others couldn't resist entering into the prevailing spirit and adding their own orgiastic touches in the dark – which actually brought a complaint from a Bishop. Christmas saw a rather more sedate production of *Die Fledermaus* with choreography (to the Blue Danube waltz) by Anthony Burke.

It was important for the Sadler's Wells Theatre Ballet to develop a distinct personality if it was to be a viable artistic unit. The company was beginning to overcome the difficult initial period, when it could be seen neither as a fully student company, nor as an independent professional group and was developing a particular identity based on a sturdy individualism of both dancer and repertory. The company already had many admirers, who found in it a warmth, energy and creative excitement that was perhaps lacking as the more familiar Sadler's Wells Ballet established itself as the national ballet at the Opera House. Much of its character came from van Praagh, who was responsible for the day-to-day running of the company, giving class, overseeing rehearsals, passing on her own infectious enthusiasm.

Ashton had been so pleased with the way that they had responded during the creation of *Valses Nobles et Sentimentales* that he offered to

Valses Nobles et Sentimentales. Anne Heaton with Donald Britton and Michael Boulton.

Photograph by Angus McBean.

revive his 1933 ballet *Les Rendezvous* which went into the repertory on Boxing Day 1947. Ashton slightly revised the choreography, restoring the game of Blindman's Buff and making small changes to the use of the four little girls in white, and William Chappell took the opportunity to make yet more revisions to his designs – far from his last thoughts on the ballet. Ashton and Fonteyn coached Fifield in the leading role, which she danced with charm and style, performing the difficult variation, created for Alicia Markova, with unflurried ease. Michael Boulton danced brilliantly in the leading male role which had been created for the formidable technique of Stanislas Idzikowski. *Les Rendezvous* was to be a mainstay of the repertory for longer than anyone at the time of its creation would have thought possible, and it rarely failed to captivate audiences. P. W. Manchester called it a 'lovely, witty, *original* thing which fourteen years later stands as an object lesson for all who care to meditate a little'.[13] Over fifty years after its creation that is still true.

As early as 1914, Lilian Baylis had established school matinées of Shakespeare, which not only guaranteed her a regular income from the London County Council education authority, but also meant that her theatres could claim an educational role and so were exempt from Entertainment Tax. Now, in 1947 the LCC discussed with the Sadler's Wells management the possibility of adding ballet visits to the school curriculum. As a result, over 8,000 schoolchildren attended five matinées of a special programme – *Valses Nobles et Sentimentales*, *Carnaval*, the *pas de trois* from *Le Lac des Cygnes*, *Tritsch-Tratsch* and *Les Rendezvous*. Van Praagh introduced the programmes, sketching the background to each work, outlining the theme, drawing attention to the importance of the imagination in interpretation, and giving her audience some idea of how ballets were revived.

Performing to an audience of children having an afternoon off school can be a daunting experience; some of their reactions are unexpected, others are only too predictable, but all are uninhibited. Although it can be difficult to hold their attention throughout what is, for the majority, a very unfamiliar experience, their general reaction is to cheer everything with gusto. P. W. Manchester caught one of the matinées and found it 'a most exhilarating afternoon'.[14] The children decided that *Carnaval* was a comedy, that the *pas de trois* from *Swan Lake* was uninteresting (children being rarely interested in pure classical dancing), were surprisingly responsive to *Valses Nobles* and adored *Tritsch-Tratsch*. The undisputed hit of the afternoon, however, was *Les Rendezvous*. School matinées were to be a feature of London and touring programmes from that time onwards.

Burke's second ballet for the company, *Parures*, was premièred on 21 January 1948. Set to Tchaikovsky's Theme and Variations from the Suite in G major, it was an attempt at a technically demanding abstract ballet in the grand manner, perhaps the most difficult genre for the young choreographer. It was a brave attempt, but the main interest lay in the performance rather than the choreography, the young Fifield and Lane performing the bravura passages with youthful assurance, and Kersley, Boulton and Poole attacking their brilliant solos with vigour.

Meanwhile John Cranko had not been idle. As there were few opportunities for producing ballets for the company, he had been working for the Royal Academy of Dancing (RAD) Production Club.[15] Here de Valois saw *Morçeaux Enfantins*, set to Debussy's suite of the same name, and took it into the Theatre Ballet repertory. Now called *Children's*

Corner and with new designs from the well-known children's book illustrator, Jan le Witt[16] it joined the repertory on 6 April. It was light and unpretentious, reflecting, through its cast of dolls, various moods and memories of childhood and making ingenious use of small, pizzicato steps to emphasize the doll-like characters. It had all Cranko's musical sensitivity, sense of character, and, most importantly, unforced invention and indications of a completely personal style of expression. If it sometimes veered towards sentimentality, that too was characteristic. Poole ran away with all the notices as the Golliwog, with support from Jane Shore as the Wooden Doll, Miller and MacMillan as Mlle Piquant and her Great Admirer and tiny Annette Page as The Monkey of Ukuababa.

By the end of the season the fewer performances meant that the company deficit was reduced to £1 2s 9d, and it was clear that more performances could be risked in future.

At the end of April 1948 the company embarked on its longest tour to date, fifteen weeks, including three weeks in Ireland, accompanied by the full orchestra. The tour was rapturously received, even in venues that did not usually have large audiences, like Peterborough and Norwich. Norwich was to remain loyal throughout the ups and downs of the company's history. In the regular venues the press enjoyed seeing the new works and monitoring the progress of the dancers, particularly those with local connections. Especially enthusiastic were audiences in Dublin and Belfast where, once again, the pleasure of seeing a company with full orchestra was remarked upon, although the *Northern Whig* noted that the pleasure would have been greater without the humming and whistling accompaniment from the audience.[17] In Dublin, however, the orchestra was criticized for low standards, another complaint that would run like an undercurrent through the history of the company. At the Gaiety Theatre in Dublin they attracted the greatest number of curtain calls that the *Evening Herald* could remember, and there were loud complaints at the unfairness of Belfast having a two week visit and Dublin only one. De Valois was present at the last performance in Belfast to see a packed house full of young people, and she expressed her thanks from the stage for the warmth of the reception.

Two new items were introduced during the tour – *Jota Toledana* and *Farruca del Sacro Monte* – Spanish dance solos choreographed by Angelo Andes for Pirmin Trecu. They were a great success with audiences, especially the Jota, which was later expanded into an often-encored pas de deux for Trecu and Sheilah O'Reilly. The only person with whom they were not a smash hit was Trecu himself, who didn't like being thought of primarily as a Spanish dancer, although he did admit that he enjoyed the applause.

There was nothing like a long tour for welding the already close company into a compact cohesive unit. Here the family feeling already begun at the school was reinforced by the common experiences of touring and the constant challenge of different audiences, so unlike their loyal, over-indulgent home audience. It was sometimes hard to tell one town from another, and life became reduced to a succession of rehearsal rooms, theatres and digs. Rehearsal rooms were always cold – dirty, drab church halls, gymnasia, pub back rooms, scout huts, the occasional ballroom with the inevitable slippery floor. Here the dancers took the daily class, rehearsed new works and the regular repertory breaking in the many cast changes needed as injury and illness took their toll. At one point seven of the twenty-eight dancers were ill or injured, and it looked as though the tour would have to be abandoned.

Theatres were often run down. The days of the large touring companies that could keep a theatre open all year round were coming to an end, and there were no profits for refurbishment or modernization, even if the building restrictions had not precluded improvements at this time. At least the dressing-rooms were relatively warm, and here in their few breaks the dancers virtually lived, creating their own personal territory set with their belongings, as generations of touring dancers have done before and since. Here, between class, rehearsal and performance they spent their days, cleaning and darning shoes, curling eyelashes, doing their laundry, writing home – the thousand traditional theatre chores. Despite the surroundings, only the highest standards of stage presentation and grooming were allowed – 'Dirty clothes, dirty dancing' de Valois used to say.[18]

Digs were merely glimpsed late at night and first thing in the morning, which was all to the good, for many were depressing, cold and inadequate. Most were found through the official Equity accommodation lists, and old hands like Kersley could be relied upon to find the best, where landladies knew their regular customers and would book them in as soon as they saw a show advertised; they understood theatrical hours and the need to provide meals after the theatre when few provincial restaurants were open. But others were filthy, with greasy meals, cat's hair in the milk and damp bedrooms (although it is good to know that the much maligned baked bean, which also turned up in quantity, has since been designated a most nutritious food). With rationing still in force meals were hardly plentiful anyway, although even so there were always those on the inevitable diet; their rations were gratefully seized upon by their less figure-conscious colleagues.

Under such conditions the youth of the company was again an asset and to many it was all part of a marvellous adventure, although the gloss did begin to wear a bit thin after years on the road. Cold was the great problem. Sunday was, and is, a frustrating time to travel, and journeys would take all day in freezing unheated trains, after which, on arriving in an often unfamiliar town the dancers would be faced with the grim task of actually finding their digs. When they eventually found them they were equally freezing. Sometimes there was good reason and one member of the stage staff found himself sleeping in a room with a large hole in the wall. Touring got slightly better the more experienced the dancers became, but it would always be depressing for those on their first tours. To many, however, it merely added spice to the excitement of belonging to the company and being able to perform continuously.

The danger of long tours was not only the increased risk of overwork and injury, but that, deprived of proper conditions for daily class, the edge began to wear off hard won technique. Thus, at the end of each tour, classes were arranged with guest teachers, and the dancers remember the marvellous teaching of Karsavina, Lydia Kyasht, Vera Volkova, Harold Turner, Errol Addison and later Anton Dolin. To keep the various ballets in good shape the choreographers themselves would, whenever possible, be on hand, and a de Valois or Ashton ballet was never revived without them coming down to add the finishing touches to rehearsals.

The dancers who now began to emerge were to establish the character of the Theatre Ballet as people remember it. The girls were headed by Fifield. There was the lovely Miller, her cool delicacy proving at once her particular charm and her limitation. Lane was a promising classical dancer with a strong fluid technique, who would later reveal a sensitive dramatic talent. Sheilah O'Reilly was another dramatic dancer, with a child-like but fiery quality that made her a haunting exponent of her own particular repertory.

The boys were even more individual – like de Valois, van Praagh always had a soft spot for the boys and was inclined to be less strict with them than with the girls, possibly because she knew that ballet would always be a harder career for the girls and they must learn to cope with the greater competition. The boys were led by the irrepressible Kersley, whose personality was in contrast to the more gentlemanly qualities of Poole. Kersley described the boys as a 'bit of roughs and toughs' and

In the rehearsal room at Sadler's Wells: Barbara Fewster, Peggy van Praagh, Ursula Moreton and Frederick Ashton.

Photograph by Roger Wood.

undoubtedly this rugged individualism was encouraged. Boulton was a more lyrical, precise dancer, with above average elevation. Trecu had great verve and dash overlaid with a *gamin* exoticism that came from his Basque background. MacMillan had a beautifully lyrical style which held great promise for a career in the classics and among the youngest boys was the immensely promising David Blair whose naturally buoyant, cheerful nature, and formidable all-round technique, were eventually to be given perfect expression by Ashton in the role of Colas in *La Fille mal gardée*.

The dancers look back on this period with nostalgia. There was practically no time that any dancer was left without something to do, a gloriously busy, creative time, when they all felt one hundred percent needed and a vital part of the organisation. It was a small company averaging about thirty, so that each dancer could be given individual attention, and at rehearsals van Praagh was always constructive, trying to get the maximum out of each of them. The repertory also stressed the importance of individuality, built as it was around small works, in which each dancer had an important part to play; the real *corps de ballet* works at this time were limited to *Les Sylphides*, to be joined later by Act II of *Le Lac des Cygnes*. This does not mean that each dancer was only out for himself – personalities and personal ideas were respected and encouraged, but there was a unified approach to the work and the aim to make that manifest on stage. Perhaps this is why there was relatively little jealousy in the company. They were all ambitious, and doubtless most had their sights set on Covent Garden, but for the time being they were in the midst of something so creative and exciting that Covent Garden could wait. 'Dancing holds a bright and provocative future for them', wrote Cranko, 'A future not in any way dulled by overwork, frustration, or the thousand bitternesses which so often seem to overtake the "old stagers". Perhaps it never will'.[19] Their enthusiasm and love of their work spilled over into their performing, often causing the over-ebullience at which some hardened critics complained. It was a winning combination, however, and endeared them to experienced and inexperienced ballet-goers alike, as well as being a perfect quality for a company that would spend more and more time bringing ballet to places that had little other chance to see it.

Chapter III

The company journeyed to Manchester in September 1948 to appear in the opera ballets with the Sadler's Wells Opera. On their return they were joined by a new leading dancer, Hans Zullig from the Ballets Jooss. A handsome, sensitive dancer-mime, Zullig had limited classical technique but, like so many dancers trained by Jooss, an exceptionally expressive body. Also joining the company at the end of his military service was Stanley Holden, whose very individual comic talent would find a more sympathetic repertory at the Wells than at Covent Garden where he had started his career.

After the opening of the Sadler's Wells season on 2 October, the *Dancing Times* noted approvingly how much the company had improved, and that they were beginning to acquire a sense of style and line. This was particularly noticeable in Ashton's revival of his delightful *Capriol Suite*, originally choreographed for the Marie Rambert Dancers in 1930. For the Theatre Ballet Ashton increased the four couples to six 'for the sake of convenience in the entrées, and a slight rearrangement of the finale'.[1] The contrasting styles of boisterous folk and formal court dances were well caught by the dancers, Shore, Poole and Zullig being particularly successful in the Pavane and Boulton, Blair, Trecu and David Gill attacking Mattachins with gusto. Although a youthful work, P. W. Manchester commented that Ashton's particular qualities were already there – 'The observation, taste, invention, wit, feeling for beauty of a young and inexperienced choreographer who had much to learn but already knew ;all the things that really matter, those things that can never be taught'.[2] It was in this ballet that the company made its first appearance at Covent Garden in April, 1949, in a Gala in aid of the Sadler's Wells Ballet Benevolent Fund.

The major creation for the autumn season of 1948 was premièred on 16 November, a new work by Andrée Howard to music by Rossini arranged by Guy Warrack with designs by Peter Williams.[3] *Selina* told of a poet, unable to find inspiration, even with the help of a vision of the eponymous heroine. The vision becomes reality and he falls in love with her, but she and her brother, Tom, are pursued by their stepfather, Lord Ravensgarth, who tries to steal a locket belonging to their late mother. A surprisingly inept witch, Agnes, confuses everyone, but in the end good triumphs over evil in a charming tableau. The designs, evoking a nineteenth-century lithograph, set a suitably Romantic mood, and it was some time before the audience realised that it was seeing not a pastiche but a parody of the conventions of the Romantic Ballet and settled down to enjoy itself immensely. Howard mixed genuine affection for the Romantic era, parody and caricature, with references to *Giselle* and *La Sylphide*. Some, however, were confused, and Richard Buckle came across one 'faint-hearted fellow of fugitive and cloistered virtue' outraged at the idea that ballet should laugh at itself.

Fifield as Selina was a charming conventional heroine and Zullig a handsomely ardent poet-lover; Trecu was Selina's brother, Tom, and David Gill a suitably villainous Lord Ravensgarth. Running away with the ballet, as no doubt Howard intended, was Holden as Agnes; Agnes, wrote Caryl Brahms 'is clearly to become the Queen Lear of the Ballet ... her lunacy, as ineffably enacted by Stanley Holden, is utter ... Her gait is that of the ebbing tide. Her gaze has the vacancy of a burst bubble. Her malevolence has all the wistfulness of an ageing wit'.[4] Howard herself later played the role with a gentle vagueness and bewilderment that by its very understatement was as effective as Holden's more extrovert approach. Laughter and charm so subtly mixed was bound to be a hit, although, sadly, the ballet did coarsen in later performances, usually after it had been performed on tour, where audiences could not be expected to see the subtle parodies (having had no chance to see the works being satirised), and the dancers had to overplay to get laughs in the right places.

The season was punctuated by what were to be the last of the short tours to two pianos, one week in the autumn to Darlington, and one to a town that was to be for many years a traditional spring venue – Stratford-upon-Avon.

The 1949 spring season at the Wells brought, on 15 March, the production of the abstract *Etude*, choreographed by Nancy McNaught, a reworking of her ballet *Mirages*, first given at the RAD Production

Club. Antony Hopkins orchestrated his original two-piano score and Vivienne Kernot provided the designs. The work was, however, overlong, and derivative and 'swamped by large intentions',[5] the dancers working themselves into a frenzy of emotion for no obvious reason, and despite some imaginative groupings, the overall impression was as grey as its costuming.

The company embarked upon a ten week tour in May beginning in Cambridge. Here on 16 May they took another step forward with the production of Act II of *Le Lac des Cygnes*. At this stage, Fifield's technique was in advance of her emotional development, and the depths of Odette's tragedy were beyond her, but she was young and her promise was unmistakeable. Poole was a noble and sympathetic partner. The *corps de ballet* had yet to weld themselves into a cohesive unit, and it must have been hard for them to suppress their individuality.

By the end of the month the dancers had arrived in the Potteries, at the Theatre Royal, Hanley, the local press bemoaning the meagre week that the town had been allocated. The *Evening Sentinel* admitted that, even though they had heard of the wonders of the Covent Garden company which they were never likely to see 'it would be folly to sacrifice a moment of present pleasure to a legend. And how much superior can the principal company be'?[6]

Digs, however, were even worse than usual, and the company was advised to leave all their belongings in the theatre. A group of dancers were staying with that particular annoying character, the jokey landlord, who kept regaling them with tall stories. On the morning of 3 June he greeted them with 'You needn't hurry this morning, the theatre's burnt down'. The dancers greeted this sally with a dutiful 'Ha, ha' and set out as usual. But for once he had not been joking. They arrived to find a smoking ruin – the fire, started by faulty wiring, had been discovered shortly before 5 a.m. An hour later, despite the efforts of ten fire engines and two turntables the roof collapsed. The interior was completely destroyed, and only the entrance foyer and offices of the last theatre in the Potteries remained. No salvage operation had been possible. The company had lost its entire repertory, scenery and costumes, the dancers had lost all but what they stood up in, musicians had lost their instruments and the music scores, including several in manuscript, were sodden.

The company was stunned but undaunted and meetings were held to assess the losses and discuss immediate plans. A statement was issued that 'rehearsals of the other ballets in the company repertory would go on from tomorrow afternoon and into the night if necessary. The company would travel to Hull on Sunday'.[7] Within hours they were rehearsing a new set of ballets in the Tabernacle Schoolroom, wearing their street clothes, for their practice clothes and shoes had also been destroyed. At the same time offers of help were pouring in from organisations and individuals, and arrangements to replace the lost repertory were put in hand. The Opera House wardrobe made a complete set of new *Sylphides* dresses, and the Opera House lent the old Leslie Hurry set for Act 2 of *Le Lac des Cygnes*. Covent Garden also undertook the painting of a new *Façade* set, using the original John Armstrong design, and William Chappell supervised the remaking of the costumes. *Les Rendezvous* would be performed for the time being with the *Promenade* backcloth and new gates, and Chappell took the opportunity to make yet more changes to the costumes.[8] Alick Johnstone would repaint the *Selina* set and the only three dresses that were lost were quickly replaced. Angelo Andes lent O'Reilly a dress for the Jota and Covent Garden set about making a new costume for Trecu. Fifield would temporarily dance Odette in Fonteyn's tutu and headdress and Alexandra Danilova's shoes. Rambert offered to lend her productions of *Capriol Suite*, *Façade* and *Le Lac des Cygnes*, although in the end only a few costumes for *Carnaval* were needed. The insurance provided for the replacement of the lost ballets, and *The Haunted Ballroom* and *La Fête étrange* would be back for the autumn season.

The sodden scores were rescued from the band room and dried out at a local paper factory. They were then sent to London, where a team of twelve ironed out the pages and recollated them. Boosey and Hawkes and Henri Selmer offered replacement instruments and the orchestra returned to London to rehearse the new repertory.

A few tights and shoes and even fewer personal possessions were rescued from the less badly damaged dressing-rooms. Fonteyn and her colleagues in London sent parcels of tights and shoes, and strangers sent outdoor clothes. An anonymous donor sent £5 and an eleven-year-old Liverpool ballet student 4s od. An American ballet school cabled 'Can we help?' and local people did all they could.

By 10 June, Moreton and the Musical Director, Guy Warrack, could write to the papers expressing their gratitude to organisations and individuals who offered help 'in ways too numerous to mention … We should like to add that if it had not been for these offers of help, and, not least, for the inspiration we have drawn from the spirit informing them, it would have been almost impossible to overcome our difficulties and to mount, as we did, a full ballet programme last night'.[9] Not surprisingly, the fire had given the Theatre Ballet its most extensive press coverage to date.

Miraculously the company was ready for Hull the following week, though, to add insult to injury, a rail strike threatened to prevent them from getting there, and they had to make the journey by coach. They noted with relief on arrival that the theatre was next door to the fire station. Not all the productions were yet back to full strength. Barbara Fewster remembers giving her only performance as von Rothbart in *Le Lac des Cygnes*; wearing tights on her arms to simulate wings, and 'frillies' on her head she flapped away in silhouette on the backcloth.[10] Make-up was still a problem, but a small amount was somehow obtained and shared around among the dancers.

It was a tribute to the company spirit and organisation that a disaster on this scale could be turned into a triumphant resurrection, and to the dancers and the staff that it could be carried through with such indomitable spirit and no dampening of enthusiasm. The tour continued as though nothing had happened and by the time the company left for Ireland on 10 July *Les Sylphides*, *Le Lac des Cygnes*, *Les Rendezvous*, *Façade*, *Selina*, and *Jota Toledana* were back in the repertory.

Amid all the upheaval, Cranko had been rehearsing his first major original work for the company, *Sea Change*, to be premièred in Dublin on 18 July. The theme was simple. Fishermen bid farewell to their wives and families and set out to sea. There is a storm, and the women wait anxiously on the quay. The boat returns, but one fisherman, a young married man, has been lost, and his widow is left inconsolable. The idea had come to Cranko while he was on holiday in Cassis, where he had been fascinated by the fishermen working on their nets. For the music he turned to Sibelius, eventually choosing *En Saga*. From his days in South Africa he had been an admirer of John Piper, and de Valois introduced them – the beginning of a distinguished partnership. Piper's impressionistic set was highly successful, using the minimum of symbols to express the working environment of the fishing community.

Lighting in those days was usually left to the stage manager (though the company had an exceptionally gifted and sensitive one, Jess Titcombe, who had worked with the Ballets Jooss), but for *Sea Change* de Valois asked Tyrone Guthrie, the distinguished theatre director, to work out the lighting plot and it contributed much to the brooding, sea-like quality of the work. Especially effective was the night scene, with the waiting women illuminated by the slowly turning beam of a lighthouse.

Cranko's choreography had all his hallmarks, save one. His innate musicality could not overcome the selection of an essentially epic score for such an emotive and realistic theme. The choreography had its origin in everyday movements — Cranko had acutely observed the Cassis fishermen — and the lament was based upon sea shanty steps. The work made greater demands than any so far upon his use of group movement. Perhaps he had not yet found a way to integrate natural features with the stylized classical ballet which formed his basic vocabulary, but it was a sincere and often deeply moving work that held its place in the repertory. It showed that Cranko's choreographic ability was also infused with theatrical sense, and that he was developing his own personal language. For its first performance at Sadler's Wells in the autumn, he made major revisions taking the girls off point, working out more varied group sequences and cutting out the role of the Pastor.

The dancers rewarded Cranko with committed performances. Poole was the Skipper with Shore as an Old Woman and Blair as her Son. O'Reilly scored a great personal success as the young Wife, developing from a joyous young bride to anxious wife and finally from 'distraught impassioned agony to hopeless sorrow'.[11]

Cranko is remembered by all who worked with him for his boundless vitality and enthusiasm for anything and everything that caught his attention. He was at the mercy of his moods, up one minute and down the next, but 'his energy was sunshine, brilliant sunshine. Somehow when he was in a really excited mood, or had found something new he was like a child with a new toy, and couldn't get on fast enough with it'.[12] He had his own friends within the company, mainly other South Africans, on whom he would try out his choreography, but he had a particular rapport with van Praagh, whose encouragement and influence upon his development at this time cannot be overestimated. Already he was developing a method of working that he would take through his life, notably a close involvement with his casts, sharing with them as well as his collaborators, the thrill of creation, and firing them with his own enthusiasm. He could make the most mundane events exciting, and not for a moment was his lively mind idle. He was greedy for experience — art exhibitions, concerts, theatre — and avid for work. He would gather his cast around him at his home, where a great stock pot stood permanently on the stove, and discuss the new work, their part in it and what he thought about it. From this, as well as from their performances, he learnt what the dancers had to contribute and what qualities he could use and develop. He made increasing demands upon them, pushing them to undertake feats they would have thought beyond them in his search for his own expression. He knew how fortunate he was in having a company that, although individuals, also understood teamwork and gave their utmost to each choreographer.

By this time it was clear to de Valois that Cranko was the most talented of the young choreographers, and she decided to concentrate upon him. He had an obvious choreographic ability, an exceptional and catholic response to music ('and consequently he was sometimes pretty reckless as to what use he put it to'[13]), courage to try and to fail, a true theatre sense and an eye for design. De Valois offered practical advice about style and staging – not that he always took it, although he usually had to admit later that she was right.

Performances at the Wells were still limited to one a week, but while the Sadler's Wells Ballet was conquering New York in the autumn of 1949 they were increased to two. Three new works were to be added during the coming season. Richard Buckle observed that the repertory was a judicious compromise between what the public wanted and what the management wanted them to have. 'Let them never forget that Lilian Baylis did not give the public what she knew it wanted, but what she hoped it would have the good sense to see it had been wanting all the time'.[14] It was Buckle who first brought Anton Dolin to see the company in October 1949 and Dolin was so delighted that he returned several times and recorded his impressions in *Ballet*. Ever practical, he also offered to give *pas de deux* coaching, and there was a noticeable improvement in partnering among the boys.

Although Dolin did not find all of the repertory well performed (especially *Carnaval*), he was impressed by the overall standard and the individual dancers. He was struck by the good, strong bearing of the male dancers and the clean lines of the girls. 'What a splendid young company they are! Beautifully disciplined, good to look at, and they know how to dance'.[15] He praised Poole as Pierrot and his stage manners in *Le Lac des Cygnes*. He admired Fifield, while admitting that she had much to learn, and Lane's brilliance and sense of style. Most of all it was the young male dancers who impressed him, especially Blair, for whom he prophesied a great future as a 'true *premier danseur noble*' and Trecu who reminded him of Volinine 'the same ease, *ballon* and quiet, masculine charm'.[16] He also noted the noble looks and charming stage manners of a young ex-Jooss dancer, Peter Wright. For some of the ballets he sat with de Valois 'her enthusiasm . . . as fresh and spontaneous as that of the large audience. How proud – and rightly so – she must feel!'[17]

With the Covent Garden company away, the Theatre Ballet attracted more attention than usual, and some of the Covent Garden regulars even found their way to Rosebery Avenue for the first time. The Covent Garden company had by now settled into their new home and if they had grown established and successful, and some felt that complacency was beginning to creep in, they still maintained the highest standards which other English companies could only hope to emulate at that time. For many, however, the Theatre Ballet represented the true popular theatre, enjoyed by *aficionado* and casual balletgoer alike. Not that there was not plenty of competition around – 'Ballet in a theatre, in a cinema, in a skating-rink. Ballet in Islington and Earl's Court; ballet in Hammersmith and Kilburn. Young ballet, old ballet, black ballet, French ballet, bad ballet, sad ballet. Whatever it is, wherever it is, the public laps it up. Only the critic who has to cover ever larger tracts of London gets tired of finding the same conventions at the end of every journey'.[18] Against such competition the Theatre Ballet's qualities were rated highly.

Cranko followed *Sea Change*, his largest work to date, with a return to the small-scale. *Beauty and the Beast* was set to Ravel's *Mother Goose* suite, with designs by Margaret Kaye. Although an extended *pas de deux*, this was a complete ballet, and his most successful to date. In it came together his means of expression, his theme, his music and his intention, and he balanced the stylization of classical ballet and realistic movement as he had not been able to do in *Sea Change*. The ballet was particularly praised for its flowing lyricism and the creation of atmosphere. The simple well-known story was carried entirely by the dance and, though a fairy-story, was adult in its treatment of loneliness, revulsion, compassion and love. The occasional over-realistic gesture could still mar the gentle atmosphere, but *Dance and Dancers* noted that 'one feels that for the first time he has really created the ballet he set out to'.[19] As Beauty, Cranko gave Miller her best role, infusing her cool but expressive lyricism with a delicate romanticism, as well as, John Percival recalled, giving her all the things she couldn't do – like sustained balances.[20] Poole was a heartrending, sympathetic Beast.

Casse-Noisette was revived for Christmas, using the 1937 Mstislav Doboujinsky designs. Here could be seen the results of Dolin's coaching of Blair, whose partnering now displayed something of Dolin's own self-effacing consideration. Markova too had been brought in to coach dancers as the Sugar Plum Fairy, although none could hope to attain her purity of style and brilliance in the role.

The New Year saw another work cashing in on the current craze for Spanish dancing, Angelo Andes' *El Destino* to music by Manuel Lazareno and designs by Hugh Stevenson. There was a slight theme, of a Sevillian boy who is lured away by a fortune-teller from a local girl towards one of Aragon, but this was no more than an excuse for dances contrasting the styles of the two provinces. Audiences at the time could be guaranteed to applaud anything vaguely Spanish, whether authentic or not, and the most Spanish things about *El Destino* were its costumes and music, the choreography never getting beyond a display of the stylistic externals.

(*Opposite*) Patricia Miller as Beauty and David Poole as The Beast in *Beauty and the Beast*.

Chapter IV

By 1949 the Sadler's Wells Governors had exhausted their reserves in building up the opera company, the ballet company and establishing the school at Colet Gardens. Bound by their charter to present performances at 'popular prices' for the working population they were unable to raise seat prices to realistic levels. Few performances and a high proportion of new works made the Theatre Ballet an uneconomic company. The Arts Council grant had risen from £10,000 in 1945–6 to £40,000 for the present season, but over the same period Covent Garden's had increased from £25,000 to £145,000, and that with the relatively profitable Sadler's Wells Ballet at their disposal, so generously handed over by the Wells Governors. It was a good thing that they could not see into the future and the sums that would be brought back as that company embarked upon its lucrative American tours. The four years of the original 'loan' of the Sadler's Wells Ballet had expired on the last day of 1949, but it was obvious that there was no possibility of it reverting back to the Wells and provision had already been made for the extension of the lease.

On 2 February 1950, *The Times* published a leader on the state of opera and ballet at the two theatres, calling for a reconsideration of subsidies to compensate the Wells for all it had given to the Garden, and to ensure the proper future grounding for dancers and audiences at the Wells. Covent Garden, the leader admitted, had to operate on a proper scale befitting a national opera house, but it must not make the error of mistaking opulence, especially in opera, for art.

This was followed by a letter from Sir George Dyson setting out the Wells' position. At the time of the hand-over of the Sadler's Wells Ballet the Governors of the Wells received about £15,000 a year from profits

44

on the ballet. As both Covent Garden and Sadler's Wells were appointed by CEMA (the forerunner of the Arts Council) it had been assumed that funds would be properly apportioned to take into account the serious financial loss of the company to the Wells, but after four years this was obviously not to be, and the Governors had now lost their entire reserves, amounting to £75,000. 'The whole ballet structure', continued Sir George, 'should be examined and integrated, so that it may be regarded as a combined national endeavour, controlling its own income, whether from the public or the State, and shouldering its own responsibilities, both those of public performance and those of education and training'. And Sadler's Wells should receive special recompense for money 'it has so generously contributed, money which originally came in great measure from private or charitable sources'.

It was a revelation to the public that the close connection they had assumed between the two ballet companies did not, in fact, exist. Admittedly Covent Garden did hand over a sum to help support the school, but in 1949 that sum was considerably less than that spent upon the notorious Peter Brook-Salvador Dalí production of Richard Strauss's opera *Salome*. The battle was already being seen as the popular ballet at Sadler's Wells versus the elite at Covent Garden, and even more it was felt, then as now, that ballet at both Covent Garden and Sadler's Wells was being sacrificed to the opera. The Governors of Sadler's Wells might have been justified in feeling a little sour as they had watched large sums being poured into the Opera House to support what was, at this stage, a very uneven opera company, while they poured in their own unseen subsidy in the form of dancers and the school. Despite their charter, the Governors had no option but to raise the seat prices a little. From May 1950 the top price was raised from 9s 0d to 10s 6d, the gallery from 1s 0d to 1s 6d and other parts of the house were increased by 1s 0d. The pit remained at 3s 6d and 4s 6d.

The whole problem was overshadowed, however, by the gala performance held at Sadler's Wells on 15 May to celebrate the twenty-first anniversary of the first ballet given by the embryo Sadler's Wells Ballet in December 1928, *Les Petits Riens*; the celebrations had had to be postponed from the previous autumn because of the Covent Garden company's absence in New York. The publicity surrounding the event concentrated on de Valois, the phenomenon she had created and the importance of ensuring its continuity when she would no longer be there.

The Theatre Ballet appeared in the small roles and as Ghosts in a mixed cast of *The Haunted Ballroom*, with Helpmann as the Master of Treginnis and Fonteyn as the Young Treginnis. Princess Margaret presented de Valois with a silver salver. 'I have never in my life enjoyed an evening as I have tonight', she said in reply. 'English ballet has won through on its discipline, its comradeship, and putting its art before itself. I do assure you this is no one-man show. This is my chance to thank the artists from my heart for allowing me to help them to get there'.

Despite the financial crisis at the Wells, the new works continued. 28 March brought Michael Somes' choreographic debut – *Summer Interlude*, a charming unpretentious work set to Respighi's *Ancient Airs and Dances*, with designs by Sophie Fedorovitch. A village boy and girl are picnicking on a Mediterranean beach. They become involved with a party of rich bathers and one of the girls flirts with the village boy to the despair of his girl friend. The bathers lend her a swimsuit, and transformed, she attracts one of the rich boys. She departs with him leaving the village boy alone. It was an astonishingly assured first work. It was musical, the simple theme was sensitively expressed in pure dance terms, the dancing flowed easily from the action, and the natural movements of the villagers and the more sophisticated movements of the bathers were well contrasted. 'His *pas de deux* were lyrical, his *soli* clear and exciting, his *ensembles* rather too busy and distracting. The company had served him well for they dance with a freshness, vigour and gaiety that was enchanting ... it would be a good ballet from the hands of an experienced master'.[1]

Somes showed particular insight into the qualities of his cast; Miller was a charming village girl and Trecu's particular *gaminerie* was effectively used as the boy. Unexpectedly, he cast Fifield as the rich bather, and she rewarded him with a portrait of a perfectly heartless and sophisticated vamp. Although the music was perhaps a little archaic for a contemporary theme, and the designs were not Fedorovitch at her best, the critics were full of praise and anxious for the next work to see how far Somes' choreographic talent extended. They are still waiting.

The company were fortunate in being part of an established organisation, with a home base and a subsidy, which meant that they were not completely dependent upon box office success for their survival. Others were not so fortunate and one of the most interesting of the young English ballet companies, Metropolitan Ballet, had recently been forced to close. It had numbered among its dancers Celia Franca, Erik Bruhn and a ravishing eighteen-year-old dancer of Lithuanian extraction, Svetlana Beriosova. Her father was the well-known former dancer and ballet master Nicholas Beriosoff, and her dance pedigree was impeccable. After her father her teachers had included Olga Preobrajenska, the former Diaghilev dancers Anatole Vilzak and Ludmilla Schollar, and Volkova. At fourteen she had joined the Ottawa Ballet, then the Grand Ballet de Monte Carlo and, at sixteen, Metropolitan Ballet. On 20 May, the last performance of the 1949–50 season, she joined the Sadler's Wells Theatre Ballet, dancing Odette. Her serene elegance, and amplitude of style had yet to reach its glorious maturity, and she had not yet developed the gracious warmth that was to lay adoring audiences at her feet, but it was clear that here was a ballerina in the making. There were the perhaps inevitable criticisms levelled at the management for bringing in a 'foreign' dancer, but many welcomed it as an insurance against insularity, and Beriosova settled down to become an integral part of the Sadler's Wells Ballet organisation. Ironically, her restrained elegance and beautiful line were to become perhaps the most perfect example of what the company style could be.

The summer tour took the Theatre Ballet to towns where they were now a welcome annual event. With the abandonment of the mid-season tours with two pianos the smaller towns were dropped, and others were not willing to find the relatively high guarantee asked by the company if they could not be certain of full houses. There was, however, a great deal of local enthusiasm and the company was building up its own following in their regular dates. In Peterborough the *Advertiser* added a plea for programme notes – 'we are a growing band of ballet lovers in this district, but our knowledge ought not to be over-rated'.[2]

Earlier in 1950, George Balanchine had mounted *Ballet Imperial* for the Covent Garden company. An exchange was now arranged by which he would mount a work on the Theatre Ballet and Cranko would create one for New York City Ballet. *Trumpet Concerto*, Balanchine's only creation for an English company, was a military exercise set to Haydn's Trumpet Concerto and with designs in drum majorette style by Vivienne Kernot. It was premièred in Manchester on 14 September, where the company were on tour with the Sadler's Wells Opera.

Five days later, almost the whole of New York City Ballet, which had been performing at Covent Garden, was in the audience at Sadler's Wells to see the first London performance. It was a work that would have suited their physiques better than those of the Theatre Ballet dancers, being full of marching on pointe, saluting, 'strutting about with that unnatural little swing of the arms always used by principal boys in a defiant mood'[3] and the general feeling was that Balanchine had done it all better before. The *corps de ballet* did their best to inject gaiety into the proceedings with their imitation of a chorus line, but the hard brilliance of the leading role was not for Beriosova. Miller later displayed a pertness which suited it better, but on the whole the ballet was a disappointment.

From the beginning of the 1950–51 season John Cranko was appointed Resident Choreographer, which would allow him to produce a series of works and to experiment. He was entering upon one of his most fertile and creative periods, when he seemed almost drunk with choreography, and the problem was to curb his enthusiasm, and get him to simplify rather than embellish his work. It was here that de Valois and van Praagh were of particular help to him.

It was perhaps fortunate that Cranko's invention was flowing so easily, for the first of his new works that season was composed almost at the last minute. It had been hoped to mount his creation for New York City Ballet, *The Witch*, but Ravel's brother had objected to the use of the Piano Concerto outside the concert hall, and the ballet had to be abandoned after only a few performances. Undaunted, Cranko set about creating an entirely new ballet for the Theatre Ballet, treating three aspects of love – innocence, love triumphant and the sadness after – in an eighteenth-century setting. He had wanted to use Scarlatti, but the music could not be orchestrated in time, so he settled on Mozart's Divertimento No. 2. Hugh Stevenson designed the costumes, and for the first performances they resurrected the unused set for *Adieu*, which had never been seen in London, Stevenson's new set being seen later.

Pastorale was premièred on 19 December. The theme was not unduly stressed, the choreography was witty, gay and stylish, and the focus was entirely upon the dancing. Miller and Trecu as Phillida and Corydon were perfectly matched in a warm, loving *pas de deux* and Beriosova as Lamilia had an interesting *pas de trois* with Poole and Blair, full of lifts suggesting 'flying' time. Cranko had been asked to feature Fifield, and he created for her a frothy, heedless character – the too demurely innocent Diaphenia.

In the New Year, De Valois revived her ballet *The Prospect Before Us*, which had not been seen since the Sadler's Wells Ballet's last Sadler's Wells season in 1945. Her hilarious account of the rivalry between two eighteenth-century theatre managers, immortalized in Rowlandson's satires of the same name, had lost none of its power to amuse. As the Theatre Ballet was smaller than the Sadler's Wells Ballet of 1945, some

John Cranko rehearsing Pauline Harrop with Maryon Lane.

Photograph by Roger Wood.

changes in numbers were inevitable, and de Valois took the opportunity to make some slight alterations and prune some ten minutes from the ballet as well.

While being in no sense a one-man work, the ballet rose or fell on the character of Mr O'Reilly, hallowed in the memories of all as one of Robert Helpmann's most brilliant creations. Helpmann came back to the Wells to dance the first three performances, to the delight of the public and critics alike, who took them as his final performances with the Sadler's Wells organisation. 'To say that he is superb, stupendous, riotously and excruciatingly funny is to sound almost grudging of praise',[4] extolled P. W. Manchester, and Arnold Haskell reflected how 'Helpmann's clowning must have rejoiced the spirit of Grimaldi'.[5] The company as a whole did not, however, go unnoticed, and if they had yet to realise the full Rowlandson spirit, de Valois had carefully coached them in their placing and timing – 'What a joy it is to see a company rising to the exacting demands of our major English choreographer'.[6] The recreation of stage life was as potent as ever, and Fifield was a charming Mlle. Theodore and Miller delightful as Cupid. Beriosova, cast as the Street Dancer, was unexpectedly good, if lacking in vulgarity. At the end of the performance de Valois took her curtain call to great acclaim, for this was her first public appearance since the announcement of her DBE in the New Year's Honours List.

The question of what would happen to the ballet when Helpmann was not there was answered when Holden took over as O'Reilly and infused the part with his own broad Cockney humour. A much less flamboyant performance, it nonetheless built up gradually and inevitably to the drunk dance with good feeling for the character and its place in the overall scheme of the ballet.

1951 had been designated Festival of Britain, that government insti-gated shindig designed to show the world that Britain had made it, and to inspire the belief in the British people themselves that the Age of Austerity was over, and a new era was in sight. If all things British was to be the aim of the Festival then Cranko's next work could not have been more apt. 1950 had seen expiry of copyright on the music of Arthur Sullivan, and devotees were waiting with trepidation to see what use would be made of his scores. It was Charles Mackerras, then a junior conductor with the Sadler's Wells Opera, who suggested to van Praagh the possibility of a Sullivan ballet, although according to Cyril Beau-mont[7] Cranko had the same idea at about the same time. Mackerras dissuaded him from using the lesser-known compositions, insisting that the strongest and best music would be found in the Savoy Operas.

Once that had been decided, Cranko naturally turned for his scenario to W. S. Gilbert. In the *Bab Ballads* he found the story of Pineapple Poll, the middle-aged bumboat woman and her unrequited love for the handsome Captain Belaye of HMS *Hot Cross Bun*; disguised as a sailor she enlisted among his crew, only to find that the Captain was already married, and the whole crew was made up of other equally love-lorn Portsmouth maidens. With a few alterations, this became the scenario for *Pineapple Poll*. Poll became a young woman and acquired her own devoted admirer, Jasper, and the Captain's wife became his fiancée Blanche, with a chaperone-aunt, Mrs Dimple. John Piper suggested Osbert Lancaster as designer; he had never worked for the theatre before, but his ability to capture the essence of any architectural period or place with wit and style was well known from his books and cartoons.

With these ingredients the ballet had to be a comedy, and the flavour inescapably English. There is nothing more difficult to create than comedy, and during rehearsals Cranko was in despair, convinced that audiences would not find it in the least funny. There was also the anxiety over how audiences would react to the use of the music of the Savoy Operas, which many regarded as sacrosanct.

Cranko need not have worried. From the moment that the curtain rose on 13 March, revealing Lancaster's delicious evocation of Portsmouth, the 'theatre suddenly seems filled with the invigorating whiff of sea air'[8], and as the sailors with their sweethearts, wives 'and others' swept onto the stage it was obvious that the company had a hit at its feet. A synopsis was unnecessary, the plot was clear, the characterisation presented through the movement, the action and choreography beautifully paced and timed. The choreography was based on a breezy, open style, full of turns and sways taken from the sailor's hornpipe and the inventiveness flowed effortlessly throughout. Especially memorable were Belaye's hornpipe, Poll's love-sick solo, the yearning of her high arabesques belied by the drooping head and the sudden drop of the hand, and the 'chatter' *pas de trois* for Belaye, Blanche and Mrs Dimple. Here was all the wit, style and robust Englishness of Gilbert and Sullivan translated into dance. Gilbertian also was the leavening of pathos and sentiment in the character of Jasper, especially moving in his *pas de deux* with Poll's dress after he thinks she has drowned herself. The gaiety was infectious and irresistible from the opening bars to the final tableau when Mrs Dimple is transformed into Britannia – an episode suggested by Lancaster.

(*Above*) David Blair as Captain Belaye in *Pineapple Poll*.

Photograph by Roger Wood.

'After all the mimsey muslin milliner's daintiness that still occludes so much ballet, this is like a fresh breeze from the briny',[9] wrote Philip Hope-Wallace, while Arnold Haskell reflected, 'The *ballet bouffe*, as Fokine so often told me, is the most difficult of all works to handle. It needs controlled craziness, a sense of character, a sense of style. All these Cranko possessed and he added to them a rare inventiveness that arose out of the situation and was not superimposed for its own sake'.[10] It was also that rarity, a true marriage of choreography, music and design.

Cranko used a *corps de ballet* of six couples, larger than any he had handled before outside the opera ballets. It was, however, a *corps de ballet* of individual characterizations that always threatened to get out of hand, but never quite did so. There is nothing like taking part in a

---

(*Opposite*) Elaine Fifield in the title role of *Pineapple Poll*.

Photograph by Denis de Marney. From the collections of the Theatre Museum. Reproduced by courtesy of the Board of Trustees of the Victoria and Albert Museum.

smash hit, and it must have been extra rewarding for a company that had lavished the same gaiety and enthusiasm upon the duds in its repertory as upon its successes and they entered into 'the spirit of (*Poll*) so well that its liveliness makes the slickest musical appear like a funeral dirge'.[11]

For his leading dancers, Cranko created the roles of a lifetime. Poll, like Swanilda, suits the pure classical dancer as well as the natural soubrette, and Fifield was perfect. Technically sure and strong, she performed the choreography as written, with no self-conscious interpretation, by turns gay, love-lorn, comic and touching, dancing the love-sick solos with a seriousness that made them affectionately comic. Many saw it as a major step in her development – 'The bud had begun to flower',[12] wrote Cyril Beaumont. As Jasper, Poole had a rich character to portray, winning sympathy for the downtrodden little man, especially in his dance with Poll's dress, and the subtle touch at the end as he donned the Captain's cast-off coat, and took from it the natural authority and appeal inbuilt into any uniform. Stella Claire was a vacuously silly Blanche, and O'Reilly was Mrs Dimple, her garrulousness and agitation expressed in fast pattering little steps, her never-still hands and the nodding head. Above all there was the dashing figure of Blair as Captain Belaye, mixing bored conceit with a natural breeziness and vigour, yet retaining an inborn breeding and authority that made his constant upstaging by his bride-to-be and her aunt all the funnier. His dancing of the hornpipe in the first scene remains a key image in people's memories of Blair, and it is a role in which he has never been surpassed.

Poll was to be that most valuable of all ballets, one that almost defies a bad performance. Over the years it may have been under-rehearsed or overplayed, but it is performance-proof and can stand almost any amount of indifferent performance. Even now, nearly forty years later, as soon as the curtain goes up the audience is automatically put into a good humour. Like many of Cranko's ballets it does not require 'interpretation', the humour is in the choreography, and will play itself, which has not stopped dancers from embellishing it. Many have danced the leading roles, but perhaps Doreen Wells has come nearest to Fifield in understanding that in comedy less is more, and understatement is needed if the humour is to make its full effect. Brenda Last's speed, attack and vitality made her the most memorable of the soubrettes in the role. Johaar Mosaval, with his air of bewildered, dog-like devotion, has been the most notable of later Jaspers.[13]

Cranko's third ballet in less than five months was premièred on

David Blair as Harlequin and Patricia Miller as Columbine in *Harlequin in April*.

Photograph by Baron.

8 May 1951. For *Harlequin in April*, he commissioned his first score, from Richard Arnell, providing him with a detailed synopsis and timings. For his designer he again turned to John Piper. One of the major successes of *Harlequin in April* was the way in which 'three of our most fertile brains in their respective spheres' as the press release resoundingly put it, worked together to produce a ballet in which choreography, music and design were perfectly blended in its expression of 'Man's search for love and happiness, and his almost inevitable frustration'.[14] It was Cranko's most ambitious and intensely personal work yet.

The set was a burnt-out proscenium arch with tattered curtains, inspired by the Hanley fire.[15] Pierrot, the human muddler, enters and tries to entertain the audience with a song, but no sound emerges, and he creeps away. From blindfold plant-like forms rises blind Harlequin – human aspiration. Pierrot gives him his multicoloured coat and magic bat, and he realises his full strength. He searches for his ideal mate among the plants, but his chosen one withers away. He pursues a unicorn, traditional guardian of chastity, and it leads him to his ideal love, Columbine. Her guardian unicorn is lulled to sleep, and she and Harlequin dance their awakening love; Pierrot, jealous of the lovers, awakens the unicorn, and it magically multiplies to guard Columbine. They bear her away leaving behind an effigy, for ideal love is without substance. The plants return, and Harlequin sinks back into the earth, leaving behind his magic coat. Pierrot takes it and the magic bat, hoping their power will work for him, but in vain. To aspire to higher things exists even in the most unlikely men.

Cranko prefaced the synopsis with the first ten lines of T S Eliot's *The Waste Land*, although he later assured Clive Barnes that the ballet bore no relation to the poem. His original inspiration was the engravings of Paul Gavarni, whose seedy, mysterious *commedia dell'arte* figures fascinated Cranko, who saw them as 'tremendously rich in images and metaphors',[16] and immediately recognisable symbols to an audience – Harlequin as Man, Columbine as ideal love, and Pierrot as the well-meaning but pathetic blunderer, the eternal butt of Harlequin's humours. There were multiple layers of symbolism and meaning, which many found impossible to disentangle, but the sincerity and depth of feeling compensated for much of the obscurity, and, miraculously, the ballet avoided pretentiousness. It was, first and foremost a ballet. Cranko expressed his ideas in dance, and his choreography was always interesting and often outstanding. Especially praised were the tendril-like movements of the plants and the birth of Harlequin, the romantic *pas de deux* for Harlequin and Columbine, the magical duplications of the unicorns, which showed Cranko's growing mastery of group movement, and the whole conception of Pierrot. The characters of Harlequin and Pierrot, two aspects of human aspiration doomed to failure, were beautifully differentiated.

If all Cranko's previous work could be said to have its roots in the work of other choreographers he had worked with and observed – *Pastorale* was likened to Balanchine, *Pineapple Poll* to Massine – in *Harlequin in April* he spoke with a recognisably individual voice, and came to a new maturity as choreographer. His collaborators served him well. 'Mr Arnell', wrote Arnold Haskell 'has written real ballet music avoiding the all too usual temptation of writing a symphony or of keeping an eye on posterity'.[17] Piper's sombre, disturbing set caught the prevailing mood of uncertainty, and Peter Williams reflected, 'Not since the death of Christian Bérard have I seen designs that so enhanced the choreography and music without dominating either'.[18]

No less successful was Cranko's use of his three leading dancers. Miller's remote coolness was perfect in expressing the unattainability of Columbine, and she had great poignancy as the leading plant in the first scene. Holden had the right mixture of comedy and pathos as Pierrot. Coming hard upon his success as Belaye, Blair as Harlequin revealed a new interpretative force, a brash vigour in the early scene tempered by an awakening sensitivity in his relationship with Columbine. The role had been intended for Trecu, but he was replaced as a punishment for refusing to understudy the role of Jasper in *Pineapple Poll* (he had wanted to understudy Belaye);[19] however he was later a Harlequin of 'fierce, yet bewildered anguish'.[20]

Harlequin in April was an adult ballet which repaid repeated viewings, although it was never a general favourite. It was revived at Covent Garden in 1959, but its intensity was lost on the larger stage, and it has never found a permanent place in the repertory.

Cranko's appointment as Resident Choreographer did not mean that there were no opportunities for others. For Purcell's opera *Dido and Aeneas* on 22 May, the choreographer was Alfred Rodrigues, a soloist with the Covent Garden company, who, like Cranko, had begun his choreographic career in his native South Africa. The opera was produced in the style of a court masque, with the chorus relegated to the orchestra pit and only the solo singers on stage, with the dancers moving around them in stylized steps with elaborate courtly gestures. No one was going to make or break a reputation in the opera ballets, but they were a useful indication of possible talent for the future.

Chapter V

The company had reached a new maturity and, unknowingly, it stood on the brink of a new phase in its development. Sol Hurok, the impresario who had been responsible for the smash-hit tours of the Sadler's Wells Ballet in America, had discovered that his dollar spinner had a younger sister, and he determined to take the Theatre Ballet on its own tour of the States. It was scheduled for autumn 1951 and would last six months, during which they would play all the principal cities of North America and Canada. Not unexpectedly, for one with so much experience of promoting ballet in America, Hurok had very definite ideas of what audiences would want, and, like the American tours of the sister company, the tour was to have far-reaching effects upon the Theatre Ballet's future.

Because of the pressures of the tour, the company was increased from twenty-eight to forty-one dancers, including some former members of the company, and the problem was to imbue them with the company personality and style. They were also joined by Britton, returning from his military service not to Covent Garden, but to the Theatre Ballet, where he replaced Kersley. There were always a number of dancers taken from the Theatre Ballet to Covent Garden who did not fit easily into the repertory, or found too few opportunities for performing and who were glad to return to the Wells.

A three-week season at Sadler's Wells in the autumn of 1951 was based on the works that would be taken to America. It was little enough time since the creation of *Harlequin in April* in May to undertake a new elaborate opera ballet, a summer tour and mount two major revivals, *Casse-Noisette* and the company's first full-length classic, *Coppélia*. It was fortunate that, among the many qualities instilled into dancers by their training in the school and company was the ability to learn quickly (an ability which they still have today).

Coppélia had its first performance on September 4. It had been selected partly because the three-act version was relatively unknown in America, but it was an obvious first full-length classic for the company, relying as it did on *demi-caractère* qualities, but also providing a challenge in the classical *divertissement* of the last act. The production closely followed the Ivanov-Cecchetti version familiar at Covent Garden, but it lacked a strong dramatic framework. Also Loudon Sainthill's designs were drab, insensitive to the spirit of the story – 'As well try to create a mysterious atmosphere in Sainthill's second-act décor as swim the Channel bound hand and foot',[1] wrote Richard Buckle – and did not help to give the visual sparkle the production needed.

The company could field three Swanildas, Fifield, Beriosova and Lane, and three Franz, Blair, Trecu and Britton, with David Poole and Holden as Dr Coppélius. In reserve as Swanilda were Miller and O'Reilly and as Coppélius, David Gill. Hurok was keeping a close eye on the company and was in the audience on the first night. He was full of enthusiasm for Fifield – 'She sets you alight. I have managed all the great ones – Pavlova, Danilova. She is in that class', he told John Barber of the *Daily Express*.[2] Each Swanilda, however, had her supporters. Clive Barnes extolled Beriosova – 'the most delicious Swanilda to be seen in London for years'[3] – for her gaiety and vivacious charm, her naughty but good natured reading of Act II and her tender maturity in the last act. Others warmed to Lane, in her biggest role to date, with her musicality, quiet fun, candid characterization and bright clarity of movement. Franz with his brash, cocky ebullience, suited the Theatre Ballet men, and Blair, Trecu and Britton all gave individual and promising performances, and, as Lionel Bradley observed, the inevitable rivalry would ensure that none ever gave less than his best.[4] As Coppélius, Poole added another remarkable reading to his gallery of characterizations, a fully rounded figure eschewing the comedy in favour of a tragic presentation of a man not far removed from madness. Holden stressed the comedy more, and aimed at pathos rather than tragedy.

The first night also saw the appearance of a new chief conductor – John Lanchbery. He had conducted for Metropolitan Ballet, and later for BBC television, where he met van Praagh, who suggested that he should join the Theatre Ballet. He was to be an invaluable part of the organization until he moved to Covent Garden in 1959.

On 11 September, 'Mayfair dined early . . . and drove out to Islington.

Why? To see the new suit of clothes which their favourite photographer Cecil Beaton had provided for Sadler's Wells Theatre Ballet's new production of two scenes from the old classic *Casse-Noisette*.[5] Ashton had revived and augmented the Kingdom of Snow and the Kingdom of Sweets to form a *divertissement* in homage to the classical school of Petipa and Ivanov. For Beriosova as the Snow Queen he created a *pas de deux* exploiting her magnificent extension and lyrical line and she gave a performance of true Russian style and grandeur. He rearranged the Kingdom of Sweets, notably giving Lane an excellent solo as a leading Crystallized Flower in the *Valse des Fleurs*. Fifield and Blair danced the Sugar Plum Fairy and her Prince; she now only needed the final touch of authority to bring her to true ballerinadom.

Beaton's designs were not particularly well received. The snow scene was entirely in black and white, the backcloth a design of sketchy trees overloaded with snow. The predominant colours for the Kingdom of Sweets were Chartreuse green (the dancers had a shorter and much less pleasant term for the colour) and claret. Individual costumes were charming but the overall impression was one of Edwardian over-indulgence which reminded Peter Williams of a Rockingham fruit dish,[6] and Richard Buckle described the backcloth as 'an elementary essay in Hairdresser's Rococo'.[7]

Other productions were enlarged for America. HMS *Hot Cross Bun* acquired two extra crew, with sweethearts in tow. The *corps de ballet* in Act II of *Le Lac des Cygnes* was increased from eight to twelve Swans, and four to six Huntsmen, while the Prince's entourage gained a First Huntsman, who danced the *pas de trois* with two Swan Princesses.

Everyone was wondering how the company would fare in America in the wake of the sensation created by the Sadler's Wells Ballet on their 1950–51 coast-to-coast tour. London admirers understood that the Theatre Ballet stood for very different qualities from the first company, and wondered if individuality, youthful exuberance and promise would be enough. Against the first company's reputation in the classics they had to offer mainly modern works, a part of the Sadler's Wells Ballet repertory that had never been particularly admired in America, and

Svetlana Beriosova as Swanilda and David Blair as Franz in *Coppélia*.

three classical ballets, in two of which they were relatively inexperienced. The proposed schedule was gruelling, and it was feared that it might kill the company's vitality and enthusiasm. It was a great responsibility for a company whose average age was only nineteen. Indeed a chaperone was felt to be desirable, and Mrs Doris Thellusson, former School Secretary of the Sadler's Wells Ballet School, was taken on to look after their welfare and social engagements.

From the earliest discussions, de Valois insisted that the publicity must make clear that the Theatre Ballet did not stand for the same policy as the Sadler's Wells Ballet. The dancers should be presented as young, promising artists, not as finished, experienced performers. Preferably they should only play the smaller theatres in America, and places where the first company had not been seen. This advice was not taken, and the Theatre Ballet's final itinerary included many cities already visited by the Sadler's Wells Ballet. Hurok wanted to strengthen the upper ranks by taking Nerina or Violetta Elvin, but de Valois would not consent to the balance of the company being so upset.

Though Hurok's admiration for the company was quite genuine, it is also true that his first wild enthusiasm became more tempered as he realised the impracticality of touring the Sadler's Wells Theatre Ballet as a viable proposition in the USA as it was. Though remaining enthusiastic, he obviously got cold feet about the repertory, and it was he who suggested enlarging the company and mounting *Coppélia* and *Casse-Noisette*, both of which he knew would find favour in America. Thus the character of the company was to be irrevocably altered. Probably what Hurok envisaged was two equal companies, so that he could, every year, present a Sadler's Wells company in America.

The final repertory was *Coppélia*, *Casse-Noisette* and *Le Lac des Cygnes* Act II for the classics, *Khadra*, *Pineapple Poll*, *Beauty and the Beast*, *Harlequin in April*, *Pastorale* and *Assembly Ball*, representing ballets created for the company, and *The Haunted Ballroom*, *The Prospect Before Us*, *Façade*, and *Les Rendezvous* the repertory inherited from the senior company. In addition they took *Capriol Suite*, and the *divertissements Tritsch-Tratsch*, the *Giselle* peasant *pas de deux* and *Jota Toledana*.

Even Hurok admitted, 'It is a moot question just what the public and the press of America expected from the Sadler's Wells Theatre Ballet'.[8] His publicity machine had been at work for a year, emphasizing the differences and similar roots of the companies, but it was a subtle distinction, even for many English people, and the only thing that anyone in America was likely to notice were the magic words 'Sadler's

Wells'. Even in Hurok's own publicity 'Sadler's Wells' figured much larger than 'Theatre Ballet' and local managers sometimes left out the word 'Theatre'. Hurok had done his original work too well and in the American mind 'Sadler's Wells' was synonymous with spectacular productions, Fonteyn and Shearer. There were also linguistic differences between England and America, and the management was advised to stop referring to the company as 'junior', as in America this meant a dancing school ensemble giving student performances.

The dancers had their own worries. Packing for a tour was always a problem. They were supposed to look their best at all times, and have the correct clothes for any social occasion – difficult enough when clothing had only just come off coupons. For this tour, however, they would need wardrobes to take them from the beginning of winter in the North American states, to the mildness of California and Florida.

Like the Sadler's Wells Ballet before them, the Theatre Ballet girls were kitted out by the cream of British manufacturers, anxious to use the company as a shop window for British goods. Each girl was given thirty pairs of nylons, three pairs of shoes, two dresses, a scarf, a mackintosh made of 'Zyl-con-ette' (with a special proofing that stood up to dry cleaning), and a musical umbrella that, when opened, played 'I'm Gonna Wash That Man Right Out Of My Hair'. The boys got only a pair of shoes apiece.

Meanwhile, the stage staff checked out 30 tons of scenery, 4,000 pairs of ballet shoes, 500 costumes, 15 crates of props, 10 baskets of make up and 600 lbs of music.

De Valois sailed with the company on 25 September 1951 from Liverpool on the *Empress of France*. It was a miserable journey. The weather was appalling, and many dancers were incapacitated and kept to their cabins – a sad beginning to what was for many their first trip out of England. On the morning of 1 October, they arrived in the St Lawrence River, and docked in Quebec. They were met by Hurok, who booked them into the best hotels in the city. One of the most welcome features of the tour were the luxury hotels in which the dancers stayed, a happy contrast to digs in England.

There was standing room only in Quebec for the opening performance of *Coppélia* on 5 October, but the audience reaction was very cool, and at subsequent performances even *Pineapple Poll* was received in stony silence. Although Fifield was acclaimed by the press, the dancers were very disconcerted and only slightly comforted on hearing that Quebec audiences were notoriously unemotional, and even Pavlova had been indifferently received there. Things began to improve in Ottawa. They were bowled over by the enthusiasm and kindness of people 'even before seeing the company perform, and more at the fall of the curtain!'[9] Montreal was even better. 'Apparently we are the best thing Montreal has ever seen', wrote Britton to his parents. 'We've had wonderful houses and they make a fuss of us!'[10] It was inevitable, after the years of rationing, that the quantity of good food available should have its effect upon restriction-starved stomachs, and there was an outbreak of gastric trouble in the company. Celia Franca was waiting to greet them in Toronto, where she was trying to set up a ballet company. Toronto audiences and the press were equally welcoming and most enthusiastic. De Valois had by now returned to England, leaving the running of the tour in the hands of van Praagh.

Decked out in newly acquired check shirts and jeans, the company entered the USA on 21 October, and headed for Buffalo. They were to be the first British ballet company many towns had seen, and there was, by accident or design, a great playing down of the words 'Theatre Ballet' in local publicity. However much audiences enjoyed the company, there was bound to be disappointment and resentment among the huge audiences many of whom had been unable to get tickets for the Sadler's Wells Ballet tour, or in towns which the first company had not visited, and who believed they had booked for them. Those who most enjoyed the Theatre Ballet were either totally ignorant about ballet, or knowledgeable enough to know the differences between the companies; those who knew only enough to equate Sadler's Wells with *The Sleeping Beauty*, Fonteyn or Shearer, were bound to be disappointed, and they felt that the company was somehow pulling a fast one.

Working conditions were very different for the company in America. They had all had to join the American performing union for the duration of the tour, and abide by its rules. These allowed for a much shorter working day than they had been used to, and led to their discovery of a wonderful new experience called 'overtime' which was unheard of in British ballet at this time. It is only fair to record that no dancers applied for overtime when they returned to England.

The company, with its American orchestra, headed across the northern United States aboard the 13-car 'Ballet Special' train on a series of one-night stands. Allowing for one free day a week, the routine became performance, overnight train, class, rehearsal, a meal grabbed in a drug store, performance and onto the train again. Partly because of the number of one-night stands, the tour is not remembered for entertaining, as the Covent Garden company's had been, although there is a lingering memory of slightly formal English Speaking Union receptions, at which the main fare seems to have been baked beans and scrambled eggs. However there were parties whenever the company was in one place for any length of time. Whether hostesses were sure who they were entertaining was a different matter, and one lady arrived at the stage door demanding to see 'Miss Sally Wells' to discuss arrangements. In Detroit the company threw their own coca-cola and hot dogs party to celebrate Fifield's twenty-first birthday.

Fifield was the great success of the tour so far with rave notices, and the press particularly enjoyed seeing her switch from the cool purity of the Sugar Plum Fairy to the sparkling comedy of Pineapple Poll. She danced, said a Denver paper 'with all the freshness of a May posy'. 'The balletomane's dream of a sparkling ballerina', raved Oregon. 'The most graceful elegant creature you will ever see this side of dreaming', extolled Salt Lake City.[11] Beriosova and Blair were also praised and fast improving was Donald Britton. As had been foreseen, audiences preferred the classics, and the critics raved about all the Swanildas. *The Stage* received a batch of enthusiastic press cuttings, which suggested that the company was far from an anti-climax, and that the male dancers were better than those from the Covent Garden company. Audiences were impressed by the quality, team spirit and vitality of all the dancers, and although the company realised that they were often performing to audiences who did not see much ballet, it was a gratifying reaction. Many small American towns were used to touring companies with minimum scenery and costumes, so the high quality of the Theatre Ballet's designs were much appreciated.

By East Lansing winter was beginning to set in; by Minneapolis the temperature was not far above zero and snow was falling in Milwaukee. This did not deter Chicago balletomanes making the journey to Milwaukee, even when they had to abandon their cars in the snowdrifts and continue by train. However, 'the British charmers were able to project across the vast (Pabst Theatre) Auditorium and before the end of *Coppélia* the fans were anything but sorry they had come'.[12]

There were many such huge auditoria on the tour and it became a luxury to play in a proper theatre. Towns were now beginning to look alike --

so much so that I cannot even remember the date to put at the head of this letter, one doesn't live from week to week any more, but almost from hour to hour with hardly ever a stop to break up the hours ... so many people, whose generosity has been almost unbelievable ... the reception has been more than anyone's wildest dreams could have expected. The press has raved from the beginning, we never perform before less than 6,000 people per performance, and often it is nearer 10,000. Their reaction is quite spontaneous: they will often applaud right through a variation. There is a marked tendency of appreciation towards the classics (The press are continually complaining they cannot understand *Harlequin in April*.) ... the only thing that worries me, is the continued lack of sleep, the last week I don't think I have had more than four hours sleep a night ...[13]

Salt Lake City was one place that the company was not packed out, but even there audiences improved after the first night and an editorial in the local paper ran: 'All those people who grouse about aid to England can just go sail their boats. If the Sadler's Wells is what they do over there, every cent we spend is well worth it. What a treat!'[14]

In Vancouver the company had its greatest triumph so far, making box-office history by being sold out for the entire week at the highest prices ever charged there. There was a rumour that two women had come to blows at the box office over a single returned ticket, and *Coppélia* had twelve curtains on the opening night. One Madame Valda closed her studio in Calgary, some 800 miles away, to spend a week at the ballet, and many came from even further away. In Portland and Seattle, both notorious for unresponsive audiences, records were broken in auditoria holding over 5,000 people.

The company travelled on to California, opening at the Memorial Opera House, San Francisco, on 3 December. The company had been warned of the severity of the local critics, but even so the bad notices for the opening programme of *Casse-Noisette*, *Harlequin in April* and *Pineapple Poll* came as a severe shock. Things improved slightly when Beriosova danced *Coppélia*, but most ballets were dismissed as not worth commenting on, and there was only grudging praise for one or two of the dancers, notably Trecu. The company hoped the press would improve, but it didn't, so they just gave up buying the papers. However, Alfred Frankenstein, the leading San Francisco critic, did soften and later admitted:

It took no more than two performances for the Theater (sic) Ballet to establish itself as an organisation with a delightful style, personality and atmosphere all its own. One must go back to the Monte Carlo company of the early 1930s to find its equal ... The new Sadler's Wells brings back the litheness, simplicity and artistic innocence that prevail when no one in a ballet company is a split second older than 20 ... [15]

However, from San Francisco the company was bussed out to nearby towns, where the reception reminded them of the loyal Sadler's Wells gallery audience.

The last performance before the Christmas break was on 17 December. Afterwards the company split up for a five day holiday, some electing to remain on the California beaches others taking a trip into Mexico. On the 20 December the British Consul in Los Angeles threw a cocktail party where the company met Douglas Fairbanks and the Ronald Colmans, while Lane drove around Hollywood with Father Christmas. The Governors of Sadler's Wells arranged a Christmas lunch for the company on 25 December, which they could hardly enjoy with the prospect of the opening that night, nor were nerves helped by a slight earth tremor in the afternoon. Press reaction in Los Angeles was good, however, and the dancers had the additional boost of audiences full of movie stars, including Gene Kelly on the opening night.

George Chamberlain, Clerk to the Governors of Sadler's Wells visited the company in Los Angeles, and reported them in good form. 'As a company the Ballet have improved enormously. It is not so much that their dancing has improved but their experience has broadened through giving eight performances a week in auditoriums twice the size of Sadler's Wells'.[16]

By the New Year, half way through the tour, *Variety*, the American stage trade paper, carried a headline 'Unknown Troupe Sock 750G in 12 Weeks', (that is to say the gross takings were about $750,000), Although *Variety* felt that the company had been sold on the combination of 'Sadler's Wells' and 'Sol Hurok' (and no one should ever doubt the drawing power of Hurok's name as presenter of any company) it admitted that it was making a strong impression and doing 'SRO biz' (Sold Right Out business) almost everywhere. 'In the face of bad times generally and a sharp slump in concert biz specifically, the showing is more remarkable'.[17]

After ten days in Los Angeles the company set off on the long haul to Texas. By now exhaustion had set in and most dancers opted for bed rather than another party, and Mrs Thellusson was forced to take token groups to functions. In Dallas, the great ballerina Alexandra Danilova who was teaching in the city, attended all the performances, and was reported to be most enthusiastic. 'In the other towns the strongest memory is of so many dancers seemingly fumbling their ways along the roads after overnight train journeys, trying to kill time until the show'.[18] It was in Texas that a group of boys, asked by the locals what they did, replied that they were with Sadler's Wells, and were hailed as friends because 'we're in the oil business too'.[19]

By 20 January the company had reached Chicago, relieved to be in one place for a week. The opening was well received by a large and very smart audience but the notices were not particularly good, several critics referring to it as a second-rate company. However, there were rave notices and a real ovation two days after for *Coppélia* with Beriosova and Blair. Ann Barzel, writing in *Dance Magazine*, saw the company as indicative of the real trend of dance in England, and admired the dancers' flexibility and versatility which she felt made for a livelier company than the Sadler's Wells Ballet. She also admired the boys, and their compact physiques which produced their notable *ballon*. The company's feet, particularly Fifield's 'most fabulously arched feet in the profession'[20] were also remarked upon. The name Sadler's Wells Theatre Ballet was still causing confusion, and it was in Chicago that the press dubbed them the 'Don't-Call-Me-Junior' Company.

From Chicago the company zig-zagged down the States via St Louis, Nashville and Atlanta to New Orleans, and then down to Florida. All the dates in Florida were most successful, the company enjoying packed houses and benefiting from the sea and sunshine. In Daytona they were given a police escort on their way to meet the mayor at a civic reception, and be given the freedom of the city for the day. Van Praagh realised the need to allow a little relaxation; rehearsals were cut to a minimum, and Hurok arranged bathing and fishing parties. A film for advance publicity was made of an impromptu 'class' on the beach, the company impressing the technicians by their co-operation and enthusiasm, especially the boys – the cameramen confessed later that they hadn't realised male dancers could be such 'regular boys'. Lane had her twenty-first birthday in Miami, and the company threw an all night barbecue on the beach to celebrate.

The strain of the tour was beginning to tell, and there were plenty of minor injuries, bringing Miller into *Pineapple Poll*, Britton into *Les Rendezvous* and a crop of younger dancers into solo roles, including Annette Page as Khadra and the leading Mirleton, and Doreen Tempest in the *pas de trois* in *Le Lac des Cygnes*. The company was standing up well on the whole to the strain of the one-night stands, but was looking forward to going home. Hurok, however, encouraged by the general reception, had decided to extend the tour by three weeks to take in Boston and, even more worryingly, New York. It would be a final formidable challenge for an already tired company.

Meanwhile, Washington was impressed by the company as an ensemble. 'There is a fresh look we like in ballet, and marks of the fine training',[21] reported the *Washington Post*, although the *Sunday Graphic* recorded a comment from a member of the audience: 'This is just a cheap job. A bunch of dames dancing around on their toes. Why don't they go and get some taller dames?'[22]

The Academy of Music in Philadelphia, with its interior based on La Scala, was a welcome relief after so many bleak auditoria. It was a notoriously hard town to please, and audiences came ready to be disappointed that the company was not the 'fabulous' Sadler's Wells Ballet that they had seen in 1950. It was a miracle that by this time the company had any charm or enthusiasm left, but they were still giving far from routine performances, and there was thunderous applause, good reviews and disappointed crowds turned away. Some of the audience were even heard to voice the opinion that the younger company was better than the Sadler's Wells Ballet.

De Valois rejoined the company for the final weeks of the tour. As soon as she arrived she began pulling everyone to pieces, determined that they would be on their mettle for New York. It would have been a daunting prospect even if conditions had been ideal but Hurok had booked them into the Warner Theatre, a former cinema, with a typical cinema stage, wider than it was deep, and a huge auditorium, making audience contact difficult. There was also considerable resentment that Hurok had set a $6 top, the same that had been charged for the Sadler's Wells Ballet at the Metropolitan Opera House; this gave the impression that he was equating the two companies, although his charges were based rather upon the cost of importing the company and did not reflect quality (company expenses in America were between £10,000 and £12,000 a week). But it was an additional grudge that the company would have to overcome.

Frederick Ashton escorted Nora Kaye to the opening on 25 March; also noted in the audience were Markova, Cecil Beaton and Gloria Vanderbilt with her husband Leopold Stokowski. Once again the company won through on dancing, youth and commitment. Many of the ballets were severely criticized, both thematically and especially for a lack of choreographic interest in a city where form is often felt to be more important than content. The good basic training was noted, especially the beautiful feet, but there was felt to be a lack of subtlety and company style, most obviously in the classics. The expression of character through movement and mime was, however, admired, and the men were especially appreciated, Chujoy going so far as to call them 'much better than in any ballet company seen here in years – strong, well built, masculine, handsome, good technique if straining to acquire finesse'.[23] The company had matured enormously over the last few months and, it could be argued, were now better equipped to appear in New York than if they had appeared there at the beginning of the tour.

Individual dancers were praised, although New York found Beriosova cold. Above all it was Fifield who created a sensation. 'Just when we'd thought that our own New York City Ballet had captured one of every type of ballerina in existence, along comes Elaine Fifield with a whole new combination of ingredients unified into a truly endearing performer',[24] wrote Doris Hering, while Francis Mason hailed her as both classicist and soubrette, 'the rare performer who can genuinely arouse interest with her potentialities because they appear limitless as you watch what she already is.[25] John Martin extolled her in the *New York Times* as a second Fonteyn.

It was left to John Martin to sum up the positive attributes of the company after all the hard things had been disposed of.

A more engaging group of young artists in the making should be difficult to find, and if none of them is yet a star who wows the customers, that is not to imply that several of them are not clearly destined to be, but rather testifies to the thoroughness and the security of the British system. With a lifetime career ahead of them, these young dancers need not hurry; they can take their time to learn their craft and their art without having to crash through to overnight success on the peril of starving. They are carefully taught, carefully guided, carefully groomed for as bright a future as their native talents will allow.[26]

Lillian Moore added her own tribute to van Praagh 'for the magnificent way in which she held the company together throughout the hazards of a difficult and lengthy tour'.[27]

Before the tour started David Poole had written, 'It is as though we are throwing off the uneasiness of adolescence'[28] and indeed many of the dancers had matured as artists during the tour. It had been an especial success for Fifield, Beriosova, Blair and Trecu, and Britton had made up all the ground he had lost during his military service. *Coppélia* had been the most successful production, but *Casse-Noisette* had not been much admired. The Ashton repertory was felt to be lightweight, although the work of a master, but de Valois' ballets were not to the taste of the American audiences, though they appreciated the humour of *The Prospect Before Us*, even if they did not fully understand the background. Cranko's ballets had been enjoyed, particularly *Pastorale*, and *Harlequin in April* had been received with respect, but *Pineapple Poll* was a little too English to travel, and the Americans were not familiar with the Britannia image (known to all in Britain from the reverse of the pre-decimal penny), and thus the end of the ballet came as a puzzling anti-climax for them.

The final statistics of the tour were 189 performances in 67 cities, taking over £700,000 at the box office, and bringing back a small profit, although nothing like that brought back by the first company. On their tour, the first company had given 153 performances in only 32 cities, taking over $2.5m and bringing back over $450.000. Even today the dancers seem dubious as to whether the tour was a success or not, but they felt that they had, on the whole, won audiences over. Hurok had an option to take the company back in 1953, but instead it was the Covent Garden company that made the tour.

It was a wiser and more experienced company that returned home. The tour had welded them together even further, and had broken them into a full-length classic with a vengeance. But it had also been a watershed in the development of the company, and things would never be quite the same again. It remained a larger company and the introduction of *Coppélia* was an irreversible step in altering the character of the repertory. Also the group could no longer be considered just as a 'graduation class' as dancers who would never be taken to the Opera House matured beyond the promising stage.

After six months of learning to project across barn-like auditoria, it was not surprising that the company looked a little cramped and that there were complaints about over-projecting when they opened a short summer season at Sadler's Wells on 24 April. While their new maturity was appreciated, a tendency towards greater sophistication was not.

There was no time for relaxation. During the season the company appeared four times a week besides dancing in the opera ballet, notably in a new production of *Eugene Onegin* with choreography by Cranko. Their main energies were directed towards the mounting of de Valois' *The Rake's Progress* on 18 June. Created in 1935, the ballet had been taken to Covent Garden by the first company, but it had never been happy on the larger stage, and the company had fallen into a rather refined way of playing it. There was nothing refined about the Theatre Ballet's interpretation – indeed several critics expressed concern at how convincing the dancers appeared in the Brothel scene, with Stella Claire 'the blowsiest trollop that can have graced the Wells stage since its last period of decline'.[29] Alexander Grant came from Covent Garden to appear as the Rake, although his innate interpretative powers could not compensate for a lack of period feeling. O'Reilly and Lane alternated as the Betrayed Girl, the one stressing the sentiment, the other the drama of the character. Filled as it was with splendid cameo roles, *The Rake's Progress* would always suit the distinct personalities of the company. It was a special favourite with provincial audiences, and especially with school parties, who responded enthusiastically to the full-blooded characters and drama. Both Blair and Trecu were to be interesting Rakes, although the most notable later interpreters have been David Wall and Stephen Jefferies, with their instinctive response to the development of the character and the final shattering decline into madness.

De Valois was a great believer in the company as a repository of the works created for the Sadler's Wells Ballet in the 1930s – the Sadler's Wells Ballet had established its own styles and traditions of which the young company, as well as its elder, were the guardians. It was too easy, she felt, for young dancers to have the luxury of appearing only in ballets created especially for them where they would automatically appear at their best and they needed the challenge of established works if they were to develop fully as artists.

The end of the season on 5 July saw Beriosova's last performance with the company before her transfer to Covent Garden, while MacMillan, whose promising dancing career had been interrupted by terrifying bouts of stage fright, moved back; it was felt that, in the more relaxed atmosphere of the Wells, he might overcome his fears. Also joining the company was one of Ballet Rambert's leading artists, Margaret Hill, a dancer with a very individual style and personality.

Chapter VI

The Theatre Ballet opened the 1952–53 season at the Edinburgh Festival, at the Empire, a fairly typical provincial theatre, with the dressing rooms on the fifth floor and no lift. Here they presented a brightened up revival of *Coppélia* and a new work by Cranko. *Reflection*, premièred on 21 August had a commissioned score from John Gardner and designs by Keith New, and was a dire warning of what could happen if Cranko was allowed to over indulge himself. The basic theme 'seems to be the conflicting aspects of a man's nature, the aggressive and tender moods that hold alternate supremacy and each annihilate the identity established by the other',[1] overlaid onto the myth of Narcissus and Echo. The choreography was not without merit, and the dancers, 'loyal to the tradition and honour of the Sadler's Wells organisation'[2] did all they could to convince the audience that they knew what it was about, but the theme defeated balletic expression.

The company returned to the Wells, and a major change in its administration. From September, Ursula Moreton took charge, with Ailne Phillips, of ballet tuition at the Sadler's Wells Ballet School, and van Praagh was appointed Assistant Director of the Theatre Ballet in her place. This was really recognition of a *fait accompli*, for van Praagh had long been responsible for the day to day running of the company and all its tours. Since 1950 she had been designated Producer to the company, which recognised her special talent for bringing out the best in a performer and teaching him how to manifest it in theatrical terms. From her customary seat on the barre, her feet on a chair beneath, she encouraged in rehearsal full-blooded true dancing performances from the dancers, not just the performance of steps. She also put great emphasis on facial expression.

Reflection was to be Cranko's last ballet for the company for nearly eighteen months, and the frantic creativity of the past year began to lessen. The problem was now to find other choreographers if the flow of new works was not to dry up completely. De Valois believed in the slow but steady development of choreographers, and was not in favour of allowing everyone to 'have a go'. In the *Dancing Times* of August 1952 she wrote:

> ... however much energy is spent encouraging everyone to attempt the production of ballet, we must remember the very few real choreographers who emerge, and each one of importance must have some form of security offered ... the single production is not of great use to a young artist, and can prove to be an upsetting element in the company. The new choreographer of merit needs to produce at least *two productions per annum in the same environment and with the same artists for a considerable period of time ... No country can really produce more than three or four serious choreographers in twenty years.*[3]

The choreographer to be offered the two works in the coming season was Alfred Rodrigues. The first, *Ile des Sirènes*, was a reworking of a ballet choreographed for Fonteyn and Helpmann and their concert group in 1950. Set to Debussy's *Petite Suite de Concert* and with effective seaweedy sets and costumes from Loudon Sainthill, it retold the legend of mariners enticed to their deaths by the Sirens. It revealed a strong dramatic sense and the choreography was full of suitably aquatic fin-like and darting movements. There was an excellent role for Fifield as the leading Siren, revealing in her a new incisive interpretative power, while Blair was the young Mariner.

Most of autumn 1952 was taken up with a provincial tour. Not surprisingly, there had been rumblings of discontent from British towns. The Covent Garden company, with year-round commitments at the Opera House and under pressure to make more financially rewarding tours of America, had virtually stopped touring in England. The Theatre Ballet had only toured for fifteen weeks since 1949. Now it was to build up its provincial touring, filling the gap left by the first company by taking over the larger towns and cities which meant dropping some of the smaller venues. The pattern of the year changed from a long season at the Wells with a summer tour to several short London seasons, punctuated by autumn, winter and spring tours.

The provinces welcomed the company once more. Leeds was on their itinerary for the first time, and Ernest Bradbury in the *Yorkshire Post* summed up the general feeling: 'So often, in the provinces, are we made to feel that a visiting company are passing off work that would not be tolerated for a moment in London, that it is a pleasure to note the artistry and sense of striving that these young and gifted dancers suggest in their work ... Their reputation, as it were, goes with them; they are proud of it and give the impression that they intend it to stay that way'.[4] There was a fundamental difference in approach to evaluating performances between London, seeing so much, and the provinces, seeing relatively little. London audiences could afford to judge from the highest standards downwards – the provinces had to judge from the lowest upwards. This could be summed up in the London critic's view that things could always be better, while the provincial reviewer was always aware that things could be worse and was positively grateful for high standards and aims.

21 January, 1953 saw the choreographic début at the Wells of Margaret Dale, a former Sadler's Wells Ballet principal, who was now making a name for herself as a producer of television ballets. The idea for *The Great Detective* came from its composer, Richard Arnell, who saw possibilities in a Sherlock Holmes ballet. Dale, however, came up with a plot so far removed from Conan Doyle that, had the Great Detective (Conan Doyle's original names were not used) not had his by now customary Inverness cape deerstalker and pipe, it is unlikely that anyone would have guessed the connection. Unsuitably bright colours and cartoon style from designer Brian Robb failed to establish a Victorian atmosphere. The highlight of a restless and muddled work was MacMillan, doubling as the Great Detective and the Infamous Professor embarking upon a ten minute chase with himself.

The ballet highlighted the perennial problem of inexperienced choreographers. No one doubted the importance of their work, but it was asked whether it should take place before an audience 'who have every right to expect a certain standard of maturity'.[5] It was Theatre Ballet policy to encourage young choreographers, but it could not give a stage to the absolute beginner. Within the Sadler's Wells Ballet and the Theatre Ballet, were those who wanted to try their hands at choreography, so de Valois suggested that they set up their own workshops. Preferably, there should be no designs, but scenery and costumes from ballets no longer in the repertory could be used. The venture was under the direction of David Poole, and finance was provided by de Valois, who raised the money by endorsing an advertisement to the effect that she smoked Craven A cigarettes exclusively.[6]

The first performance of the Sadler's Wells Choreographic Group took place before an invited audience on 1 February. Although critics had been asked not to review, it soon became known that there had been one especially promising item – *Somnambulism* by Kenneth MacMillan set to a score by the American jazz band leader Stan Kenton. It showed various fears expressed in dreams – Anxiety (MacMillan, substituting for the injured Margaret Hill), Premonition (Lane) and Monotony (Poole). Anxiety was full of shudders and twitches, ending with Mac-Millan walking as if along a tightrope in fear of falling. In Monotony, Poole had a solo of slow shuffling steps, while in Premonition Lane was surrounded by hands stretching out from the wings; on grabbing one a body fell dead at her feet. MacMillan had approached the difficult score with unfailing musical sense, and admirably reflected its restless stridency. It was an astonishing first work, with an intuitive command of mood and stage technique, the choreography was inventive without straining after effect, and already showed clear indication of a very individual choreographic mind.

Dance and Dancers summed up the enigma of MacMillan's career to date: 'MacMillan has been rather the lost sheep of ballet ... doing several things well but there has always been the feeling that there was something he could do superbly. Choreography may be it'.[7]

During April the company paid its first visit to Europe, dancing in Holland, Belgium and Germany. Some confusion with the Sadler's Wells Ballet, which had toured in the 1940s, was perhaps to be expected. Holland was used to visits from many different dance companies, and had its own very definite, if not long-established, dance traditions. Even at this stage they valued experiment and 'modernism' in choreography, and found much of the repertory choreographically unadventurous and lacking in originality. Holland was not to find its dance salvation out of the classical vocabulary. Most admired were *The Rake's Progress* and *Harlequin in April*. Germany was equally restrained, *Abendzeitung* summing up the Munich appearances as 'a well-earned success for the ballet, whose achievements cannot yet be evaluated with superlatives, but with comparatives'.[8] The real failure was *Pineapple Poll*, whose gutsy, English music-hall vitality was looked on askance by the continental press and audiences. Particular triumphs were recorded by O'Reilly and especially Miller, who was invited back to Germany as guest artist.

The company returned to Sadler's Wells for the Coronation season in May and June. The opening of the season on 8 May, was poorly attended, although audiences did improve, especially after the première of Rodrigues' new ballet *Blood Wedding* on 5 June. Based on the Lorca play, the ballet had a commissioned score from Denis ApIvor and designs by Isabel Lambert. Leonardo, a married man, secretly meets a young Bride-to-be; after her wedding they steal away, followed by the Bridegroom. The two men fight and kill each other. Intertwined into the story were the unsatisfactory figures of the Moon, longing for blood to warm his cold heart, and Death, who brings about the tragedy to fulfil that longing.

Rodrigues was criticised for having attempted the subject at all. It did, indeed, reduce tragedy to melodrama, but so convincingly that the ballet created its own dramatic references. If the choreographic vocabulary was limited, the Spanish flavour was introduced with great skill. The story was told with utmost clarity, the characters were well evoked in movement, and the ballet had passion and blazing intensity, and provided magnificent dramatic roles. The low-key but tense ending, with the children unconsciously mimicking the wedding that has just brought such tragedy, was especially effective. As Leonardo, Poole was all fire and passion, while Fifield as the Bride developed 'a sort of smouldering intensity in her performance, suggesting that the character is carried away by forces beyond her control'.[9] It was a role with which Maryon Lane later had a particular affinity. As the Bridegroom Trecu had gaiety and fire until the loss of his bride transformed him into 'a primitive hunter',[10] and the tragedy became unavoidable. Among several excellent cameo performances, Margaret Hill stood out as Leonardo's Mother.

The ballet was notable for the unity between the elements. ApIvor's powerful score had the right balance of emotion and drama, and Lambert's set with its stormy, oppressive colours admirably reflected the rhythmic throb of the movements. Even those who disapproved of the subject had to admit that it was effective theatre and it was to have a long and steady life in the repertory. Indeed, the popularity of such works, and the scarcity of good ones, often led to them being performed long after their natural life was over.

The 1952–53 season ended with a two-week visit to Bulawayo, as part of the Rhodes centenary celebrations. The venue was a huge temporary structure, the biggest of its kind in Africa, holding 3,500. From the first they were beset by illness; it was the African winter, the temperature dropped 40°F every evening, and almost all the company suffered from bad colds or influenza. Eventually each dancer was given a blanket for

backstage use and extra heating was installed in the dressing-rooms and orchestra pit.

There was no time for sightseeing. In less than a fortnight they danced sixteen performances of ten ballets to audiences totalling almost 50,000 and 'kept each ballet bubbling with vitality: their weariness was there before and after each performance; it was never apparent onstage'.[11] The stage was hard and there were many minor injuries to add to the epidemic of colds.

Press and audiences were full of praise for the repertory, the productions and above all the dancers. JNF in the *Chronicle* described them as 'charged with luminous personality'[12] and *The Star* praised the general teamwork 'without which the finest performers would be powerless to make a full impact'.[13] Also in the Festival were local African dancers; one evening a village chief told van Praagh, 'I just wanted to tell you how beautiful your ballet was and that it was one of the most wonderful things I have ever seen. I know I shall not see it again, not in this life at least, but perhaps in Heaven'.[14]

Chapter VII

Autumn found the company again at the Edinburgh Festival. There were complaints that this prestigious event was being denied the Sadler's Wells Ballet (which had been a regular guest since the foundation of the Festival in 1947), but the *Scotsman* noted that the Theatre Ballet had improved over the last year and 'viewed from whatever angle, they presented on Monday night the most finished performance of any ballet company this year'.[1] This was high praise in a Festival that had included American Ballet Theatre, but the press admired the more varied repertory of the Theatre Ballet, and that 'they have enough young blood to change their casts without the audience thinking that they have been cheated of the best'.[2]

Carte Blanche by one of British ballet's most original talents, Walter Gore, was premièred at the Festival on 10 September. The designer was a promising young Australian, Kenneth Rowell, who had previously designed Gore's *Winter Night* for Ballet Rambert, and the composer was John Addison. The ballet was summed up in its title. It was a lighthearted *divertissement* set in a circus tent where anything went; there was a knockabout pantomime horse, a satirical waltz for staid dancers, a burlesque bacchanal, a 'shaggy dog' story and a delightful sentimental *pas de deux*. It was good to see an unpretentious, inconsequential entertainment, full of wit and invention, although Richard Buckle observed that 'it is quite extraordinary to what lengths Gore will go to avoid letting his dancers dance'.[3] Gore revelled in using the large company – most of his ballets had been done for relatively small groups – and made excellent use of individual talents, notably Hill, deliciously funny as the Equestrienne, Britton as a Trapeze Artist and Johaar Mosaval, whimsical and enigmatic in the Prelude and Postlude.

Once the Festival was over Fifield went on maternity leave, but, after the birth of a daughter the following year, she transferred to the Sadler's Wells Ballet. Slowly the established principals of the Theatre Ballet were being stripped away, leaving serious gaps that would take time to fill. Lane and Miller were the natural successors to most of Fifield's roles, and younger dancers, like Page and Tempest, were now brought forward, but there was a worrying shortage of potential principal dancers to equal those that the company had lost.

What the young soloists needed were plenty of performances, and that was just what they were going to get for over the next two years the length of time spent on tour increased by twenty-five percent, taking in more of the major towns and cities. Now was laid the foundations of a touring circuit that has not changed much over the years – Oxford, Bournemouth, Bristol, Cardiff, Brighton, Birmingham, Stratford, Wolverhampton, Nottingham, Manchester, Liverpool, Leeds, Hull, Newcastle, Glasgow and Edinburgh. There was still confusion between the two Sadler's Wells companies, but publicity always pointed out that the Theatre Ballet had its own personality and a growing independent reputation at home and abroad. Its importance in producing new works was stressed, but it was those very works that became increasingly difficult to sell out of London – only *Pineapple Poll* was to become a draw in its own right. Although the press quickly tired of reviewing endless *Les Sylphides* and *Le Lac des Cygnes* Act II, audiences clung to the familiar. Seeing so little ballet each year, and with only limited funds, they could not afford to risk not enjoying themselves. A familiar name was their guarantee.

The demand for the Covent Garden company to tour in England was never to lessen. The belief that, because it was Covent Garden it must be better, died hard, and few saw that the companies were not better than one another but *different*. 'Ballet companies, like individuals, have their own personalities and should be treated on their own merits', wrote Eileen Anstey in Nottingham, which was to become one of the most discerning and loyal audiences over the years. 'If you look for an imitation of Covent Garden you will be disappointed. You may well miss the fire and gaiety which is the unique contribution of these highly trained enthusiastic young dancers, if you go to compare irrelevantly instead of to enter into the spirit of their entertainment'.[4] It would take time to establish discriminating ballet audiences everywhere out of London, for most towns saw too little to build a very precise critical judgement.

At the beginning of 1954 a new Cranko ballet was in rehearsal. *The Lady and the Fool*, which had its première in Oxford on 25 February, was a comment on love and friendship. A society beauty, La Capricciosa, rejects her wealthy suitors and the empty glitter of her life for the love of a clown, Moondog. This love threatens to destroy his friendship with his partner and companion Bootface, but all ends happily. Charles Mackerras carved a score out of the ballet music from Verdi's operas, which made for a robust, lively accompaniment, if one with rather more climaxes than the choreography required. Richard Beer's costumes were pretty and colourful, but his sketchy sets had no particular character and were unrealistic. The guiding hand that Cranko often needed did not seem to have been much in evidence, and the simple theme was almost submerged in sub-plots and incidental characters. The most effective choreography was the *pas de quatre* for La Capricciosa and her three suitors, as they strip away the masks that hide her spiritual emptiness, the symbolic dance for the two clowns as they dispute the possession of a rose, and a romantic, passionate *pas de deux* for the Beauty and Moondog. There were also effective solos for two minor characters that almost threw the ballet off balance.

The ballet was beautifully cast. As La Capricciosa, Miller showed a new warm, romantic maturity. For Moondog and Bootface, Cranko cleverly used the physical difference between the tall MacMillan and the short Mosaval as part of the clowns' characters. By a judicious use of restraint and sincerity they just managed to keep the ballet from drowning in its own sentiment, particularly Mosaval as Bootface, with his spaniel-eyes, waif-like personality and heartbreaking humility.

The ballet was immediately popular, and was soon taken over by the Sadler's Wells Ballet – the first of the Theatre Ballet works to be transferred. Cranko took advantage of this to make certain revisions, cutting out several incidental characters and reassigning the male solos to La Capricciosa's suitors, the one full of flash for the wealthy Signor Midas, the other full of dash for the handsome Captain Adoncino. In its revised form, the ballet was later taken back into the touring repertory, when Beriosova danced it, her tragic beauty and expressive yearning style lending extra poignancy to the leading character. Later distinguished interpreters have included Vyvyan Lorrayne and Margaret Barbieri. As Bootface both Ronald Emblen and David Morse understood the balance between sentiment and pathos, while Poole was, not surprisingly, the most effective successor to MacMillan.

Twelve weeks of 1954 were spent in South Africa on what was to be the

company's most successful overseas tour to date, visiting Johannesburg, Durban, to coincide with the city's centenary celebrations, and Cape Town. This would be the first chance for South Africa to see how its children had developed since leaving over seven years before. There were no less than six South African dancers on the tour, including the principals, Lane, Miller and Poole, and works by two choreographers, Cranko and Rodrigues. Rodrigues had been working on a new ballet, *Café des sports*, which would have its première in Johannesburg.

There was the luxury of a two week sea voyage out to Cape Town, although after the ship passed the Canary Islands the crew rigged up temporary barres and classes resumed. They docked in Cape Town on 22 April, where they embarked upon a series of civic receptions, hotly pursued by droves of photographers. In the afternoon they flew to Johannesburg, where the welcoming process began all over again.

The first night in Johannesburg was an important social occasion and the audience's warmth and enthusiasm had the usual effect on the company and they excelled themselves. The altitude was to prove trying, however, and oxygen was on hand at all times. The season was a smash-hit and was extended to seven weeks – the longest single run of a non-musical in the history of theatre in Johannesburg and there were packed houses at every performance. South Africa had several small amateur ballet societies of high standard, but the city had not seen a professional company for eighteen years, and happily went ballet mad.

Interest focused on Rodrigues' *Café des Sports*, premièred on 24 May. The action centred around a town square somewhere in the South of France, and its café, patronized by a cross section of artistic types – including Hedonists, Essentialist artists and Absinthe-drinkers – while the Bourgeoisie looked on askance. It was the day of the great cycle race and the excitement was seen through the eyes of a ragged Urchin. She fell in love with the youngest cyclist and, when he was injured, took his place and won the race.

The Lady and the Fool. Patricia Miller as La Capricciosa, Peter Wright as Capitano Adoncino, David Poole as the Prince of Arragonza and David Gill as Signor Midas.

It was an unpretentious, amusing work, with a score by Antony Hopkins full of familiar and popular tunes that might have been played in such a café. The bright, primitive designs were by the 'Sunday painter' Jack Taylor, whose work Rodrigues had admired at the Redfern Gallery. Rodrigues had a lively sense of movement, introducing various kinds of social dance for the different characters, including a jive entry for the Hedonists, a suitably introverted *pas de trois* for the pseudo-artists and an elegiac blues number. His experience in the commercial theatre (he had worked on a number of successful musicals and revues) had given him an understanding of pace and timing and how to make effects without labouring them. He exploited Lane's perky, loose-limbed expressiveness as the Urchin, and her wide-eyed ragamuffin was one of the most endearing roles she ever had. The ballet was a tremendous success and added to the general feeling of euphoria.

In Durban and Cape Town, the company were received with equal enthusiasm. Their success was absolute. They were fêted everywhere and lavishly entertained and understandably the success began to go to their heads a little. They had spent too long living in the shadow of their big sister at Covent Garden, always compared, usually unfavourably, with her. Here they were a success in their own right.

Also, they began to find personal finances tight. They were not highly paid, the top salary being £18 a week. As they knew, they were paid less than the dancers at Covent Garden because they were still regarded as a 'graduate' company. Now some of them began to ask if this was quite fair. They were being asked to fulfil the responsibilities of a national company without recognition or recompense. Touring brought expenses over and above accommodation and food, which were covered by a touring allowance. De Valois insisted that the company was smartly turned out at all times, which for the girls meant suits with all the accessories and at least a cocktail dress. The dancers themselves wanted to be a credit to the company, but this was difficult on the lower salaries, which averaged about £8 a week. There also began to be a sneaking suspicion that someone, somewhere, was making a great deal of money out of their efforts.

Before leaving Cape Town some of the senior dancers approached van Praagh, saying that, as they had worked long hours to assure the success of the tour, they felt entitled to a bonus in addition to their regular wages. Van Praagh advised them to put their request to the Sadler's Wells management. The company returned to England for their summer break, while van Praagh stopped off en route for her annual holiday. In London the company spokesmen approached Equity, the theatre Trades Union, and the first the management knew was an official Equity letter endorsing the dancers' demand for an across the board increase of £2 a week. The management was somewhat taken aback. They had always negotiated with Equity on the basic rate, but after that it was understood that they should negotiate with each dancer and salary increases be apportioned according to individual merit. On this basis, they had prepared contracts offering increases in salary between 10s 0d and £2. Equity reduced its demands to a minimum rise of £1 10s all round, but the Management stuck to its right to base increases on merit alone – 'The Directors of the (Sadler's Wells) Trust cannot regard dancers merely as wage-earning units, indistinguishable one from another, whose salaries can be fixed collectively', wrote Patricia Strauss.[5]

The Governors of Sadler's Wells offered to meet the Director of Equity, but Equity refused. De Valois invited the company to see her, but Equity told her that they would meet her only at Equity offices in the presence of the Equity secretary. Not unexpectedly, she refused. It was the first time that either company had acted without consulting her first, and it must have been a hurtful personal blow. De Valois may have been abrupt and often intimidating to young dancers, but she would always listen, think and, if she felt a complaint was justified, change her mind. It was not that she did not believe in dancers earning a living wage, but money was not something she understood, being quite alien to what she wanted from life. She was also angry with van Praagh for not having been with the company when the claim was put to Equity.

Amid the greatest publicity the company had ever had, the crisis escalated, and the September season at Sadler's Wells was cancelled. The press made comparisons between the wages paid to other companies and to dancers in the West End, where a chorus girl could earn on average £10 and the salaries of ex-Theatre Ballet dancers now appearing in revues were as much as £30 a week. The management reminded Equity that the Theatre Ballet dancers had security, being contracted for fifty-two weeks of the year, forty-six of them on full pay, the remainder on holiday and rehearsal pay. They also had arrangements for sick pay, benevolent funds and far more free tuition than the basic laid down in Equity contracts.

By mid-August there was talk of the company disbanding. Then came an ultimatum – unless the dancers signed their contracts by 23 August the autumn provincial tour would be cancelled and the whole future of the company be at risk.

On 17 August Equity published its own statement. It pointed out that the company's salaries had failed to keep pace with its development, especially in view of the success they had had in South Africa. Some dancers were still receiving the national minimum of £7 after two years with the company, and others no more than £8 10s after six years. Also, the dancers' salaries were not compatible with those of the Sadler's Wells Opera singers at the same levels. Equity denied that it was making itself the judge of individual dancers, but felt 'the request of the dancers is moderate and reasonable and that the all-round increase which they require is fully justified by the status of the company, irrespective of any additional increases which the management may feel justified in offering to individual dancers in accordance with their personal merits'. Equity believed, rightly, that the general public was unaware of the low salaries paid to dancers in view of the hard work, discipline, dedication and relative shortness of their professional life.

25 August was now the deadline for the settlement if the tour was still to go ahead. On 26 August, however, a compromise was reached.

The company did not achieve anything like their full demands. Salaries were raised by a minimum of £1 per week and on average over £1 10s a week but there was no all-round flat-rate increase. The basic salary would still be £7, but now rising by 10s 0d every six months to a maximum of £9 a week. Equity undertook to review the entire structure of ballet salaries, and the management to consider contracts at full salary for fifty-two weeks a year. The dancers issued a statement thanking the public for their sympathy and support and assuring them of their desire to serve their audiences, but also to safeguard their living standards.

Not everyone had been sympathetic. The dancers at Covent Garden were horrified. One vociferous lobby felt that the dancers were being unbelievably presumptuous, cushioned as they were from the insecurities of the general theatrical profession, without the fear of unemployment between jobs, agents' fees and job seeking. 'The management alone', wrote Arnold Haskell, 'can know the value of any particular individual. So long as the salary does not fall below a reasonable living wage the intrusion of any third party is essentially destructive, and it should be beneath the dignity of artists to evoke such help ... Artistic socialism is a contradiction in terms'.[6] The dispute was shocking and unheard of at a time when strikes were the ultimate resort of industry. Neither side had really won, and the battle had partly been one of principle and discipline.

The last word came from de Valois in a letter to the *New Statesman*, published on 2 October, in which she reiterated the position and policy of the Theatre Ballet. The function of the company was to develop young dancers, choreographers and designers 'who must start their work in the more intimate atmosphere of Sadler's Wells', and promotion to Covent Garden could be expected over the years. A principal at the Wells equalled a soloist at Covent Garden, a soloist the *corps de ballet* and so on – 'This tradition is taken in good part and with complete understanding by the young artistes concerned'. She rejected comparisons that had been made with other companies for they were independent in their own right and 'not a younger sister of an existing major company'. She also reiterated the important role that the Theatre Ballet had to play in the Sadler's Wells organisation.

It was a difficult situation, especially for those dancers who were growing older and more experienced without any hope of getting to Covent Garden. There had never been much movement between the lower orders of the two companies – Theatre Ballet dancers who felt they would get no further had usually left – and it became obvious that only potential principals would be taken to Covent Garden. Thus it was difficult for a dancer to envisage a permanent career with the company. It must have been even more frustrating for those who had transferred back to the company because they were more suited to its repertory. Perhaps none of this had mattered when the company was small and buoyed up by its youthful enthusiasm, when everyone had their own roles and felt an important part of a great adventure. Now, with the larger company there were dancers who just did not have enough to do. The company was still needed as part of the Sadler's Wells ideal of a People's Theatre, to cater for those who could not afford Covent Garden, and its vitality could 'provide an insurance policy against the lethargy which inevitably threatens to overtake every state institution'.[7]

The pay for young dancers was still comparatively low and was to remain so. About two years later, a survey was done on the lowest paid *corps de ballet* dancers, who by then were earning £10 a week. After allowing for expenses connected with their professional lives – digs, taxis (so necessary to find digs in unfamiliar towns), make up, laundry, tips, stationery and stamps to find digs, baths, luggage and practice clothes – they were left with an average of 12s od a week. It was noted that all six of the dancers surveyed still relied upon their parents for help with extra living expenses.

In September the company set out upon its delayed provincial tour. The publicity they had received during the wage dispute did the box

Maryon Lane, Donald Britton and David Poole in *Danses Concertantes*.

Photograph by Denis de Marney. From the collections of the Theatre Museum.
Reproduced by courtesy of the Board of Trustees of the Victoria and Albert Museum.

office no harm, and they were received enthusiastically everywhere. Over the year they were to tour more than ever before, and so the company could no longer fulfil its obligations to the Sadler's Wells Opera. Thus, while it was on tour, a group of student dancers under Harold Turner and Judy Laraman was organised to appear in the opera ballets. The links with the past were slowly being broken.

The Theatre Ballet was not alone on the road. London's Festival Ballet[8] was now well established and Ballet Rambert was building up a repertory of larger works than the chamber ballets on which it had made its name. Because of a lack of a central touring policy (and it would seem the companies' inability actually to talk to each other) they trailed each other around the country, playing the same circuits at the same time of the year and often appearing in one town within weeks or even days of each other, to nobody's advantage. There were too many chasing a limited audience with limited means over too short a period.

Having already lost Blair, over the next season the company also lost two of its most individual talents, Trecu, to Covent Garden, and Holden to teach temporarily in South Africa. In return Covent Garden transferred Michael Boulton back to the Theatre Ballet, and the Czech-born Miro Zolan was brought forward. Russian-trained, he had appeared as Miroslav Zlochovsky and Miro Zloch with Ballet Rambert on their Australian tour of 1948, with the Borovansky Ballet and in England with International Ballet. He was not a virtuoso dancer, but had a strength and directness that blended well with the other Theatre Ballet men, and he was an experienced partner.

Despite all the changes the company still looked strong. Its 'powers of assimilation of new personnel seem equal to its recuperative ability after the loss of older members. Its freshness remains, its zest no less than it was, its spirit unimpaired'.[9]

Also unimpaired was its creative output as on 18 January 1955 MacMillan choreographed his first ballet for the company. He had suggested Stravinsky's *Le Baiser de la Fée*, but the Wells could not meet its orchestral demands, so he settled upon the same composer's *Danses Concertantes*. Tradition has it that the ballet was financed by another de Valois advertisement, this time for a chair in America.

'If I was to satisfy myself it was essential that my choreography should have a style of its own'.[10] MacMillan later wrote, and satisfied he must have been. A unique choreographic style was there from the first, owing to nothing but his own understanding of Stravinsky's elegant, astringent, witty score with its complex rhythms. He devised a pure dance work with an angular, asymmetric style, the parts of the body moving in opposition to each other, the arms and legs reflecting the spikiness of the music. He twisted and contorted the basic classical vocabulary, augmenting it with jazz steps, and matched the percussive quality of the score with stabbing pointe work and off balance movements. The angularity was accented by his brilliant use of pointed fingers, often using them to frame the eyes like strange barbed masks. MacMillan always had an eye for the choreographic possibilities in normal everyday movements – in *Danses Concertantes* it was dancers resting on chairs. The ballet might have been plotless, but there were undertones of a disturbing menace and foreboding. It was wildly inventive, but never for invention's sake, and not just a promising first work, but a good work by any standards.

The première at Sadler's Wells was exciting, not just because this was the first choreographer to have come entirely from within the Sadler's Wells organisation, but also for the début of a new designer. De Valois had introduced MacMillan to William Coldstream, Principal of the Slade School, and here MacMillan met a young Greek designer, Nicholas Georgiadis, who had already designed ballet for Trudy Goth's choreographic workshop in New York. Their collaboration on *Danses Concertantes* was to develop into an outstanding partnership that carried on the traditional high design standards of the Sadler's Wells Ballet. His work showed mastery of colour and line. Over the glowing blue and green backcloth and wings, were streaked black architectural features and small winged sphinxes. Sphinxes also decorated the chairs that were the only props. The men were dressed in brilliantly coloured all-over tights – peacock blue, orange, lime green and yellow ochre – banded with narrow black lines and arrowheads, the girls in short-skirted matching costumes. Their heads were encased in closefitting urchin-cut black wigs topped with neat double-winged ornaments or finials. 'The effect is of brilliantly plumaged birds dipping, darting and turning in a gaudy cage'.[11] It was an excitingly original concept which heightened the strange mood of the choreography and the brittle, acid score.

MacMillan's understanding of the complexities of the score was transferred to his choreography, and the dancers found it easy to feel the music through the steps. Like all good choreographers, he brought out previously unsuspected qualities in his dancers. His chosen muse in his early works was Lane, and he revealed in her a new sophistication as well as displaying to the full her musicality, marvellous precision and speed. Britton had a difficult extrovert solo, full of unexpected changes of direction, performed with an insouciant ease that no one else has ever matched. In contrast, Poole performed 'like a mournful Picasso *saltimbanque*'.[12] Among the rest of the cast Sara Neil had an elegant chic in her solo passages, and in the small ensemble a young good-looking boy named Donald MacLeary caught the eye.

The press was full of praise for MacMillan's originality and invention, and astonished by the nonchalant ease with which he handled a difficult score. The public found more difficulty in adjusting to this strange new choreographic world especially outside London where both chor- eography and the Stravinsky score seemed exceptionally avant-garde, but the ballet has held its place in the repertory over the years, even if no one has quite equalled its first cast.

Following the success of the ballet MacMillan resigned as a principal dancer with the company and accepted de Valois' offer of the post of Resident Choreographer, his salary dropping from £14 to £13 a week in the process.

Chapter VIII

Despite the popularity of the Theatre Ballet, audiences at both the Wells and in the provinces were sometimes disappointing. In London they had a faithful following, but at times the company seemed under publicized, and there were often clashes with ballet performances at Covent Garden, to the detriment of audiences at the Wells. The great ballet boom of the post-war period was over.

Conditions on tour were getting no better. Rehearsal rooms were inadequate, small and insufficiently heated. Thus, in Wolverhampton on the 1955 spring tour, having endured the intense cold of the local Labour Club during the morning, the dancers closed the windows over lunch to allow the room to warm up. At rehearsal that afternoon fifteen dancers fainted and several others were in a state of collapse. Lethal carbon monoxide fumes from the coke-fired boiler had leaked into the room. The dancers were rushed to hospital, where four of them were detained. The performance that night went on as usual, although with some very groggy dancers, and van Praagh had to appear in *The Rake's Progress* to make up the numbers. Unfortunately, amid all the panic, no one had informed London what had happened, and de Valois was not pleased to learn about the episode from her evening paper.

In return for *The Lady and the Fool*, Covent Garden restored Ashton's *Les Patineurs* to Sadler's Wells; it was to continue in the Covent Garden repertory, although it never looked its best on the larger stage and the older company approached it with a touch too much sophistication. The Theatre Ballet danced it with all the vigour and enthusiasm of which they were capable. Britton, with his cocky attack, and Boulton with a cheeky humour, were both admirable Blue Skaters, while Neil and Tempest were assured Blue Girls. The ballet was a popular addition to the repertory, and allowed the stalwart *Les Rendezvous* to be rested from time to time.

A month later, on 26 May, MacMillan produced *House of Birds*, a narrative ballet based, at Cranko's suggestion, on the Grimms' fairy tale *Jorinda and Joringel*. A Bird Woman traps girls and transforms them into birds. She entices a girl into her house and tries to turn her into a bird, but her Lover releases her and they set free the other enchanted girls, who peck the Bird Woman to death. John Lanchbery suggested the Spanish composer Federics Mompou, and orchestrated a selection of his piano pieces that had the right blend of mystery and magic.

House of Birds was at once a fascinating and repelling work, 'a chilling fairy-tale for grown-up children, and like his earlier work it leaves behind a tremendous impression of originality, power and compelling oddity'.[1] MacMillan's translation of bird behaviour into dance had all the disturbing menace that Hitchcock later put into his film *The Birds* (1963), made more frightening because of the girls' caged, helpless flutterings. Dressed in a black and white skeletal costume with a large scarlet beak over her face, the Bird Woman, with her jerky, pecking movements was a genuinely frightening creation, and the ending, as she was destroyed by the freed birds had all the horror and realism of the Brothers Grimm. In contrast, the romantic *pas de deux* for the Lovers showed assured command of fluent classical dance, as well as introducing some of the complicated lifts which were to become such a feature of MacMillan's work. Just as encouragingly, the ballet showed an understanding of structure and true sense of theatre.

Once again Georgiadis caught the exact mood of the choreography. His colours – hot reds, pinks, blues, greens and oranges – were like exotic birds' plumage, and intensified the sense of power inherent in the choreography. The bird costumes with their practical wings, masks and cages built over the heads had a strange beauty. This was no pretty world of caged birds, but one of frustrated strength. In its fusion of theme and design the ballet showed how much MacMillan had learned from watching the Ballets des Champs-Elysées in his student days.

The ballet was dominated by Tempest and later Hill as the Bird Woman, a characterization all the more disturbing because her behaviour seemed entirely instinctive. Lane and Poole as the Lovers created genuine characters, and MacMillan took advantage of Poole's skill as a partner to introduce acrobatic lifts into the *pas de deux*.

The season was rife with rumours. They were not unfounded. Before its end an announcement was made that, from September 1955, the

Theatre Ballet would spend most of its time on tour, returning to Sadler's Wells only for occasional continuous seasons, and no longer performing in repertory with the Sadler's Wells Opera. The Sadler's Wells management had found it almost impossible to run opera and ballet in repertory as an economic proposition, even for short seasons. Separate seasons and more touring were the answer, although as always happened on these occasions, the opera would get the lion's share of London performances and the ballet would spend most of its time on the road.

The reasons behind the decision were partly financial and partly political. The Arts Council had been under pressure to show more of the major subsidized companies in the provinces. Sadler's Wells Ballet's commitments at the Opera House meant that it was almost impossible for them to be out of London for any length of time, and their productions were all geared to the Covent Garden stage, which was much bigger than most of those in the provinces. The Theatre Ballet had a touring repertory and the youth and versatility to cope. But they would lose the benefits of the Wells as a home base, with proper rehearsal facilities and time to put back the edge blunted by long-term touring and it remained to see how, or if, new works could be produced if the company was permanently on the road.

Some dancers were not willing to undergo the rigours of the new schedule. Lane and Annette Page were among a small group taken to Covent Garden; they were to feel a little lost in the more impersonal atmosphere there and missed the careful coaching of the Theatre Ballet, where someone was always trying to get a little bit more out of every dancer. Poole, too, was offered a transfer, but he refused, and after a short period with Ballet Rambert and then the Edinburgh International Ballet, he returned to South Africa. Miller was on maternity leave, but she too decided to go back home to South Africa. Several experienced soloists, including Peter Wright and David Gill also left. Of the 'old school' only Britton and Boulton remained. There were no experienced successors within the Theatre Ballet to compensate for the loss of dancers so imbued with its traditions and spirit, and the company entered upon another period of rebuilding as young dancers like Sara Neil, Brenda Bolton, Patricia Cox and Donald MacLeary took their first steps in leading roles. Fortunately, there were no signs of decline in the over-all teamwork of the company.

From now on the company would have its own orchestra of twenty-eight players. It was, and still is, difficult to attract first class musicians to ballet, especially to companies that spend most of their time on tour, for the players are thus denied the chance of augmenting their regular salaries with teaching or session playing. The difficult and often unrewarding task of pulling an ever-changing orchestra together fell to the capable hands of John Lanchbery.

It was now out of the question for the Theatre Ballet to fulfil any obligations to the Opera Company, and so a completely new Sadler's Wells Opera Ballet was formed under Peter Wright. This would still draw upon senior students from the school for its recruits, and, as in ,the past, give them the chance of professional stage experience before being transferred to one of the companies. As walk-ons in *Hansel and Gretel* at Christmas 1955 (for which Poole did the choreography), Wright selected three senior students, Lynn Seymour, Christopher Gable and Elizabeth Anderton, all of whom joined the Opera Ballet the following year. They were not delighted, for the Opera Ballet was considered a 'dead end', but Seymour remembered that Wright 'treated the opera *corps* with respectful affection, and built up a sense of camaraderie. We never once felt like "rejects"'.[2]

Many theatre managements were not willing to risk booking companies as large as the Theatre Ballet; most profitable for them were plays with star names, small casts and minimum sets, for many theatres now had only a skeleton back-stage staff, which had to be augmented by inexperienced locals for large touring companies. Many towns, like Preston, Stockton and Wolverhampton, expressed their gratitude to the Theatre Ballet for presenting first-class live entertainment, and for not being afraid to bring new and unfamiliar works to the provinces. This was balanced, however, by others wondering just what Acts I, III and IV of *Swan Lake* were like, and why if, as they read, the Sadler's Wells Ballet's reputation was based upon the full-length classics, which were necessary for the proper development of the dancers, they didn't see them out of London.

Hardly had the company assimilated the implications of the new touring policy than there came an even more devastating announcement. At the end of 1955 Peggy van Praagh would leave the Theatre Ballet. She would be succeeded by Sadler's Wells Ballet principal John Field, who would take over with the title of Resident Director. The new policy required a different approach and a different personality.

The last ballet to be produced under van Praagh's regime was *Saudades* by Alfred Rodrigues, set to a commissioned score by Denis ApIvor with the designs by Norman Adams. The title was the Portuguese for 'nostalgia', and the ballet told of a king (Donald MacLeary in his first created leading role), who brings from the north a beautiful young princess (Maureen Bruce) to be his queen. In the heat of the south she falls ill, until revived by the snow of blossoms in the spring. The simple story and well-drawn main characters were almost swamped by a large cast of warriors, eunuchs, dancing girls and attendants, and the turbulent score suggested violence rather than gentle nostalgia. Rodrigues made cuts before the ballet reached London the following spring, but to no avail.

Van Praagh left the company in Dublin on 17 December 1955. De Valois devised a new post for her as a kind of travelling répétiteur, reproducing ballets from the Sadler's Wells repertory for companies abroad. She had steered the company through its formative years, mothering them, inspiring dancers and choreographers alike with her own fervour and devotion, giving them a stimulating atmosphere in which to work, and developing much of the talent which was now enriching the Covent Garden company.

Van Praagh's influence and planning would be felt for some time to come, for Field had had no time to formulate his own plans. On 4 January 1956 he gave his last performance as Prince Siegfried at Covent Garden. The next day he was in Stratford-upon-Avon at the beginning of a new career.

Part 2

⚜

The Royal Ballet
Touring Company

Chapter IX

There had been nothing in John Field's career so far to indicate that he had the makings of a successful company director. Trained in his native Liverpool, and at the Vic-Wells Ballet School, he joined the Sadler's Wells Ballet in 1939, and established himself as a promising soloist before going into the RAF in 1942. On his return in 1946 his progress to principal was steady but assured. He was a handsome, virile dancer, neat and finished and an excellent partner. The last thing he wanted to do, however, was 'to rub the paint off the backcloth in a few years' time',[1] and when de Valois, with her usual perspicacity, offered him the new post he accepted. His colleagues thought he was mad, but he felt that such a chance might never come again. Even David Webster, General Administrator of the Royal Opera House, told him that he was a fool, but added, 'Remember, this is always your home, and you can always come back whilst I'm here'.[2] Field was to remember the words with gratitude in the not too distant future.

Returning at the same time was Anne Heaton. Since leaving the Theatre Ballet in 1948, she had danced a number of important roles with the Sadler's Wells Ballet, notably Giselle, which suited her mixture of dramatic intensity and lyrical flow. Her return gave the Theatre Ballet the experienced ballerina that it needed. To further strengthen the male side, Alexander Bennett joined from Ballet Rambert, a strong, lyrical dancer and a skilled partner who would be an invaluable help to the young dancers making their débuts in leading roles.

Although it had never actually been said, Field felt his job was to look at the state of the classics. He was too late, however, to do anything about the new *Coppélia* which was premièred at Stratford on 16 January 1956. De Valois supervised the production, basing it upon the version used at Covent Garden, but adapting it for the smaller company. She paid considerable attention to detail, put back some of the refreshing spirit and readjusted the relationships between the characters, which had somehow got lost in the previous production.

Having got the look of the ballet wrong once before, the company got it wrong again. Robert Medley's setting was vaguely Victorian and the costumes predominantly magenta, emerald green and dark red. The granite village and lowering mountains created a rather sombre atmosphere which the dancers did their best to overcome with their customary attack.

The first performances of Swanilda went to the younger dancers Doreen Tempest and Sara Neil, partnered by the more experienced Britton and Zolan. Zolan also appeared as Dr Coppélius, playing him as a completely crazy figure of high farce; Walter Trevor was a little too young to cope with the complexities of the part, but the company was also able to call upon Henry Legerton, their new Ballet Master, at subsequent performances. Jim Webber in the *Stratford-upon-Avon Herald*, however, sounded a warning note: 'At times one wishes that the principals were a little more adequate ... (*Coppélia*) would not have received the ovation it did without the all-round sureness and precision of the supporting dancers and the *corps de ballet*'.[3] It was hardly surprising, with Errol Addison as their teacher, that the boys were in particularly good shape, showing the virility and strength for which his pupils were notable.

Field took over a company that, despite its still excellent creative record, had slid from the peak of the early 1950s. Discipline had been allowed to slacken, and de Valois felt that the dancers had been mollycoddled by van Praagh; she wanted them to learn to work on their own and develop a tougher professionalism. The foundations of the company Field found in good shape, but performances needed a lot of polish. For the first few seasons there was a considerable gap between Heaton and the rest of the girls, and the situation was not helped as a succession of young potential principals abandoned ballet for marriage and motherhood. A number of the boys were also due to be called up for military service. Faced with a company without stars Field set about enthusiastically 'growing my own timber'.[4] For the first year he was principal dancer, director, teacher, company manager. Things got so bad that before one performance Field, in full costume and make-up, was waiting for his cue on stage and taking a telephone call as the overture was playing. This kind of situation could not continue for long, and slowly he began to build his own team, starting with two experienced members of the Covent Garden company, Lorna Mossford as his Ballet Mistress, and Henry Legerton as Ballet Master.

The thirty-one week autumn and winter tours meant that the company was not free in May 1956 to take part in the celebrations at Covent Garden to mark the twenty-fifth anniversary of the Sadler's Wells Ballet.[5] Without a break, they returned in June to Sadler's Wells, for a three week season during which they presented two new MacMillan ballets. It had been hoped that *Somnambulism* could be taken over before 29 May, but only now had Stan Kenton given permission for the music to be re-scored and the separate pieces to be integrated into a complete work. The ballet had to stand comparison with MacMillan's later creations, but it was noted how clear a genuine 'MacMillan' style had been from the very first. Hill danced the role created for her, Britton danced Monotony and Heaton Premonition. Not everybody was impressed. After the first night Lanchbery received an anonymous note, 'To John Lanchbery, Kenneth MacMillan and Stan Kenton – this is my opinion of it'; enclosed was $\frac{1}{2}$d.

It was an all-MacMillan evening on 7 June when *Solitaire* was premièred. 'The theme was a very simple one, or so I thought, of a lonely child unable to make friends – but happy in the memories of the rare times that people had befriended her.'[6] Set to Malcolm Arnold's *English Dances*, the ballet was a complete surprise to those who thought that MacMillan was only at home with the disturbing and the macabre. The choreography was light, clear and original, and refreshingly unliterary. Partly inspired by children's games, like follow-my-leader, it flowed out of the music, with wit, style and gaiety, but underlaid by the wistful sadness of the Girl, who knows that after each encounter she will again be left alone. Arnold composed two new dances, the perky Polka and the Sarabande, to which MacMillan set a charming romantic *pas de deux*, full of the gentle sadness of transient youthful love.

For the setting, MacMillan was asked to take over the backcloth designed by Desmond Heeley for a projected Cranko ballet. He did so gladly. Set against a blue-green sky was a playground of fantastic spun-sugar scaffolding, 'not the well ordered respectable sort of playground, but one of those secret playgrounds in the mind of every child'.[7] Heeley's costumes, with their asymmetric tutus and strong colours reflected the child-like directness of the theme, and the flowered 'bathing-cap' headdress for the Girl was deliciously frivolous.

The cornerstone of the ballet was the character of the Girl. Hill caught the bitter-sweet loneliness of the child peopling the stage with her imaginings without ever falling into sentimentality. Having come as a principal from Ballet Rambert, she brought to the role something of her own sense of being an 'outsider' within a close knit company. The off-beat Polka, danced with pert wit by Neil, contrasted with Britton and Boulton's rumbustious boyish approach. MacLeary in the *pas de deux* was given a more romantic persona, displaying that astonishing sureness as a partner for which he was to become famous.

MacMillan found the Theatre Ballet full of new young dancers, who flung themselves willingly and eagerly into whatever he suggested. He was a very different choreographer from Cranko, introspective where Cranko had been extrovert, working very much on his own and never sharing his creative processes with the dancers. Every step was carefully thought out, and he never explained the motivation or reason behind a particular movement, just telling the dancers to do as he asked and it would come out right; no amount of cajoling from the dancers would make him change his mind. Only occasionally would he take the sugges-tion of a new step or *enchaînement* from Errol Addison. However difficult his chosen score, he approached it with a sureness of choreographic purpose that made it easy for the dancers to follow the most complicated rhythms. He was not interested in ballet for its beauty or its charm, and he had a particular dislike of male dancers who shared his own gifts of lyrical softness. His mild and indecisive outward manner was deceptive. 'His most personal emotion – a feeling of savage alienation in a punishing world filled with contemptible desires – was expressed on stage and he was very conscious of psychological imprisonments and rejections that impose solitary confinement'.[8]

During July the Theatre Ballet flew to Spain to appear at the Granada Festival. They performed on a special stage built in the Jardines del Generalife, with no backcloth, only the vista of the snowcapped moun-tains on the horizon, the wings formed by avenues of cypress hedges. The setting was suitably romantic for their new production of *Giselle*, the second act of which was given, with Heaton and Field as Giselle and Albrecht. The two performances were seen by nearly 10,000 people, and there was a flourishing black market in tickets. At the public rehearsals the gypsies came down from their caves in the hills to watch, and after one performance the company was taken to the cave of Joaquin, where they were treated to some of the finest flamenco dancing in Granada.

They had been working hard on *Giselle*, their first production of a classic since *Coppélia* in 1951. The complete ballet was presented on 18 August, during a visit to Santander. Heaton was injured, so Nerina came to dance the first performance with her partner Alexis Rassine. Hill doubled as a gracious Bathilde and a vengeful Myrtha.

Giselle was designed by Peter Rice, who set the ballet in the Romantic *Sturm und Drang* period of *Werther* rather than in the softer Romanticism of the era of the Romantic ballet itself. Like *Coppélia*, the production had been commissioned before he took over and Field was not happy with the result. Both *Giselle* and *Coppélia* had their roots in Nicolai Sergeyev's productions for the Vic-Wells Ballet in the 1930s, which derived from the Imperial Russian Ballet. They were fortunate in having an experienced and excellent Giselle in Heaton, but alternative casts were promising rather than finished. Field, Zolan and Bennett, who shared Albrecht, spent much time steering young dancers through their first *Giselle*. Bennett was one of the most experienced men in the role – as Ballet Rambert's leading male dancer, he reckoned he must have performed Albrecht some five hundred times. After that even the Theatre Ballet seemed like a rest.[9]

The company was well received in Spain, and did not suffer too badly in comparison with the other guests at the Festival, the Paris Opera Ballet. While it was conceded that the Theatre Ballet lacked the excitement and bravura of the French dancers, they were none the less much admired for their discipline and company spirit.

During October 1956, the attention of the whole ballet world was focused on the first appearance in London of the Bolshoi Ballet and part-way through the autumn tour there was a short break to allow the Theatre Ballet to return to London to see them. Ulanova bowled everybody over, and her Giselle showed how the role could be approached with a sincerity, understanding and realism that made it live anew. De Valois was also struck by the fact that, in spite of bringing such a large contingent to London, there were more than enough dancers left behind to fulfil the company's commitments in Moscow.

On 16 January 1957 the press were summoned to the Crush Bar of the Royal Opera House to hear a statement delivered by Lord Waverley, Chairman of the Board of the Royal Opera House. He announced that the Sadler's Wells Ballet, Sadler's Wells Theatre Ballet and Sadler's Wells School had been granted a Royal Charter, bringing the three disparate organisations together under the title of The Royal Ballet. HM The Queen would be its Patron, with Princess Margaret as President. Hitherto each body had operated under its own management, held together by the voluntary co-operation of their governing bodies. The new arrangement would, it was hoped, eliminate the confusion between the companies caused by their similar names. Asked by what names the companies would now be known, Lord Waverley announced that refreshments were available, but when pressed suggested that, for the time being both companies should be called The Royal Ballet, 'formerly the Sadler's Wells Ballet from Covent Garden' and 'formerly the Sadler's Wells Theatre Ballet from the Sadler's Wells Theatre'.

The vexed question of the names of the respective companies had been exercising the minds of the governing bodies for some years, but they had seen no easy way around the problem that the Sadler's Wells Ballet bore the name of a theatre with which it now had no connection, but needed to keep that name because of the reputation and standing that it represented at home and abroad; meanwhile the Sadler's Wells Theatre Ballet suffered from possessing a name which, while it related to its theatre, was too close to the name of its sister company, thus causing confusion in the minds of casual ballet-goers.

Beyond that, de Valois had realised some years before that the companies had no existence independent of their respective theatres. The Governors of both Sadler's Wells and Covent Garden were bound to present ballet performances, but in no legal document was it specified by which companies. As the governing bodies controlled the grants to both opera and ballet companies they could, theoretically, have dispensed with both Sadler's Wells Ballet companies and been within their rights. Legally they did not exist. What was needed was for the two companies and school to be set up as 'as separate entity under a name which recognises their fundamental unity'.[10] This would be a first step in enabling the ballet companies to exist independently of the theatres and their governing bodies, which de Valois saw as essential to their preservation and growth. As usual she was planning for the future 'when the people of understanding who have watched and helped in the growth of the ballet are no longer concerned with its welfare'.[11] Thus the Royal Charter was sought.

With the current tour having been planned so far ahead, the publicity continued to announce the Sadler's Wells Theatre Ballet until they reached Sheffield in March 1957 when they became for the first time The Royal Ballet. Here de Valois came to see them and spoke about the honour and importance of the new name, and urged them to act and behave as befitted a company with such a title. That title, however, would bring its own problems. Some managements had in the past left out the significant word 'Theatre' from the company's billing, now it was easier to drop the cumbersome 'formerly ...'. It took many years for local papers and audiences to adjust to the new name, and there was still understandable confusion between the two companies.

The seven month tour was long and gruelling. Winter was never the best time to tour the English provinces. A. V. Coton criticized the current policy of long tours 'thus partly satisfying a provincial demand, and effectively hamstringing any hope of artistic growth among the young dancers who fill most of its ranks ... they are fated to dance themselves into comparatively early retirement, while gradually degenerating into dance-mechanisms incapable of a pure act of creation that every dancer needs to experience'.[12]

There was only one new work that season, Ashton's 1936 ballet, *Apparitions*, which was revived on 28 January 1957. Heaton was in Fonteyn's role of Woman in Balldress, a role she had danced at Covent Garden, and Field was the Poet. The ballet was in that uncomfortable state that overtakes all fashion – it was just not far enough away from its creation to appear other than out-of-date and it did not remain long in the repertory.

The company was to be welcomed more and more on tour, especially in cities like Plymouth, Sheffield and Peterborough which saw few first-rate companies. The touring circuit out of London was degenerating rapidly, and a typical situation was that in Plymouth, where the company was followed into the Palace by the revue *Nudes of the World*. Theatres were closing down. Audiences needed something very special to lure them into the decaying and unwelcoming places that many theatres had become. It was a downward spiral. Without the audiences to fill the theatres there was no impetus to carry out the necessary refurbishing and rebuilding to bring them up-to-date; without those alterations they could not hope to lure first class companies onto the road; without the companies they could not get the audiences. However, while one always has to take reports of full houses and audience enthusiasm with a pinch of salt, there is still plenty of evidence that the company was a welcome good deed in the naughty world of provincial touring. It was not surprising that Clive Barnes dubbed them 'the national ballet of the Provinces'.[13]

'Of the Provinces' maybe, but was that enough to sustain an international reputation? During May and June of 1957 the company undertook a European tour, appearing at festivals in Spain, Portugal, Germany and Holland. If 'formerly ... from ...' could give rise to confusion in

England it was even worse on the continent, and there was considerable disappointment and even anger in many places. The company had been properly announced, but public ignorance, or just misunderstanding, meant that audiences still expected the Covent Garden company or at least a company with known stars. Only in Orvieto, where the point of the festival was to provide the arts at reasonable prices, dancing in a large marquee before audiences who had no expectations other than to enjoy themselves, was the company an unqualified success. In Holland the organisers had fixed prices much higher than usual, and the company met with a very hostile reception. In Germany the audience took the whole mix-up to be a deliberate deception and complained that they had been subjected to little more than 'an inferior school display'.[14] The change of title was going to create more problems than it solved.

But the significance of the Charter went beyond the new name. The importance of the Theatre Ballet being established as an integral part of The Royal Ballet organization and independent from its home theatre soon became clear. In autumn 1956 James Smith, of the Sadler's Wells Governors, had written to the Arts Council warning them 'unless certain assurances could be given, the Governors of Sadler's Wells saw no alternative to closing the Theatre next year'.[15] Expenses were crippling. Most of the Wells' equipment and fittings had been bought second-hand in 1931 and there had never been the money to replace them. Now the switchboard had been condemned by the London County Council, and a new one would cost £20,000. Running costs for the coming year were estimated at £167,000, without which the theatre would close.

In March 1957 de Valois asked the Board of Directors of the Royal Opera House for clarification of the future of the Theatre Ballet if Sadler's Wells ceased to accept responsibility for it after July 'which she understood was their present intention'.[16] Lord Waverley assured her that the two companies now belonged to The Royal Ballet and, in such an eventuality responsibility would revert to The Royal Ballet council, who would make provision for it.

In April the Governors of Sadler's Wells decided not to renew the contracts of the Theatre Ballet after the end of the season. No bookings had been made for an autumn tour, and this could no longer be delayed if the company's existence was to be ensured. Whatever the ultimate cost 'Covent Garden had no alternative to intervening at this stage to ensure the company's future employment'.[17] Thus, on 21 May 1957 Covent Garden assumed responsibility for the second company. They agreed that it should be known as The Royal Ballet, and to guarantee the already commissioned ballets from Cranko, MacMillan and Peter Wright. They also booked it into Covent Garden for a Christmas season, which would help establish its credibility and give the company a goal to work for. As Field recalls, he never thought that Webster's open invitation for him to come home would extend to the entire company.

For the Opera House the taking over of the Theatre Ballet was 'at once an act of rescue and an act of faith ... For the moment we have rescued a fine organisation from possible break-up and increased our resources of talent and enthusiasm. But there can be no disguising the fact that we have added to our financial difficulties'.[18] The actual increase in personnel would be thirty-seven on an overall base of 650 in the Opera House.

With understandable apprehension the company returned to London in July 1957 for their last season at Sadler's Wells, with a repertory that summed up the Theatre Ballet years. There were the established names of de Valois (*The Rake's Progress*), Howard (*La Fête étrange*) and Ashton (*Les Patineurs*) and those developed within their ranks – MacMillan (*House of Birds* and *Solitaire*), Cranko (*Pineapple Poll* and *Beauty and the Beast*) and Rodrigues (*Blood Wedding*) as well as classics *Giselle*, *Coppélia* and *Le Lac des Cygnes* Act II. No Royal Ballet company was to set foot on that stage again for fourteen years. It was a sad farewell for Heaton, Britton and Boulton, who had grown up in the theatre and for whom it had become more familiar than home.

Many mourned the passing of the Sadler's Wells Theatre Ballet, remembering how much vitality and zest it had added to ballet-going in London, and the great contribution it had made to choreography and dance over the last decade. To this day the dancers who developed under the Theatre Ballet will tell you that there was never a company like it, with the same energy, creative drive and sheer excitement. No one could see the contribution its dancers would continue to make to British and world ballet, in South Africa (Poole and Miller), in Portugal (Trecu), Stuttgart (Cranko and Wright) and Australia (van Praagh) as choreographers, teachers and company directors. They took with them the lessons they had learned, particularly from observing de Valois. In future years many a harassed ex-Theatre Ballet dancer now director would think in a crisis, 'What would Madam have done'.

Although the repertory for their final season left no one in doubt of the company's choreographic strength, the dancers looked tired and disheartened after the criticisms of the continental tour. By the end of the season, there were reports of nearly a quarter of them leaving.

In bringing the company to Covent Garden de Valois' dream was nothing less than the fusion of the two companies into one Royal Ballet. From this body of over one hundred dancers a section could be sent out on tour, while the other performed in London. Thus would end the confusion – it would always be *The* Royal Ballet. Dancers could be interchanged between the companies, so that each would experience the benefits of a home base without stagnation and the benefits of touring without getting stale. The acquisition of the former Theatre Ballet would give Covent Garden a ready-made touring company to send out under its management and under the name of The Royal Ballet, thus stemming the constant criticism that they, a highly state subsidized theatre, did not fulfil their obligations to the majority of the British people whose taxes paid that subsidy. The company would be an extra financial burden, but it was hoped that touring, especially abroad, could be made to show a profit. Also, if the repertories were similar, there would be more chances for the Covent Garden's under-used leading dancers to appear on tour and for young dancers to appear in roles that they might otherwise have to wait years to get in London. It was expected that the company would still produce new works, but obviously the new policy would prove expensive, and something had to give.

De Valois of course recognised that full integration was not possible immediately. In *Dancing Times* she laid out in her usual clear-sighted way the policy for the future. Until fusion is complete and understood by everyone we shall most carefully distinguish between (the companies)'.[19] She hoped that future modern works would be in a form adaptable to London and to touring, and, where necessary, productions would be duplicated, especially the classics, which from now on would be common to both companies. In practical terms this meant reproducing Covent Garden designs for the road. This was obviously a long term aim, otherwise the cost would be crippling. Other productions could be shared. As de Valois saw it, the need was for a larger Royal Ballet capable of being split and thus able to fulfil the increasing demands for appearances, both at home and abroad.

It should be said at the outset that the dream of full integration was never fulfilled. The two companies were never brought together, dancers and repertories reshuffled and then different groups sent out on different tours. Despite a few small changes at *corps de ballet* or soloist level, the group on the road was essentially the one that Field had inherited, and so it remained. However much publicity might stress one Royal Ballet there were obviously two. As to the integrated repertory, the Opera

House took over *Solitaire, La Fête étrange, Dances Concertantes, Pine-apple Poll* and revived *Harlequin in April,* but none really suited the larger stage. Even if there were a single repertory it still would not be easy to transfer dancers between the two companies unless both were performing the same repertory at the same time. However, over the next few years 'integration' was to be the keyword in the Opera House policy for the company.

Only in the classics would interchange be relatively easy. The immediate plan, therefore, was to mount the Royal Opera House productions for the Touring Company, a decision that was to change its character and direction over the next few years. If The Royal Ballet ('formerly the Sadler's Wells Ballet') could not tour, then its productions would with The Royal Ballet ('formerly the Sadler's Wells Theatre Ballet'). There was, however, a danger that the company on the road would lay itself open to criticism in presenting productions geared to Covent Garden without the resources of either the company or the theatre, and it would take time for them to bring their technique up to the level demanded by a repertory based on the nineteenth-century classics.

Under the new management the company set out on its autumn tour. They had had only three weeks to rehearse twelve acts of repertory[20] as well as beginning work on the new ballets by Cranko, MacMillan and Wright. Company morale, however, was high, and was helped by good business at the box office. There was also a new Giselle in Susan Alexander, soft and pretty without, as yet, much depth, but promising in her childish, light-weight playing.

Confusion over the new name was, however, inevitable. In one paper the company was billed as Royal Festival Ballet and in another as Royal (Sadler's Wells) Ballet and even The Royal Covent Garden Opera House Ballet. In Bristol the management simply advertised 'The Royal Ballet' without the important 'formerly Sadler's Wells Theatre Ballet'. Press and public were expecting to see top names from Covent Garden and were disappointed at the non-appearance of the few names they did know.

De Valois, of course, had her own answer to the provincial audiences who clamoured for stars.

We have duties outside London of which we are acutely aware, and I would like to see ballet in the provinces grow to twice what it is today ... I want to see the ability to support a repertory ballet for a fortnight in these provincial towns and cities. People get to the pitch where they only want to see a name and don't even know what they are looking at.[21]

As there was no 'official' way of distinguishing between the companies (the official line being that there was only one) the press fell into the habit of referring to them as 'senior' and 'junior'. Eventually time solved the problem and 'junior' became the Royal Ballet Touring Company, although never acknowledged as such on company publicity posters and leaflets, where it was always The Royal Ballet.

Chapter X

The company opened its first Covent Garden season on Boxing Day 1957. The seat prices for the nine performances had been pitched lower than usual, and the house full signs were often out. Apart from *Giselle*, *Les Sylphides* and *Pineapple Poll*, the repertory consisted of four new works – a revival of Andrée Howard's *Veneziana*, and three world premières.

The opening performance of the season on 26 December included two of the premières, Wright's *A Blue Rose* and Cranko's *The Angels*. *A Blue Rose*, choreographed to Samuel Barber music, had a simple theme; a rose passes from owner to owner, the mood changing with each episode. These were based on popular social dances of the early twentieth century, the Schottische, the Two Step, the Waltz and the Hesitation Tango, and the choreography showed the young dancers, Susan Alexander, Edward Miller, Patricia Cox, Donald MacLeary and Audrey Farriss, to advantage. Not surprisingly, considering that the work was conceived for the Wells and that Wright had never before set foot on the Opera House stage, the ballet was criticized as being too slight for Covent Garden, but it had promise and charm. The work was a baptism of fire for the designer too. Yolanda Sonnabend was a student at the Slade School, and was faced in this her first commission with the practical problems of producing a set ideal for Covent Garden and yet adaptable for touring.

In contrast, Cranko's *The Angels*, was bedevilled by a pretentious libretto. Various human types – the Startled, the Morbid, the Strident, the Terrified, the Lyrical and the Vigorous – were paraded, and one, the Vigorous, was selected by the Angel for immortality. It gave the impression of being highly significant but to what end remained unclear

The Burrow. Donald Britton as the Joker and Edward Miller as the Outcast.

Photograph by G. B. L. Wilson. By courtesy of the Royal Academy of Dancing.

and the confused symbolism seemed to find its way into the contorted choreography.

Howard kept up her reputation for never completely finishing a ballet when she mounted *Veneziana* for the company, and she was still making changes after the first performance on 28 December. Created for the Sadler's Wells Ballet in 1953, it was a series of pleasant variations on Venetian themes, and was that invaluable type of work, an ideal opening or closing ballet. The company took to it like a gondola to the Grand Canal, with Margaret Lee as La Favorita, and Mosaval and later Holden as a genially bouncing Punchinello.

The sensation of the season came on 2 January 1958, with the première of MacMillan's *The Burrow*. To a Frank Martin concerto, MacMillan

Kenneth MacMillan with Nicholas Georgiadis and Anne Heaton at a rehearsal of *The Burrow*.

Photograph by G. B. L. Wilson. By courtesy of the Royal Academy of Dancing.

created a harrowing study of fear. People are crowded together in hiding, each bound up in himself and each personality grating upon the other. At the end a knock comes upon their prison door 'and their world is shattered'.[1] Many took it to be based upon *The Diary of Anne Frank*, but MacMillan denied that he had ever read the book; the source was, in fact, the eponymous short story by Kafka. His concern was not physical incarceration but the self imprisoned within the self by its fears; the knock at the end was the particular fear coming to claim its own.

Georgiadis set the ballet in a drab room – a suitable 'environment for lost souls',[2] – its claustrophobic atmosphere intensified by the sloping ceiling and the mood of apprehension highlighted by the warning flicker of the single light bulb. The costumes blended into the set, their drab greys and browns streaked with cross hatching and daubs of colour to suggest texture. The effect was overpoweringly real, and the emotions portrayed no less so. MacMillan wanted to break away from conventional balletic themes into a world of the inner man, and there were many who felt such themes were incapable of balletic expression.

He was rewarded by stunning performances from his dancers, particularly Heaton as the neurotic woman of faded gentility, Britton as the relentless Joker, at first amusing, but after a while irritating, Edward Miller as the Outcast, morose and turned in upon himself, and Noreen Sopwith as the carefree Child. As the Lovers, who find a brief glimpse of happiness even in such a hostile environment, were MacLeary and a young dancer that MacMillan had picked out of the *corps de ballet* only two weeks after her joining from the Sadler's Wells Opera Ballet – Lynn Seymour. It was a modern theme tackled with imagination and courage, and if the choreography came in for criticism as being unoriginal, it was none the less expressive of the individual characters. The choreography was, however, overshadowed by the subject. 'Here', announced Clive Barnes, 'is the first British ballet to express the feelings of the post-war, H-bomb-ridden generation, and it was they who were cheering'.[3]

Andrew Porter appraised the season: 'One of the wonders of Dame Ninette's regime is that her company seems always on the verge of still greater achievements. Though we grumbled, last year, that the Theatre Ballet seemed to be below form, set to work on recreations of old ballets instead of being developed, as dancers must be, on new ones written for them, now the "Junior Company" seems to have recovered all its vigour, to be filled with exceptional dancers, to foretell still greater days for the single Royal Ballet that is to come'.[4] The dancers had risen to the challenge of the Opera House, and the audience received them with encouraging cheers. It was a far cry from the dispirited band that had left Sadler's Wells Theatre only a few months before.

From January to June 1958 the company was on the road with only one week rehearsal break. *The Burrow* certainly had a shock effect on tour. The reaction of most people was one of respect, but others were perplexed when faced with a ballet that disturbed rather than entertained. Occasionally the company was joined by dancers from Covent Garden, notably Beriosova and Bryan Ashbridge who appeared in Belfast, at a gala performance in the presence of the Queen Mother.

The gala was a highlight amid the drudgery of winter touring, zig-zagging across Britain on the slow, draughty Sunday trains. The dancers spent the journeys stretching cramped limbs in the corridors, playing cards, reading, gossiping and sleeping – as generations of touring dancers have done before and since – each dancer 'lugging one large scuffed suitcase with an entire life stuffed inside'.[5] It was almost impossible to get anything to eat on Sunday trains, or at railway stations, and the dancers would bring food with them, ranging from simple sandwiches to full scale meals with a tablecloth and wine. The extremes of prevailing conditions are summed up in the stage management reports. The Palace in Plymouth was – 'A scruffy place ... The offices were still pervaded by the smell of cheap haircream. Samuel's electric razor was stolen whilst we were there, and the supply of toilet paper and hot water needed constant chivvying. Desultory stage crew too. The week in no way brilliant'.[6] In contrast was the Grand in Blackpool, an excellently run immaculate theatre, where the stage was washed every day and 'Mr Egan, the House Manager, thanked us for bringing culture to Blackpool'.[7] The back-up of publicity and block booking arrangements, were all handled from Covent Garden, which was often out of touch with conditions on the road, so the success of the tour often depended upon the efficiency of the local theatre. Good managements meant good business and a regular theatregoing audience. But too often the stage management reports tell the sad tale of poor business and managers, unsatisfactory stage floors and incompetent stage crews.

There were increasing problems with transporting the scenery by rail. Trucks would fail to arrive on time to load up, and there was always the chance of missing the connection to the next date. Scenery trucks were very large and their couplings only fitted steam trains, which were themselves getting rarer as electrification spread throughout the rail network. Eventually the management began to investigate the possibilities of road transport, and by the mid 1960s all scenery and equipment were moved by road.

To most dancers, cities took on a dreadful sameness – rehearsal room, theatre and digs. There was, as in all touring companies, a close family atmosphere, built out of sharing the same experiences, conditions, anxieties, hopes and fears; in the case of The Royal Ballet, where most of the dancers had been together since their schooldays, the closeness was even stronger than usual. They were together much more than the Resident Company dancers, who had the luxury of proper home lives at the end of the day. The closeness extended to their technical staff, although it was always difficult to get to know the orchestra, as their working hours were different and orchestra calls were rare.

The theatres were not exactly a home from home. In the days before the company toured its own washing-machines and spin-driers, every dressing-room was festooned with washing. The theatres were old and inconvenient, and one boy calculated that he had to climb up and down eight hundred steps during *The Sleeping Beauty* in Manchester. Each theatre had different lighting equipment, meaning lamps in unexpected places, which could have a great effect upon dancing. Stages came in many different shapes and sizes and all kinds of floors, including some cinema floors built over concrete, and with and without rakes. Rakes were a hazard not only for the dancers' balance but also for the sets, giving rise to leaning walls and sticking doors.

During the 1958 spring tour the company was joined by Ailne Phillips, who was to set the full-length *Swan Lake*. It was given an Opera House first night on 27 June during a brief visit to London, when the company managed to cram six ballets into four performances.

The production had been mounted under less than ideal conditions, and the dancers only had ten days between the end of their tour and their opening at the Opera House. With Heaton suffering from foot problems, there were no experienced principals in the touring section yet capable of carrying a full-length ballet, so Odette-Odile and Prince Siegfried were danced by Covent Garden principals Rowena Jackson and Philip Chatfield; Anya Linden and David Blair were also scheduled to appear on tour. The production and designs by Leslie Hurry were copies of those in use at Covent Garden, another link in forging the companies into a single unit. All went well 'considering, ... but we should not have to consider so many difficulties and problems when watching a company with such a proud title',[8] although it was recognised that the failings were due to the conditions under which the production had been mounted.

The ballet made greater demands upon the whole company than *Coppélia* or *Giselle*, and only time would instil the necessary discipline and finish into the *corps de ballet*, though there was no lack of enthusiasm among the dancers for whom the ballet still had the freshness of novelty. The company was maturing and the classics gave the audience the chance to measure its progress. The traditionally anonymous critic of the *Times Educational Supplement* summed up the general feeling: 'More than anything else this *Swan Lake* revealed the high standard of technique and theatrical know-how bequeathed by the school to its students past and present. But the triumph is not unmixed ... one could wish that in future the school would rank acting and expression equal with technique in the education it gives'.[9]

Dancers like Bennett, used to Rambert's more emotional approach, found rehearsals at this time very clinical and he was struck by the emphasis put on technique. Dancers were meticulously prepared for their performances and Field was adept at passing on his own partnering skills. De Valois and Field were determined that the Royal Ballet should not be faulted technically, and that it should live up to its name and reputation as part of the national ballet company. Field, Legerton and Mossford were always out front, to pick up errors and correct them before they turned into bad habits. There was great emphasis on the perfection of the *corps de ballet* – straight lines, beautifully pointed feet, unified movement – the hallmarks of The Royal Ballet on which its reputation had been based and which they were at pains to maintain.

In the autumn of 1958 the touring section set out on its longest tour to date, seven months in Australia and New Zealand. Here, appearing in theatres for up to two months of continuous performances they had more chance to settle than ever before. Two months were to be spent in Sydney and Melbourne, a month in Adelaide and Brisbane, a week in Dunedin and thirteen days each in Christchurch, Wellington and Auckland. The repertory consisted of the full length *Swan Lake*, *Giselle*, *Coppélia* (which from now on would be performed in the same pretty Osbert Lancaster designs as at Covent Garden), *Veneziana*, *Blood Wedding*, *Pineapple Poll*, *Les Sylphides*, *The Burrow*, *A Blue Rose*, *Façade*, *The Rake's Progress*, *Les Patineurs*, *Hamlet* and a number of classical *divertissements*. While they were away, the Covent Garden company made a short tour to Bristol, Manchester and Oxford, the last time they would tour the provinces for over a decade.

The company of fifty-four was led by Jackson (a New Zealander) and Chatfield, and all the Covent Garden principals, except Nerina, were to appear during the tour. Robert Helpmann, who had been acting in Australia in Noël Coward's *Nude with Violin*, joined the company to make his first appearances in Australia as a dancer since he had left in 1933 to join the Vic-Wells Ballet; he would also revive his ballet *Hamlet* for the company. About ten dancers were similarly going home.

Australia was used to first-class ballet and had been for many years. Adeline Genée and Anna Pavlova had both toured there, the De Basil Ballets Russes had scored a particular success in the 1930s and 1940s, as had Ballet Rambert in 1947–8. The country boasted one major ballet company, the Borovansky Ballet, as well as several small ones. Australian audiences were known to be extremely discriminating, and the dancers were warned not to imagine that they were going out as pioneers.

The flight out took four days. On arrival in Sydney, the company was met by de Valois, who had gone ahead to promote the tour, John Tooley, David Webster's assistant, and Kathleen Gorham, a former member of the Theatre Ballet who was now dancing with the Borovansky Ballet. They settled in happily to the Empire Theatre, which reminded them of a larger version of Sadler's Wells.

They opened on 11 September with *Swan Lake*. The company danced well, Jackson excelling herself technically, but the press were cool, feeling that the dancers were too restrained and that the performance lacked magic. There was also an unspoken but definite undercurrent of feeling that this was a 'second' company. De Valois made a speech referring to 'the commonwealth of English-speaking dancers' and thanking the country for the wealth of talent that it had sent to enrich British ballet. She then continued her promotional tour, exhorting people to attend as many performances by as many different companies as possible so that they could see how varied an art ballet could be. She found the Australians inclined to be star-conscious, and urged her audiences to see the company as a whole: 'The great dancer helps to make a great company, but the great company also makes the great dancer. Either is incomplete without the other'.[10]

The tour really took off with the arrival of Beriosova and Ashbridge. Sydney went wild over her and more than anything it was her success that tipped the scales in the company's favour. After she had joined them, the whole tour was seen in a different light and people returned to see the other dancers and ballets. The modern works were particularly well received, especially *Blood Wedding* and *The Burrow*, (though both must have been far from normal Australian experience), in which Heaton and Britton were much admired. Beriosova's success continued, but Jackson more than held her own. Not surprisingly, Helpmann, appearing twenty-five times in twelve days, was acclaimed as the Rake, Dr Coppélius and in *Façade*, to which the Nocturne Peruvienne had been restored especially for him.

The Sydney season built up to a rapturous finale, ending with a traditional Australian streamer-throwing farewell on the last night, leaving the stage ankle-deep in pink, green, blue and yellow strips. Field made a speech paying tribute to Helpmann and Helpmann replied with a speech praising the company. John Tooley reported to the Ballet Sub-Committee in London that the visit ended in 'a blaze of glory, and that the box office takings had greatly improved'.

It was in Sydney that de Valois told Seymour that, after only fifteen months in the company, she was to study Odette-Odile. She was understandably alarmed, for she had never danced the lead in a one-act ballet, or even a lengthy classical adagio. She had to fit learning the role into her normal rehearsal schedule and to break her into the classical showpieces she was made to do the *Don Quixote pas de deux* first. Beriosova and Blair, who had arrived with Anya Linden for the Melbourne season, both encouraged her, as did Robert Helpmann. From the beginning of her career Seymour strove to find the emotional truth of every role, and Helpmann, with his actor's attitude to dancing, was of great help to her as she worked her way into the part.

The opening of the Melbourne season on 10 November was an exciting, full dress occasion, and there was an ovation for Jackson, Chatfield and the whole company. Melbourne as a city was quieter and more dignified than Sydney, but the company was warmly received and entertained. Linden and Blair quickly established themselves as favourites, her delicate allure being especially admired as Swanilda. To everyone's delight Blair was dancing Captain Belaye again, with no diminution in dash and charm.

The Canadian flag flew over Her Majesty's Theatre on 12 November to signal Seymour's début as Odette-Odile. After the performance she sent a laconic telegram to her parents in Vancouver simply saying 'Performance successful. Relief.' – an understatement to put it mildly. She was praised both by the press and her fellow dancers. She had a beautiful supple back, eloquent arms and lovely feet, and her limpid style and fluid line made her a natural Odette, but few could have expected the strength and brilliance of her Odile. She already had the makings of a completely personal reading of the role, very different from the refined elegance of Fonteyn that set the standard for most Royal Ballet dancers, for Seymour's was a very sensuous and, as MacMillan described it 'very luscious' style. Blair partnered her, and she was later to dance the ballet with MacLeary, making his own impressive début as Prince Siegfried.

Adelaide gave the company the warmest welcome yet when they opened at the Theatre Royal on 7 January 1959. It was Helpmann's home town, and he was dancing there for the first time in thirty years. It was now the height of the Australian summer, and the heat rose to about 110°F, which meant a good ten degrees higher on stage. The press reception was equally warm, likening the company's success to that of the De Basil Ballets Russes over twenty years before. Here Alexander danced her first Odette-Odile. The variety of the repertory was much appreciated and the many opportunities it gave to the dancers and here, as elsewhere on the tour, the high standard of design was especially commented on. *Hamlet*, in particular, stunned the audience into temporary silence before a tumultuous reception, and Harold Tidemann in the *Adelaide Advertiser* hailed it as 'one of the most overwhelming pieces of theatre ever devised ... Leslie Hurry's scenery and costumes are as fantastically vivid as the dramatic choreography, the intensity of which does not let up for 17 minutes'.[12]

The company further endeared themselves to Adelaide by mounting a special midnight gala in aid of the Mayor's bushfire appeal as 'a gesture of the company's appreciation of its happy time in Australia',[13] and the fund benefited by over £2,000. As everywhere on the tour, Field invited local teachers and senior students to attend company classes, a gesture that was much appreciated.

The dancers travelled by air from city to city, the sets leap-frogging ahead to the next destination as soon as they were finished with in each. Unfortunately one of the trucks transporting the shoes and some costumes, scenery and electrics got lost between Adelaide and Brisbane, and the Brisbane first night on 3 February had a rather make-shift air. The wardrobe hastily concocted an Odile tutu for Jackson using the *Veneziana* La Favorita costume, the peasants had to do without wigs, props were improvised and shoes had to be hurriedly supplied from a local shop. It did nothing to mar the success of the visit, however, and Field was quoted in the *Sydney Morning Herald* as saying that Brisbane 'has more interest in ballet than any other city we have come across in years ... we have found nothing to touch its degree of interest outside London, New York and Paris'.[14]

The Australian reception was nothing to the mania that was building up in New Zealand, where the excitement centered around the performances to be given by Fonteyn and Somes – their first visit to the island. The company opened in Dunedin on 4 March with *Swan Lake*, causing the local critic to bemoan the fact that visiting companies so underestimated the capacity of audiences, 'I ask only that one day some overseas company will give us just a taste of the new currents and trends which are sweeping the world of dance in Europe and America today'.[15] But the high overall standard was welcomed, for New Zealand did not see as much first-class ballet as Australia. The Royal Ballet performances were eagerly looked forward to as a yardstick by which future companies could be measured and there was understandable local pride in the success of native dancers, like Jackson and Alexander Grant.

Everywhere there was a sense of occasion. In Christchurch twenty people worked on the flowers decorating the Theatre Royal for two days before the opening on 9 March. It was again a glittering first night and full evening dress was worn by an audience that had got used to casual dressing for the theatre. Jackson had added depth and humanity to her Odette-Odile, and Grant and Farriss were almost hysterically received in the Neapolitan dance. The dancers, as usual, responded to the warmth and fervour of the audience and excelled themselves.

Excitement was mounting to Fonteyn's first appearance in *Giselle* on 19 March. People queued for an unheard of three days for tickets and many were turned away. The press reflected the sense of occasion amounting almost to awe that her presence inspired. Police had to be called out to keep roads clear outside the theatre. The critics polished up their superlatives 'incomparable ... a creature apart, falling not far short of divinity'.[16] 'A thrilling occasion, one to haunt the Theatre Royal ever more ... she gave her audience the very ecstasy of discovering love – and thrust into it every anguish of despair. She made magic'.[17] After the performance the audience rushed from the theatre to the stage door and crowds lined the streets to watch her drive away. Over 2,000 packed the Town Hall for a Civic Lunch in her honour on 24 March, at which she was welcomed by the Mayor and the Prime Minister, Mr Nash.

The company moved on to Wellington, tired and strained after the long tour, although there was no sign of it on stage. The 'zest and gaiety evident among the whole company ... speaks much for their morale', recorded JJC in the *Wellington Evening Post*. Once again most critics had eyes for others in the company besides Fonteyn, and Heaton's Giselle was acclaimed as 'masterly ... delicate as a lily and as seductive as moonlight on a silver sea'.[18]

Fonteyn-mania was at its height. On the way to Auckland she and Somes made a brief non-dancing stopover in Masterton, where over 1,000 people turned out to see them, and there was an official welcome by the Mayor at their hotel. Auckland, where they opened on 6 April, was the final date on the tour. Audiences were not to be disappointed. 'It is the finest company which has visited New Zealand in twenty years', declared the *Auckland Star*. 'It is a ballet up to the highest standards within the limitations of numbers and space; and it can set a standard for lovers of the art in New Zealand who have no opportunity to travel abroad'.[19] A packed house gave them an emotional farewell on 18 April, 'the atmosphere charged by the pride of New Zealanders in the virtuosity of Rowena Jackson and Alexander Grant and supercharged by the gaiety and abandon of the entire company'.[20]

The company took back to England memories of a triumph, but they left behind several married couples, including Jackson and Chatfield, Sara Neil and Walter Trevor, and Patricia Cox and Leslie White, all of whom had decided to settle in Australasia. It had taken time for audiences to respond to the company and to the unfamiliar ballets, but, once accepted, the enthusiasm had been overwhelming, and it had been the most acclaimed foreign company since the De Basil Ballets Russes in the 1940s. Many ballets had rivalled the classics in popularity, especially *Blood Wedding* and *The Rake's Progress*. The company, particularly the enlarged *corps de ballet*, had matured into a spirited cohesive unit. There is nothing like a long and successful tour for bringing on young dancers, and de Valois was so pleased that she proposed giving Seymour and Alexander the chance of dancing leading roles with the Covent Garden company.

Thus in the few days between their return and setting out on the provincial spring tour, Seymour and MacLeary made their Opera House débuts in *Swan Lake*, and Alexander danced *Coppélia* with Britton and *Giselle* with Bennett. Seymour astounded the London audience by the maturity and the depth of emotion that she could already pour into the role. At Covent Garden it could have taken several years for her to do nine performances of the role, so she was already a veteran by Resident Company standards.

There was no time for the company to rest on its laurels, however, before it was off on a six-week provincial tour and a return to the 'second company' carping and the hopes that, once the companies were fully integrated it would be possible to split it into two groups of equal standard. It was difficult to make everyone understand that a company on the road would always be different from a company with a home base, and that constant interchange between the two could only have an unsettling effect and would result in two unstable companies of lower, not higher, standard. Again Covent Garden supplied the principals for *Swan Lake*, and on 17 June Beriosova and MacLeary danced together for the first time, the beginning of a distinguished partnership. Nerina was also on the road, and Annette Page and Ronald Hynd, made their débuts as Odette-Odile and Prince Siegfried.

After the summer break the company moved back to Covent Garden for the first, much-heralded, 'joint' season by both Royal Ballets – over a hundred dancers with Fonteyn and Grey as Guest Artists. Only *Swan*

Lake and *The Rake's Progress* had truly mixed casts, otherwise each company performed its own repertory with the occasional exchange of dancers. The problem was to bring the company up to a single standard of performance and there was especial criticism of the immaturity of the male dancers, although MacLeary was one of the major successes of the season, especially his partnership with Beriosova. Seymour and Alexander both made their débuts in the Covent Garden revised production of *The Sleeping Beauty*. Among the young dancers who began to attract attention were Elizabeth Anderton and a good-looking young boy named Christopher Gable.

For the 'second company' and many of the audience, the season was mixed with sadness, for Heaton had been forced to give up dancing by an arthritic foot, which had dogged her career for the last few years. She made her farewell as the Betrayed Girl in *The Rake's Progress* and at the end, surrounded by flowers, received a great ovation.

After a month a section of the Royal Ballet which bore a strong resemblance to that of the Touring Company of the previous tour, left for the provinces. On the opening night of the tour, in Leeds on 14 September, they faced their biggest test to date, the full *The Sleeping Beauty* using the same Oliver Messel designs as the Resident Company. The first Aurora was Linden, partnered by Bryan Ashbridge. The first of the Touring Company dancers to essay Princess Aurora on tour was Alexander, partnered by Desmond Doyle, a sunny interpretation, even if she was not yet mature enough for the grandeur of the last act.

Most of the dancers were new to their roles and, not surprisingly, the first performances were rather tentative. *The Sleeping Beauty* stretched the company up to and beyond their limits, even when no dancers were on the sick list, which was rarely on the long tours; there were only twenty-four dancers at *corps de ballet* level and twenty-two of them were needed for the Prologue. Even with the ensembles cut down, extras provided from local dancing schools and one classical variation eliminated (the Fairy of the Crystal Fountain) it was still a massive production by current touring standards and easily the most sumptuous spectacle that most provincial audiences, starved of visual splendour, would now see. No designer ever caught the fairy-tale atmosphere of the ballet as well as Messel, but though the costumes still looked good the scenery was originally at least fifteen feet too large for most provincial theatres, which meant that the proportions were completely ruined, although later the company acquired a properly rescaled set of cloths.

Now began the criticism that would last for the next decade about

The Sleeping Beauty.

the inadvisability of touring productions of the classics intended for Covent Garden. Field would, of course, have preferred to have special touring versions, but mirror-image productions were the aim. The policy gave rise to an attitude which was to gain favour with some critics and some of the management, that the classics should not be performed anywhere but in an opera house. This feeling was summed up by Clive Barnes: 'In my opinion to produce these ballets in any other circumstances cannot result in anything but a travesty of their true nature. Furthermore, I am unable to feel a great deal of respect for an artistic policy which appears to an outsider to be governed by the principle of giving the public what it wants – such a course can hardly be called a policy, it is a mere expediency'.[21]

It was perhaps also difficult for critics who could sometimes see *The Sleeping Beauty* or *Swan Lake* several times a month to realise that out of London the classics, especially *The Sleeping Beauty*, were now a novelty, and that it was not so much a matter of giving provincial audiences what they wanted as what they had rarely seen. Now for the first time a new generation had regular access to the mainsprings of the repertory, to one of the cornerstones upon which The Royal Ballet was built.

It was also a fact that, subsidy or no, box office still counted, and audience preferences could not be completely ignored. With so few visits and high seat prices, audiences still needed a guarantee that they would enjoy themselves. That meant a known name, either in the ballet, the music or the dancers. No other company at this period was touring either a full *Swan Lake* or *The Sleeping Beauty*, so there was not exactly a glut on the road. *Beauty* was not given everywhere, for some theatres were just too small, nor did the Touring Company ever dance it at the Royal Opera House.

The critics' attitude not surprisingly upset the dancers. Field had his own answer. 'My job in directing you', he told them, 'is to turn every place we perform into the best opera house in the world, with the best performance in the world being presented there. I don't care if it's just trestle tables on the village green – that is the best opera house in the world because we are giving the best performance anybody can see on it tonight. Not last night, not tomorrow night – tonight. It's not the bricks and mortar, it's what you put into the bricks and mortar'.[22]

De Valois knew the classics were important for dancers, audience and young choreographers alike, for from them they could learn both dance and stage craft. She saw no problem in adapting them for the smaller stages – 'the classics are very elastic: they hold good in different circumstances. In our early days we could give them in miniature in a small theatre, knowing that later on the small productions would prove suitable for a big theatre like Covent Garden. It is also possible to tour productions of them – indeed, for touring, the classics are extremely adaptable',[23] more adaptable, she felt than some modern works. She always refuted the suggestion that ballet audiences were innately conservative, pointing out that they were no more so than those for opera or music – indeed probably less so.

So Henry Legerton became expert at expanding and contracting the productions according to the stage. By the end of the decade he had an invaluable notebook of diagrams of 'how to get there in *Swan Lake*', starting with thirty-two swans, then thirty, twenty-four, twenty, sixteen, fourteen and even six, which the company once needed at the tiny Arts Theatre in Cambridge.

One thing *The Sleeping Beauty* did show up was the smallness of the orchestra. It was not easy to cut down Tchaikovsky to twenty-seven players and, if the provincial audiences did not know much about ballet, they often did know about music. Orchestras were always expensive, and it was getting no easier to find good musicians willing to tour. It was not only a matter of economics – the Opera House was anxious to increase the size and standards as soon as possible, but not every theatre even had an orchestra pit, let alone room for a large orchestra. Sometimes players had to be put in the stage boxes, thus playing havoc with the balance of the sound.

It was also difficult for many of the provincial theatres to find the staff to provide the back-up for a company with large productions. In Woolwich, where the company appeared in a local cinema, thirty-one additional people had to be brought in – stage hands, wardrobe staff, call boys and dressers. Lighting equipment was often insufficient, and the company had to tour its own extra lights and switchboard.

The unpopularity of the triple bills was always one of the problems exercising Boards of Directors, Sub-Committees and Directors alike. Ballets lasting a full evening have always been a bigger draw than an evening of short ballets. Audiences never quite overcame the feeling that three separate ballets somehow shortchanged them, that they were not value for money (indeed, calculated as time as money they were often under two and a half hours as against three hours of a full evening ballet). The general theatre-going audience never developed the 'concert' rather than the 'theatre' mentality, that accepted an evening made up of complete, but short, contrasted works. Indeed, many never caught up with the idea that a short ballet was complete in itself, and not just an extract from a full length work; as Patricia Ruanne later remarked, 'You get certain old ladies, you know, who are convinced that *Pineapple Poll* is the third act of *Solitaire*.'[24]

The *Liverpool Echo* reviewed the general situation. 'As a whole, the company has done well for us. It has brought a new work, two neglected ones and a number of old favourites, all well presented and including some fine dancing. It has scored on the counts of youth and vitality, and has sometimes lost a few points for the unsteadiness in the *corps-de-ballet* and bad orchestral playing'.[25]

In autumn 1959, the company briefly inherited Andrée Howard's *La*

Donald Britton as Sweeney Todd and Margaret Knoesen as Mrs Lovett in *Sweeney Todd*.

Belle Dame sans Merci, but their main energies were directed towards creating their first original ballet since *The Burrow*, two years before. Cranko's *Sweeney Todd*, premièred at Stratford-Upon-Avon on 10 December, was based on the gory tale of the Demon Barber of Fleet Street, and his part in Mrs Lovett's pie business. Malcolm Arnold provided a tuneful score and Alix Stone some delightful Victorian-pastiche designs. Cranko's presentation opted for knockabout comedy and burlesque, and if the ballet was short on finish and style the story was 'told with the zest and vulgarity of a pair of bursting stays'.[26] There were some inventive moments, like the *pas de quatre* for the heroine, Sweeney, an Indian Army Colonel and a waltzing table, the apprentice (a plaintive Mosaval) hiccuping buttons after eating one of Mrs Lovett's special pies, and a deal of slapstick chasing à la Keystone cops, but it never really added up to a satisfying whole, and there was no danger of

Elizabeth Anderton in *Solitaire*.

Photograph by G. B. L. Wilson. By courtesy of the Royal Academy of Dancing.

Pineapple Poll being pushed off its comic throne. Britton played the title role with relish and a mirthless leer and ran away with all the notices, and Elizabeth Anderton was enchanting as the beautiful heroine, Johanna. Anderton's progress in solo roles was a heartening feature of the tour. She was a notable Bluebird, and played the Girl in *Solitaire* with a wistful gentleness that was very appealing.

Chapter XI

On 30 January 1960 the company left a dreary English winter for the warmth of South Africa, where they were to make a three month tour, playing the main cities of Johannesburg, Pietermaritzburg, Durban and Cape Town to coincide with the golden jubilee of the founding of the Union of South Africa. The tour was, not unexpectedly, surrounded with controversy, mainly because Mosaval, South African born of Malaysian extraction, was at the last minute left behind, ostensibly because he was not needed for the selected repertory. He had not been included in the Theatre Ballet tour in 1954 either, and it was obvious to everyone that he was prevented by South African law from appearing there as a member of a white company. The press picked up the story and there were even questions in the House, with Tom Driberg demanding that the company be recalled from the tour, but Field's view was that they had a contract and a duty to fulfil it.

The general situation was not encouraging. There was a state of emergency in force, making travel within South Africa difficult, and natives were being held in the townships by armoured cars. The Foreign Office ensured that the company had complete protection, but they were advised never to go out alone and always to leave messages at their hotels about where they were going and how long they expected to be away. On the whole, however, everyone realised that the company had nothing to do with the internal politics, and they were welcomed everywhere. In accordance with Equity rules, they had agreed to give performances in Pietermaritzburg before mixed audiences and one performance in Johannesburg and one in Cape Town before non-European audiences.

The company was increased to seventy, and several Covent Garden principals were ferried between London and South Africa, including Beriosova, Nerina and Brian Shaw, and several younger dancers notably Antoinette Sibley and Gary Burne were seconded for the tour. Sibley had just scored a highly publicised success in *Swan Lake* at Covent Garden, and it was felt desirable for her to have the chance to develop in the classical repertory away from the pressures of London. In South Africa she made her debut as Giselle and Princess Aurora as well as appearing in a wide range of ballets.

Nerina was indisposed for part of the tour and Beryl Grey came out as Guest Artist in her place (travelling out with a replacement *corps de ballet* dancer named Alfreda Thorogood). Audiences responded to her warm personality and her expansive line and mixture of strength and lyricism were much admired. Audiences were enthusiastic and, considering how little ballet they saw, very discriminating. The standards of both ballet and teaching in South Africa had always been incredibly high, as the number and strength of South African dancers in The Royal Ballet bore witness. The company became a household name and Grey was asked to endorse a range of cosmetics. There were capacity audiences everywhere and performances were acclaimed as the most memorable and exciting that the country had seen for years. There was great interest in the young dancers, especially Sibley, and in the South Africans in the company.

The tour was relatively smooth running, the administration and the Foreign Office saw to that, but it could not avoid controversy. The performance for non-whites in Cape Town had been arranged for a Monday afternoon, which meant that most would have to lose a half day's pay to go, and the Mayor of Cape Town had to make a special appeal to employers to release as many employees as possible who wanted to attend the performance. The ban on coloureds at the Alhambra meant that the performance had to be relegated to the drab City Hall, and there were complaints that the programme included a number of excerpts, rather than complete works, and there were threats that the whole matter would be reported to Equity as not fulfilling their rules. The company made every effort to arrange a second programme in Cape Town for non-whites, but it was not possible to fit it into the schedule.

A year later South Africa became a republic and withdrew from the Commonwealth. South Africans already working in Britain were given time to acquire British nationality, but in future no South African national would be eligible to join a British ballet company. They had contributed much to the development of the second company – Cranko,

Poole, Lane, Nerina, Miller, Doyle, Rodrigues and Mosaval – and their vitality and expansive movement would be much missed once the current group of dancers had retired.

After a summer tour and their annual holiday, the dancers returned to a short London season. It was Seymour's season; her fluency of movement and glorious line were irresistible, especially in *Solitaire*, to which she brought a delicate childlike wonder. A young Resident Company soloist, Doreen Wells, made a memorable debut as Pineapple Poll, succeeding because, like Fifield before her, she just danced the role and let the character and humour come through the choreography, not through 'interpretation'.

Wells joined the company out on tour that autumn as a replacement for Alexander, who had left to get married, making her debut with them in *Swan Lake* and *The Sleeping Beauty*. Technically assured, the roles held no terrors for her, and her precision and sweet charm quickly won audiences over. Her personality was as yet undeveloped, and she needed to work on the expressive side of her dancing, but the essentials were there for what everybody felt would be a distinguished career. Nor was the company short of talent among the young soloists.

The most important night of the tour was the première on 10 November in Oxford of a new MacMillan ballet. *The Invitation* had a libretto based on Colette's *The Ripening Seed* and Beatriz Guido's *The House of the Angel*; its score had been commissioned from the Hungarian composer Mátyás Seiber, and the designs from Nicholas Georgiadis. The theme was the awakening of adolescent sexuality, in an outwardly prudish and conventional society. Two teenagers become involved with an unhappily married couple. For the boy the encounter with the wife helps him to come to terms with his sexuality, but the girl's confrontation with the husband leads to rape and her emotional crippling for life. 'The story does not resolve itself', MacMillan was quoted as saying. 'When one loses innocence and grows up it can be a shattering experience without resolution. I hope the spectators may see things in the ballet which they've felt in their lives. I'm sick to death of fairy stories. I want people to go to the theatre to be moved by something they can recognize'.[1] The ballet reflected his concern with real characters and their emotions, and if the sexual context shook audiences out of their complacency that was all to the good.

Since his early works MacMillan had come to believe that content was more important than form; he had evolved a freer, more lyrical style, and developed the *pas de deux* as expressive of human relationships.

He demanded dancers who could also act and create recognisable human beings, and his cast did not let him down. Doyle had his best role ever as the Husband, a man of raging suppressed passions. Heaton, whose foot had responded to treatment, made a welcome temporary return as the Wife, her rigid anger hiding a desperate need for affection. Gable was the Cousin, all eager gaucheness and fumbling tenderness. But it was Seymour's ballet. MacMillan loved her extraordinarily expressive body and her willingness to put emotional truth before beauty of line. As the Girl, her voluptuous innocence of the early scenes gave way to battered, bewildered incomprehension and at the end one glimpsed the life of frustrated spinsterhood that awaited her. It was also the beginning of her famous partnership with Gable; both had wonderfully expressive bodies, the minds of actors, and a commitment to emotional truth. Their naturalism in dance contrasted with the more stylized approach of the older Royal Ballet dancers; they were examples of a new generation of dancers for the new decade that was dawning.

The Invitation was an uneven work, but its power was undeniable. The *pas de deux* for the Girl and her Cousin had a tender, physical hunger, unrealised by them for what it was, and the children's dancing party at which the Girl unwittingly flirts with the Man was a neat piece of choreographic construction. Less successful was the symbolic *pas de trois* for the party entertainers dressed as a hen and two cocks, which lowered rather than raised the growing sexual tension.

Georgiadis designed a magnificent, almost impressionist, set of gauzy drapes, which suggested an over-lush, emotive environment and managed to combine evocations of Edwardian fashions with appropriate dance costumes.

The ballet was received with mixed feelings amounting to outrage in some quarters, and performances on tour were punctuated by the sound of up-ending seats as the more shocked among the audience walked out. Many resented the attempt to treat serious subjects realistically in ballet, and there were complaints that it was unsuitable for children by those who thought ballet should be no more than innocuous family enter-

---

Lynn Seymour as The Girl and Desmond Kelly as The Husband in *The Invitation*.

tainment. There was, however, a lot of publicity to be got out of the decision to announce it as 'not suitable for children' and it was actually given an X certificate by the company. Audiences remained unprepared for the ballet well into the 'swinging Sixties'; school parties were warned about the subject matter, and it was not programmed for matinées.

With the Resident Company in America over Christmas, the Touring Company moved into the Opera House for a four-month season, playing in repertory with the opera. There was less than a fortnight between the end of the tour and the London performances, during which they had to learn the far from easy Ashton *Cinderella*. Principals, including Fonteyn and Beriosova returned from America to dance the lead, but it was Seymour who captivated everyone with her performance as a shy, forlorn slattern, rising to heights of regality and wonder at the ball. Gable too, was attracting attention for his open, clean dancing and even more for his natural unaffected acting, particularly in his interpretation of the cardboard princes of the classics.

During the season Pirmin Trecu gave his last performance with The Royal Ballet in one of his most unforgettable roles, the Country Boy in *La Fête étrange*. Incessant knee trouble had forced him to give up dancing while he still had much to contribute. His distinctive personality had enlivened the Covent Garden performances as it had once the Theatre Ballet, and it was fitting that his last performance should have been with his old company's successor.

The company was also rehearsing Ashton's first ballet to be created for them since *Valses Nobles et Sentimentales*. *Les Deux Pigeons* (its name was later anglicized for touring) was appropriately premièred on St Valentine's day 1961, at a gala performance in the presence of the Queen Mother, Princess Margaret and her husband Antony Armstrong-Jones.

André Messager had composed *Les Deux Pigeons* for Louis Mérante at the Paris Opera in 1886 and Ashton now made a new and simpler libretto based on the eponymous La Fontaine fable. Lanchbery, who had moved to the Opera House in 1959, reworked and cut Messager's delicious score.

In that romantic Bohemian Paris which never existed beyond the stage door, an artist has begun to tire of his young fiancée; her charming innocence no longer appeals to him, and he falls easy victim to the flashy sensuality of a gypsy girl. Bewildered, his fiancée tries all her charms and then sadly attempts to ape the gypsy to win him back, but in vain, and he deserts her for his new love. In the gypsy camp he is tolerated at first, but the girl quickly tires of him and he is unceremoniously thrown out. Sadder and wiser he returns to his fiancée, and in one of Ashton's loveliest *pas de deux* they rebuild their shattered love, beginning in sorrow, guilt and anguish and ending in a quiet, deeper happiness than any they have known before.

The Two Pigeons was a masterpiece of storytelling in dancing. Ashton extended the punning title ('pigeon' being a French endearment) to introduce both real birds to highlight significant moments of the action, and bird motifs into the choreography, fluttering hands and feet and the use of the flexed arms to suggest beating wings. The ballet showed Ashton at his best – his superlative craftsmanship, his keen observation, his gentle humanity. It could so easily have been sentimental, no more than a charming confection, but from the basic operetta story Ashton created a deeply moving comment on love and experience. He perfectly understood the period and style of the score and never overburdened it with an emotion that it would not bear. His characters were recognisably ordinary people, brought to a fuller understanding of themselves by their experiences.

Like so many of Ashton's works, the critics originally underestimated the ballet. Even those who received it well thought it charming but shallow. Ashton was bemused at the critical response: 'They say it is not contemporary, but ballet is not primarily a matter of ideas or trends; these do not necessarily make for good choreography; and ballet is a matter of choreography'.[2] It took a long time to establish itself in public favour, especially in the provinces; de Valois, however, loved it and soon appropriated it for Covent Garden.

Coming hard upon *The Invitation*, *The Two Pigeons* likewise looked at youthful love and experience and exploited Seymour's particular talents. Her flowing pliancy enchanted Ashton, especially her beautifully arched feet, which reminded him of Pavlova's, and, as the Girl, he gave her lots of intricate, delicate footwork and complicated *enchaînements* to show them off. He exploited her willingness to look gauche and awkward in a character that was at once funny and touching. In contrast he gave Anderton as the Gypsy Girl lots of flashy virtuoso steps and jumps, which she performed with a passionate fire and sensuality. The Young Man was set on Britton, but he injured himself at the dress rehearsal, so Gable danced the first night. His coltish unformed youth and virtuoso prowess in the solos were completely expressive of a young man in the grip of a youthful emotion over which he had no control.

The strength of the ballet can be seen by the variety and number of interpreters it has encompassed. With the Touring Company, Wells was

Lynn Seymour as The Young Girl and Christopher Gable as The Young Man in *The Two Pigeons*.

Photograph by Houston Rogers. From the collections of the Theatre Museum. Reproduced by courtesy of the Board of Trustees of the Victoria and Albert Museum.

particularly successful in projecting sweetness, while Alfreda Thorogood's glorious dancing was expressive of a bewitching charm. David Wall was outstanding as the Young Man, tracing the development from youth to maturity through his marvellously lyrical virile style. No one ever quite matched Anderton as the Gypsy, with her proud sensuality, but Margaret Barbieri's spitfire ran her close, and in recent years Karen Donovan has danced it with a disdainful dash and sparkle.

In mid March John Sullivan, Technical Director of Covent Garden, flew out to Tokyo to sort out the technical problems for the company's forthcoming tour of the Far East; because of the large stages the scenery had to be specially built in Japan for the visit. The Festival Hall in Tokyo was a vast stage, but extremely modern, with everything electrically controlled, and the stage staff must have compared it enviously with the out-of-date equipment they had to contend with in Britain. It was the first visit of any major British institution to Japan, and was backed by several British firms with interests in the Far East, the first time that the company had had commercial sponsorship.

Augmented by Grey as Guest Artist, Linden and Shaw, with Fonteyn and Somes for Japan, the company arrived in Tokyo to find banners welcoming the 'Loyal' Ballet and make-up tables only eighteen inches off the ground. They also had wardrobe problems, for they had been told to expect bitter weather, but found instead a climate so mild that they needed two changes of light clothing a day.

The Tokyo opening on 17 April was a gala performance of *Giselle* with Fonteyn and Somes, in the presence of Crown Prince Akihito and Princess Michiko. Interest in ballet in Japan was intense – Tokyo had no less than nineteen regular ballet groups, which at least meant that the orchestras were familiar with some of the scores. The local critics were extremely knowledgeable, having seen a wide range of dance companies, particularly from Russia, and the notices were good. The dramatic ballets were extremely popular, especially de Valois' *Checkmate*, which they performed for the first time in Tokyo with Beryl Grey in one of her best roles as the Black Queen and Doyle as the Red Knight. So successful was the Tokyo season that the company had to return after their visit to Osaka.

In complete contrast was the visit to Hong Kong, where nothing as prepared, all the equipment seemed broken and there was no orchestra, so that performances had to be given to two pianos and against black drapes. Fonteyn and Somes had returned to London and matters were not helped by their names being erroneously included in the posters.

Under these circumstances the company hardly felt it was being seen at its best, although audiences were enthusiastic.

In Manila, however, no expense had been spared. The presenter had been to see the company in Japan and the whole backstage area of the Rizal Theatre had been reconstructed with new dressing-rooms, showers and air conditioning. Even the orchestra volunteered to do extra unpaid rehearsals to get the music up to standard. The first night was memorable, and after the performance the police stopped the traffic around the theatre to allow the company to get to the many receptions organized in their honour. Most spectacular party of the three day visit was at the Polo Club, with cha-chaing until 3 a.m. and a lavish buffet, with a centre piece of a huge block of ice in which was embedded all kinds of seafood.

Autumn 1961 began with a visit to the Middle East, to perform at the Baalbek Festival and in Athens, slipping in a visit to a British Trade Fair in Damascus in between. Baalbek was a very prestigious Festival, taking place when visitors from all over the Middle East were vacationing in the mountains, and the Foreign Office attached great importance to the visit. Fonteyn and Blair led the company, Ashton accompanied them to adapt the ballets to the historic sites which would form the settings for the performances, and for the first time on a foreign tour they took their own orchestra. It would have been easy for the grandeur of the Temple of Bacchus to overwhelm the performers, but Ashton used the site with great sensitivity and skill to enhance the ballets. The 1961 Festival was generally considered to have achieved a new standard of excellence and the Foreign Office reported that The Royal Ballet had won hands down as the most successful visit yet by any foreign company at Baalbek.

In Athens the company appeared in the Herodias Atticus, with its auditorium so steeply raked that the dancers had the impression of performing to a vast wall of people. It seated some 5,000, but such was the enthusiasm of the Athenians that the performances were overbooked and over five hundred extra people had to be accommodated in the aisles each evening. So great was the reception for the *pas de deux* in *Swan Lake* that Fonteyn actually consented to repeat it – a hitherto unheard of occurrence. Her presence was inspiring not only for audiences, but also for the dancers, most of whom had had few chances of seeing her perform.

However much Field welcomed the prestigious names from London on tour, he was determined that his dancers should not degenerate into mere background. It would have been better to have Resident Company dancers seconded for a part of a tour, but no dancer wanted to risk losing their already too few London performances. Most frequent visitors were Nerina, Beriosova, Page, Linden, Lane, Doyle, MacLeary and Hynd. Whoever else might have to cancel, Beriosova always fulfilled her commitments. Legerton remembers the company being snowed up in Taunton, but even so Beriosova got through. It was not surprising that her following in the provinces was as loyal and enthusiastic as her London audience. Seymour had now moved to Covent Garden, although she was still dancing on tour. It looked as though the old pattern, of the most talented dancers being taken into the London company, was to continue.

Field was opposed to interchange at soloist level, as this would bar the senior *corps de ballet*, from which the next generation of soloists would come, from those roles. He knew that he had to give his dancers something to work for, and he insisted that they got their chance to appear in the classics as they became ready. Thus during the autumn tour of 1961 Shirley Grahame made her debut in both *Swan Lake* and *The Sleeping Beauty*. The company, however, was touring more modern works than before and at least one and if possible two triple bills were presented each week. Field abhorred the idea of a repertory only consisting of *Swan Lake* and *The Sleeping Beauty* – 'You can't expect the dancers to keep up their artistic standards on those two alone. You'd just get puppets, and pretty poor performances'.[3] The short ballets were a lifeline, especially for the youngest *corps de ballet* girls, who otherwise would have been on a treadmill of peasants, swans and court ladies, and the boys for whom the classics had even less to offer.

It was not surprising if some dancers found touring lacking in intellectual stimulation. Life centred around the theatre and performance and in most towns there was not much to see apart from the occasional art gallery. Some of these were, admittedly very splendid, but after five years of touring to the same towns even they wore thin. Meryl Chapell remembers with pleasure the university towns where there were at least good bookshops. Under these conditions it was very difficult for young performers to develop as artists and individuals.

In the 1960s very few dancers could afford to run cars, and for the majority travel still meant the Sunday train call. Every week over a hundred dancers, staff and orchestra descended upon a town. Where possible they would have booked digs in advance, but they were often booking blind and until they arrived they had no idea just where their digs might be in relation to the theatre. Over the years the more

Shirley Grahame as Odette and Alexander Bennett as Prince Siegfried in *Swan Lake*.

Photograph by Houston Rogers. From the collections of the Theatre Museum. Reproduced by courtesy of the Board of Trustees of the Victoria and Albert Museum.

experienced dancers built up contacts throughout the country, and the real old timers eventually established a chain of friends, which at least ensured them some social life outside the company. But there were always dancers left trudging round towns late on a Sunday, stories about insanitary lodgings, the girl who was attacked by her landlady and of two having to spend the night in a police cell, while Margaret Barbieri is sure she once booked into a brothel for the night.

There were, of course, some excellent digs, but throughout the 1960s they got fewer and fewer as the demands of town planning and rebuilding and the expansion of the universities in the major cities cut down the temporary accommodation available. In certain parts of the country 'theatricals' were still regarded with mistrust. Many landladies, or ordinary families who often came to the rescue, did not appreciate the special needs of dancers, like late meals after the show. Small hotels were not much better, as they did not usually provide meals after 9 p.m., and only the most expensive restaurants were open late. At one time excellent small pubs could be found, but they too faded away during the 1960s. Barbieri used to add a pathetic PS to her letters booking accommodation – 'I am South African and suffer from the cold', which usually ensured her an extra heater in her room. Dancer Hilary Cartwright once suggested that the most practical gift any dancer could receive from supportive parents was an electric blanket. 'The company', wrote George Milford-Cottam, who went out on the road with them in 1962, 'seemed to be overshadowed by an underlying unhappiness caused by miserable living conditions'.[4]

The company began to advertise in each town for 'hosts' – families willing to become 'landladies' for a week or two, but that had its problems too as Meryl Chapell recalled. 'You got people who "loved the ballet" and had a ballet daughter and it was agony. You were well looked after, and you had a nice warm home and you didn't have the hot taps sealed up and there was a plug in the bath. But you had to *talk* and when you came back after eight acts of *Swan Lake* on a Wednesday and with 10.30 class the following day you didn't want to know ...'[5]

Some dancers had their own answers. Britton and his wife Maureen Bruce had had a caravan for touring in the 1950s, and in the 1960s Jeffery Phillips and his wife, Kathleen Denley, travelled in a motor caravan. Richard Farley had a converted Volkswagen; the roof had portholes to let in the daylight and raise the height, the walls were insulated with polystyrene and the windows were shuttered. Most elaborate of the mobile homes was that of Sharon Koshley, with its William

Morris wallpaper and antique paraffin lamps. These vans were parked near the theatre, so that the dancers could use its baths, toilets and laundry facilities. Not that every theatre boasted baths or showers; Brenda Last recalled rehearsing Ashton's *Sinfonietta* on tour, after which she was so stiff that the wardrobe staff fixed for her to have a bath in the only tub available – the company twin-tub washing-machine.

The company on tour was very close – even closer than the old Theatre Ballet, which at least had its long London seasons – and it was very hard upon the more introverted members of the company. Most dancers got their relaxation at the cinema, while others developed hobbies – Colin Jones had photography, Britton model boats, Last went hunting for antiques and Kerrison Cooke for match holders. Heaton used to travel with her cat, as she found that having to feed it in the intervals kept her mind off the next ballet and was very calming. Animals were usually banned in theatres, but small creatures were smuggled in over the years, and provided some link with normality amid the upheavals of touring.

Field kept a tight rein on his company and there were strict fashion rules for his girls. They became adept at living out of suitcases, learning to carry the minimum amount of clothing that would allow them to mix and match from the warmth of early autumn to the onset of winter and from the depths of winter to the beginning of summer, when they returned to London. Trousers were frowned upon until the severe winter of 1962–63 proved the thin end of the wedge, when dancers piled on any amount of clothing to keep warm. Clothes, however, had to be immaculate and well-cared for. The era of non-crushable fabric was just coming in, making life much easier. The company was always on show, at the stage door or at civic functions at home and abroad. Consequently the dancers dressed with great care, keeping up the idea of the 'glamorous' world of ballet.

Chapter XII

On 29 December 1961 a major restructuring of the Royal Ballet was announced with the appointment of three Assistant Directors – John Field, Michael Somes and John Hart. Field continued to run the Touring Company, working closely over the transfer of dancers between the companies with Hart, who was in charge of administration at Covent Garden. Somes was responsible for rehearsing and coaching the young dancers at Covent Garden.

A company of forty-eight was quite small to carry a full classical repertory, and the nightly slog of classics, even relieved by the triple bills, meant that boredom could quickly set in. After a below par performance of *Swan Lake* or *The Sleeping Beauty*, Legerton often had to remind the dancers that these ballets were their bread and butter, on which they depended for survival.

Thus tours abroad were a welcome break in the routine even if in 1962 they were limited to a short visit to Lausanne and Munich and then to Nervi. In Lausanne the critics, used to the Paris Opera Ballet and American companies which stressed individual stars rather than the company, were unanimous in praise of the company's technique, discipline and unified style. In Munich, Wells took over twenty calls after her performance as Princess Aurora. Nervi however was a disaster. Fonteyn and Nureyev joined them to perform *Swan Lake* in the open air setting, and not surprisingly interest centred totally on them. Nureyev had eliminated almost all classical mime from his performance and his idiosyncratic naturalism contrasted oddly with the company's more traditional stylized playing. The orchestra was bad and there had been little thought given to adapting the production for the open air; there was much criticism of the careless presentation, and there were the usual

146

brickbats about publicity having suggested that it was the Covent Garden company.

To relieve pressure on the touring *corps de ballet*, in the autumn of 1962 a small group of Covent Garden *corps de ballet* dancers transferred to the Touring Company (they were replaced by eight students). The plan was to replace those eight at intervals until the whole Covent Garden *corps de ballet* had appeared on tour. In fact this was only unsettling, for a *corps de ballet* needs stability to grow into a unified group; the real answer was to increase the *corps* by two or three extra dancers, which was eventually done. However, the Covent Garden dancers enjoyed dancing every night and the chance to perform the occasional solo. One, Patricia Ruanne, liked it so much that she opted to stay with the Touring Company.

Topped up by principals from Covent Garden, the company began the 1962–63 season with a hectic scamper through Scandinavia and Germany, giving thirty-four performances in thirty-five days, visiting Oslo, Stockholm, Germany and Copenhagen. Beriosova achieved a great personal triumph, and she and the company took forty-nine curtain calls for *The Sleeping Beauty* in Hamburg. The British had always been regarded in Europe as guardians of the classics, and their approach to *The Sleeping Beauty* was much admired, *Der Tagesspiegel* concluding that the British 'don't dance fairy tales, they dance grand opera'. Berlin was indifferent to the classics, but was taken aback by the staid British producing a ballet like *The Invitation*, since Germany had always considered that the expression of the psychological in dance was their special province. They were astounded at the power of MacMillan's work and Seymour and Gable received hysterical ovations. Particularly gratifying was the warm reception in Copenhagen, although local critics noted with satisfaction that the men were not as strong as they were used to in Denmark. However, a new generation of British male dancers was developing, spearheaded by Gable, and newly inspired by Nureyev, whose example was to do so much to raise standards of male dancing in Britain over the years.

During the autumn tour of the provinces the Touring Company inherited from Covent Garden their first Bournonville, the *divertissement* from the last act of *Napoli* and the *pas de deux* from *Flower Festival at Genzano*, the basis of which they had learned in Copenhagen. They could not be said to make a substantial addition to the repertory, and indeed made for rather scrappy programming, but it was valuable experience for the dancers in a style notable for its exploitation of the male dancer and especially good for the development of elevation and footwork. Gable and the young Gary Sherwood had the makings of the bounce and open style that the choreography required, and Wells and Anderton had the right delicacy for the girls, but the company was never able to produce one overall cast of equal strength.

Much more to their style was Ashton's *La Fille mal gardée*, which had been a smash hit since its première at Covent Garden in 1960. Ashton's masterpiece came deep from his English roots, revealing at once his love of Constable country and the eighteenth-century pastoral tradition, and paying his own tribute to nature – 'My poor man's Pastoral Symphony'[1] he once called it. The ballet was reduced a little for touring – even the pony was cut (the company didn't tour live pigeons in *The Two Pigeons* either, although both birds and ponies were later restored to delight the sentimental old hearts of English audiences) – but the spirit was there. The company did not aspire to the elegant pastoral charm of the Covent Garden company, but brought its own gusto that eminently suited the ballet's rustic setting.

Nerina, Blair, Holden and Grant came to Bristol on 9 November 1962 to recreate Lise, Colas, Widow Simone and the simpleton Alain, with Legerton proving a splendid Thomas. It had originally been thought that no dancers except Nerina and Blair, for whom Lise and Colas had been created, would be able to meet the technical demands of the leading roles, but in fact they have, over the years, proved almost dancer-proof, even if no one has quite equalled that first cast. Soon the Touring Company began to produce its own crop of charming lovers, strict mothers with their hearts in the right place, and simple but moving Alains. First of the home-bred lovers were Wells and Gable, well able to hold their own, she pretty and tender if a little sophisticated, he refreshingly natural in characterization and impressive in technique. Ronald Emblen, who had joined the company from Festival Ballet in 1962, was to prove one of the best Simones of all, warmhearted if standing no nonsense, funny without vulgarity and completely endearing. There have been so many good interpreters down the years that it is almost invidious to single out from the touring Lises Brenda Last, Ann Jenner, Marion Tait and Sandra Madgwick, and from the Colases Gary Sherwood and two of the greatest interpreters of all, David Wall and Stephen Jefferies. David Morse gave an individual reading of Simone, avoiding all camp to produce a believable character and mother, not just a pantomime dame figure.

La Fille mal gardée's universal themes and glorious inventive chor-

Ronald Emblen as Widow Simone in *La Fille mal gardée*.

eography won the hearts of the touring audience as it had London's although for some time its name was against it, and it has steadfastly resisted all attempts to find an acceptable English equivalent. Its ultimate success (it has rarely been out of the repertory of either company) was gained by word of mouth, television transmissions and the popularity of the music – especially the clog dance which became well-known in its own right. There were, and still are, however, some sad souls who cannot respond to the depths in *Fille*, and regard it as a mere romp and only suitable as a substitute Christmas pantomime.

The first new work created in nearly two years was Alan Carter's *Toccata*. Since leaving the Theatre Ballet in 1947, Carter had had a varied career as choreographer and director, including five years directing the ballet in Munich, and in 1962 he had been Guest Teacher to both Royal Ballet companies. *Toccata* had its première on 14 December at the Theatre Royal in Newcastle. Set to an arrangement of Bach by Lanchbery and with designs by Peter Rice, it related Bach's rhythmic structure to both classical and various social dances, including jive, swing and the rhumba, the different styles suggested by the different costumes adopted by the performers. It was an unaffected, enjoyable work, if with leanings towards cuteness, but with too little substance to form a regular part of the touring repertory.

The company never lost its characteristic vigour and love of dancing, and did not aspire to the more elegant and pure style of the sister company. The road and its audiences simply bred a different type of dancer. A perfect example of that type joined them in January 1963. Brenda Last had been a founder member of Western Theatre Ballet, one of Britain's most innovative and creative young dance companies, where she had gained a reputation as a performer of great intelligence and strong technique. With the Royal Ballet Touring Company she developed into a virtuoso soubrette of the highest quality, notable for her speed, clarity and attack, an excellent actress with a warm, bubbling personality that made her a favourite of audiences everywhere. After her years with Western Theatre Ballet, when she often had to lend a hand with the scenery, lights and wardrobe on one night stands, a week in each place would seem luxurious. Being a 'pro' *par excellence*, she cared deeply about performing standards, and is remembered by the younger dancers for keeping a stern, but friendly, eye on their performances and grooming.

Early in 1963 de Valois announced that she would retire from the Directorship of The Royal Ballet to be succeeded by Frederick Ashton at the beginning of the 1963–64 season. As everything in her life, her retirement had been carefully planned, and she had assured Ashton adequate back-up with the appointment of the three Assistant Directors, who now had both companies running smoothly. Hers was not to be a conventional retirement – as always her eyes were set on the future, and she would now be free to devote more time to her beloved school and the development of future generations of dancers to ensure the continuation of the companies. She had always kept a severe eye on the Touring Company, and nothing had escaped her as she demanded higher and higher standards in her aim of making both companies worthy of the name they bore.

London audiences were now beginning to look forward to the Covent Garden seasons to judge the Touring Company's rising standards. The repertory for the 1963 visit was an odd assortment, including Massine's disastrous *Le Bal des Voleurs* and a revival of Ashton's *Sylvia*.

Equally ill-assorted were the guest artists imported for the season on the grounds that the company was not yet strong enough to sustain an entire season without being topped up at principal level – Grey, Carla Fracci from Milan, Melissa Hayden from New York City Ballet, Flemming Flindt, Danish trained, and ex-Festival Ballet and Paris Opera, and Lane was seconded from the Resident Company. John Gilpin was borrowed from Festival Ballet while Gable was making his New York début in *The Invitation* and he and Fracci headed the company in an exceptional revival of *Les Sylphides*, which had been thoroughly overhauled by Serge Grigoriev and Lubov Tchernicheva. The real stars of the season, however, were the *corps de ballet* who had now been welded into an excellent team by Field and his staff. Although everyone was glad and interested to see the guest artists, the company could now stand on its own, and throughout the season their sheer love of dancing, vivacity and freshness captivated audiences.

The season established Gable as a major star and audience favourite, while Lane's maturity and intelligence made her outstanding in every role. Flindt had a predictable success as Colas, but the delicacies of the Ashton style must have given Hayden many problems as Lise, and her performance had a distinct American accent. Their different styles made them a mismatched couple in the Bournonville excerpts.

Sylvia, revived on 6 May, was never the strongest of Ashton's three-act works and his pastiche of a Second Empire ballet had not stood the test of time well. Much of the choreography had been forgotten, and there was much scratching of heads by Field and other dancers who had appeared in the original as they tried to reconstruct it. Wells and Gable took the leads on the opening night, she lacking allure and authority, he stretching his acting skills to the full to make Aminta interesting and credible. The *corps de ballet*, however, were highly praised for their attack and soaring jetés as the Amazons in the first act and the conviction of their playing. Hayden later scored her greatest success of the season in the title role, her American attack admirably suiting the Amazonian aspects of the choreography.

If any ballet laid an egg that ballet was Massine's *Le Bal des Voleurs*, seen on 17 May. In return for his work on revivals at Covent Garden, he had been asked to choose one of his ballets to mount on the Touring

Company; de Valois had hoped that he would revive *Les Matelots*, but he insisted on *Le Bal des Voleurs*, which none of the Covent Garden Board had seen. Created for the Nervi Festival in 1960, to a score by Georges Auric, it had a plot so complex as to defy comprehension, so full was it of disguises and mistaken identities. Unfortunately it also had no choreography worthy of the name or musical distinction and when Fracci was injured before the sixth performance it was not thought worth while to rehearse anyone else in it and the ballet slipped quietly into oblivion.

A group of dancers from the Bolshoi Ballet were in the audience for the last matinée of the season – *La Fille mal gardée* with Last – and one of them was heard to remark how much the company had improved since Moscow – a gratifying tribute, for the Moscow company had, of course, been the resident Covent Garden company. The hard work over the years was beginning to pay high dividends.

The autumn season saw an unprecedented number of débuts – Field was fulfilling his dream of developing his own artists, while still giving performances to the Covent Garden stars, but with at least eight performances a week there were plenty of chances for all. *Giselle* was revived and Field quietly continued to tinker with the production until he felt the action was logical and real, in contrast to the Opera House's consciously over-Romantic production. Wells made her debut in the title role and an intelligent young dance-actor, Richard Farley, appeared for the first time as Albrecht.

The Touring Company dancers were primarily performers, rather than technicians, although there was a gradual increase in technical mastery. This was partly due to Erling Sunde, former dancer and Ballet Master with Western Theatre Ballet, who had become company teacher in 1962. There was little chance to work on technique in depth on tour, but Sunde got everybody into better shape under very bad conditions. 'It was very hard for the dancers to improve', explained Meryl Chapell. 'If you're working freezing cold on concrete, it's quite a talent to give a class that doesn't injure the dancers. He kept you well tuned. But he couldn't push us. Once you got in the centre you'd do what you could knowing you'd got *Swan Lake* that night'.[2]

On tour, in halls with no mirrors and wrapped up against the cold, it was easy for dancers to hide from themselves – even when in London they rarely rehearsed in studios with mirrors. 'All those years on tour', recalled Chapell, 'I never saw myself, and that's bad for a dancer'.[3] But the lack of mirrors did prevent them from developing the narcissistic

John Field in rehearsal.

Photograph by Reg Wilson.

introspection that bedevils some establishment companies, where one feels dancers are dancing to their own imagined image in the mirror rather than to an audience.

Most Touring Company class and rehearsal calls were organized by the Ballet Master, Henry Legerton (he always put the boys' class first thing in the morning, to make them get up), and he also kept a stern eye on all the performances. 'It was Mr Legerton you were terrified of if you made a mistake or a shoe came off', recalled Marion Tait. 'He was round at once. He wouldn't wait until the interval'. The dancers 'just waited to hear the jingling money in his pocket from the wings',[4] and knew that retribution had arrived. He, with Field, was in charge of the cast sheets, and made sure that rising soloists didn't get swollen headed by keeping up the old (and on touring inevitable) tradition of making them still walk-on as Court Ladies. 'You knew you were made', remembers Chapell, 'when you were let off Saturday night Court Ladies'.[5]

Once the technical foundations of the company were secure, Field was free to concentrate on the side of ballet that really interested him – the interpretation – and he would take the big production calls of the classics. It was not that Field did not stress the importance of technique, but as David Wall put it, 'performing to less (balletically) educated audiences as we were, he was conscious that they needed to be involved in theatre rather than just watching ballet steps'.[6] Many were the normal public who supported all live theatre and were not tuned to the finer points of classical ballet. How could they be with perhaps two visits a year if they were lucky? So Field concentrated on the dramatic side of the ballets, making the narrative as clear as possible, and developing a feeling for theatre and performance in his dancers. He never tried to over-simplify or deny the classical basis, but to make it interesting to the general public.

Field developed his own methods of working. Legerton and Mossford rehearsed the *corps de ballet* and soloists while he and the principals sat down to talk about the leading roles; as they became involved, the other characters would be introduced, and then the whole company would be called for the big scenes, and walk through to get the feel of the ballet and the relationships. Field encouraged the principals to experiment from performance to performance. Thus he developed a sense of involvement throughout the productions and kept his dancers' interest alive throughout endless performances of the same repertory.

In time honoured tradition, roles were handed down from dancer to dancer, taught in corners in spare moments. In the 1960s, however, dance notation came to play an increasingly important part in the company's life. The Royal Ballet used Benesh Notation, developed by former company dancer Joan Benesh and her husband, Rudolf. During the 1960s, Faith Worth came out to work with the Touring Company on new ballets and revivals. There were inevitable clashes between the notated 'bible' and the dancers who had photographic memories for ballets, and Legerton often found himself having to arbitrate between notator and company.

Fonteyn, Beriosova, Nureyev and MacLeary joined the company for a short visit to Paris in November 1963, where they gave six performances of *Swan Lake* to commemorate the fifty years of the Théâtre des Champs Elysées. There was great enthusiasm for Fonteyn and especially Nureyev, and their presence ensured an audience as glittering as the stage, including the Duke and Duchess of Windsor, Princess Soraya and the Begum Aga Khan, with an opening night party given by Yves Saint Laurent.

The less glamorous provincial audiences grew steadily and began to follow the careers of the emerging touring dancers – Wells, Grahame, Wall, Ruanne, Thorogood, Kerrison Cooke and Paul Clarke – as keenly as the Resident Company audiences followed their favourites. For every dancer that Covent Garden sent out, Field could match it with a cast of his own, more inexperienced maybe, but of distinct promise.

The pattern was now set – a spring or summer season at the Opera House, most years a European tour, usually coinciding with music festivals, and the rest of the year on tour in England. Field tried to ensure that the company established a pattern and visited each town at the same time every year. A year missed could be a disaster.

Field was in constant touch with Ashton, Webster and his assistant John Tooley. He was left to work on his own within an established framework, but as Field pointed out, if he really wanted to do something on tour that London might disapprove of, then it was often too late when the Royal Opera House found out. The company could not have operated without the backup of the Opera House, and the network of technical departments, that oversaw the productions, maintained them and always delivered new ones on time.

Over the next few years there was an average of two ballets a year mounted on the company, not always original creations, but it was a good record considering the problems in keeping the regular repertory rehearsed. Peter Wright came back to work with them in 1964 and found that:

> Mounting two new ballets on tour is an absolute revelation ... but I was amazed at how much work the Royal Ballet can accomplish on the road. In three weeks' rehearsal period before they went out with fourteen new dancers, they had to cope not only with my two ballets and prepare a full-length *Sleeping Beauty*, a Triple Bill and *La Fille mal gardée*. As if that was not enough, when they reached Oxford, where my two ballets come into the repertoire, they are adding *Giselle*, *Solitaire*, *Les Patineurs* and *The Two Pigeons*. ... They have a tougher life than anything I remember ... I simply don't know how they do it; they are a marvellous bunch of kids, and John Field does a fantastic job.[7]

The lack of new ballets meant that most of the dancers' interest lay in perfecting the basic repertory. Grahame, a lovely stylish dancer, was developing her performances in the classical repertory, as was Wells, whose naturally sunny nature could also embrace a gracious restrained aristocracy. Richard Farley was developing into an intelligent performer with a flair for the dramatic which was seen to particular advantage in the title role of *Hamlet*.

The problem for the company lay, as it always would, in the shortage of first-rate classical soloists. By late 1963 people were beginning to be aware of a young newcomer among the *corps de ballet*, as conspicuous for his clean finished technique and lively interest in what was going on as for his red hair. David Wall had arrived just in time, for Gable had finally moved over to Covent Garden at the beginning of the 1963–64 season. By the spring of 1964 he was appearing in solo roles and Clive Barnes noted his good build, modest presence and open manly style. 'If Wall lives up to even half of this promise', he wrote, 'he will be one of the most interesting male dancers the Royal Ballet has ever produced'.[8]

1964 was an unusually busy year for the company, with four new works, including two creations. MacMillan's *La Création du Monde* was premièred on 12 February 1964 at Stratford-upon-Avon using the score composed by Darius Milhaud for the Ballets Suédois in 1923. The ballet showed the Garden of Eden myth as if enacted by children, their innocence counteracted by the sophisticated pop-art designs of James Goddard. It was obviously intended to be flip and satirical, but just what was being sent up never became clear and the choreography was neither particularly outstanding nor amusing.

La Création du Monde was the Touring Company's offering at a Gala tribute to de Valois at the Royal Opera House on 7 May. At the end of the performance, the entire Royal Ballet organization, the pupils from the School, the teaching staff, the Covent Garden Opera Ballet, the Touring Company and the Covent Garden company – over four hundred in all came on stage – and finally de Valois herself entered acknowledging their homage.

In her speech, she recalled her wonderful years since leaving the Royal Ballet, 'For I have left to see the ballet continue without me and that has always been the dream of my life ... You know, as I do, that they have succeeded, and that The Royal Ballet will continue to grow and progress.'

The 1964 European tour lasted two months, through Germany and Holland, often coinciding with British trade fairs. Britain was trying to open up new markets in Europe at a time when the Common Market was making its effects felt on British exports. The company followed the Bolshoi around Germany, and the press found the gap between the companies not as wide as they had expected.

Paying surreptitious visits out to the provinces in the spring of 1964 was Rudolf Nureyev, who was fitting into his usual hectic schedule the mounting of Marius Petipa's full-length *Raymonda*. In addition to his formidable performing talents, Nureyev had a phenomenal memory, and a gift for imparting his highly developed sense of style to others. The new production of Petipa's ballet had been commissioned by the Festival of Two Worlds at Spoleto for presentation at that year's Festival as a vehicle for Fonteyn and Nureyev.

The Festival commissioned Beni Montresor to design the production, and he began working, as befitted the story, in a traditional 'historical' style. However, at the last minute, he decided that this would detract from Fonteyn and Nureyev, and substituted simple panels of colour and light, so that audiences could concentrate on the expressive powers of the performers. Meanwhile, Nureyev, who believed that the Royal Ballet were too respectful of the Petipa classics, had stripped away what he considered most of the irrelevant and extraneous mime taking much of the storyline with it. *Raymonda* had never been notable for its comprehensible narrative – the story of a Hungarian princess, her Crusader lover (who appears to her mainly in dreams) and a dastardly Saracen knight with designs upon her was only the flimsiest of excuses for the dancing – but, without it, there was barely enough to sustain interest over a full evening.

The première was scheduled for 10 July 1964 in Spoleto, but with little over a day to go it was put in jeopardy when Fonteyn suddenly had to return to England and the bedside of her husband, who had been shot the previous month in Panama. It was assumed that without her the production would have to be cancelled, but within thirty-six hours Wells, arch professional that she was, had learned the role. Not surprisingly there was a highly charged atmosphere on the first night, with the company keyed up to give of their very best. They were rewarded with fifteen curtain calls and a huge personal success for Wells. She was sparkling and elegant, and, if she lacked Fonteyn's authority, she had her own freshness and beauty of line. It was the beginning of her maturity as a ballerina.

Despite its faults, *Raymonda* would have stretched the company further in the classical repertory, and given them an extra full length work, but Ashton felt that without the drama the ballet lacked heart, that the designs were dull, and it would need drastic rethinking if it were to go into the repertory, so Covent Garden dropped the idea of buying it for the Touring Company. However, some of the choreography was too good to lose, and in 1966 Nureyev filtered out the best of Petipa from the early acts and incorporated it into the last act wedding celebrations for Raymonda and Jean de Brienne. *Raymonda Act III* became a splendid *grand divertissement*, providing challenges for the dancers at all levels with its mix of Hungarian national dances seen through the eyes of the Imperial Russian Ballet and classical variations. Barry Kay produced a magnificent Byzantine setting and sumptuous costumes of cream and gold that a quarter of a century later, still evoke welcoming applause. Kay carefully designed the sets for touring, and they managed to look equally good whatever the size of stage.

Fonteyn joined the company for the opening of their autumn tour in Coventry to compensate for the non-appearance of *Raymonda* ('technical difficulties' were given as the reason for its absence). That and the 'X' certificate ballet, as the company continued to bill *The Invitation*, ensured plenty of publicity.

In the days of the Theatre Ballet Peter Wright should not have had to wait seven years before being given another chance after *A Blue Rose*, but not until 1964 did he work with the Touring Company again. On the autumn tour of 1964 he mounted a new new, *Summer's Night*, and *Quintet*, made in 1963 for the Stuttgart Ballet, where Wright was now

Ballet Master, which were given a joint première on 29 October in Oxford.

The programme note for *Summer's Night* read: 'At a summer's night party the ghosts of lovers are awakened by a first kiss of love and borrow the affection of the young guests'. Wright concentrated on mood rather than narrative; Judith Wood's sets and costumes, all greeny gauzes, extended the amorphous quality and Poulenc's *Sinfonietta* admirably matched both with its wistful, nebulous quality. Wright now handled groups with confidence and showed off the leading dancers, Anderton and Farley as the humans, and Wells and Sherwood as the ghosts. But its rather hazy nature did not make it a strong repertory piece.

Quintet, danced to Ibert's Wind Quintet, was a short cheerful work for, as its name suggested, five dancers, matching the five musicians – a lighthearted joke between players, dancers and Judith Wood's pentagonal sets and props. The laughs arose naturally out of the dancing and, as Alexander Bland observed, the ballet 'does not aim higher than a cute charm, but hits the mark with a resounding tinkle'.[9] It made considerable technical demands upon its cast, which Last and Emblen seized upon with glee, backed up by Piers Beaumont, Mosaval and Wall.

Wright paid tribute to the company's new conductor, Ashley Lawrence, who took the trouble to get to know the dancers and their needs. Lawrence was one of a number of young conductors being tried out in an attempt to raise the company's musical standards. Things had reached such a pitch that the music critic of the *Yorkshire Post* refused to write on the Royal Ballet because 'the provincial theatre is no longer a place where touring orchestras and music critics can meet on civil terms'.[10]

Debuts continued thick and fast. Michael Coleman was an excellent Bluebird, and his open, friendly personality allied to an easy technique and good jump made him an admirable Colas. Wall was making astonishing progress. Only in his second season, he made his début as Colas and was already challenging memories of the past with his interpretation of the Rake. De Valois had specially asked that he learn the role, and he worked on it with Legerton, himself a former distinguished interpreter. It was a youthful performance, but Wall had a grasp of the development of the character and movingly showed the Rake's disintegration, from vulnerability in the first scene to a violent and frightening vacancy in the Mad House. He also danced *The Two Pigeons*, but was almost upstaged by Thorogood, one of the best of all Young Girls, with her eloquent arms, gamine heartbreaking quality and purity of style, which came from her early training under Vera Volkova.

Slowly the company was increased until, by the end of the decade, it numbered sixty-four dancers. As it grew it abandoned some of the smaller theatres, and really outgrew others – like the de Montfort Hall in Leicester, where the wings were barely wide enough to accommodate one or two portly members of the City Council who visited a performance on a fact-finding visit. The same wings had to take thirty *corps de ballet*. There were too few dressing-rooms, and dancers were to be found changing in every corner.

De Valois would have liked to see a concert touring group which would relieve the strain on the Touring Company and be able to play these smaller theatres. Ballet For All was not quite that, but it had its own part to play in the company's history during the 1960s and 1970s.

The brainchild of dance historian Peter Brinson, Ballet For All grew out of his lectures on history and aesthetics of ballet for which he often called upon students from the Royal Ballet School to demonstrate. Brinson suggested to David Webster that these should be put on a professional basis, using dancers from The Royal Ballet, as a means of educating and building a new audience. The Resident Company did not feel that it could fit it into their schedule, but John Field jumped at the idea, and his company was increased by two so that a succession of dancers could be sent out in a programme of lecture demonstrations, based on the company's repertoire, performing in community centres, town halls, festivals, small theatres and schools.

The first tour was in autumn 1964. Initially there were two dancers (Last and Sherwood were the first), a pianist, stage manager, a secretary and a director – Brinson, who also wrote and delivered the lectures and drove the van – performing mainly one night stands. In the first year the group gave 141 performances to over 70,000 people, averaging four performances a week over thirty-five weeks and travelling 17,000 miles. The group looked after its own day-to-day administration and bookings, while the Opera House provided production and administrative services. In time the lectures were rewritten as ballet plays, and delivered by actors. Productions became more ambitious as they developed the historical programmes with their own reconstructions of significant historical works, like the *Ballet Royal de la Nuit*, or *The World of Giselle*, or one related to Ashton's works. There were even occasional creations, like *A Yorkshire Marriage*. By the late 1960s the company had grown to five dancers, changing every three months, two actors, a pianist, a director and small staff.

Ballet For All was a marvellous opportunity for giving young *corps de ballet* dancers and soloists a grounding in the repertory as well as an understanding of ballet history and style. Thus Margaret Barbieri and Nicholas Johnson, when they came to take over Giselle and Albrecht overnight in 1968 were well primed in the basics of the roles from their performances with Ballet For All. They all learned a tremendous amount. Not that it did not provide additional headaches for Field, sometimes having to provide replacements for dancers over a hundred miles away for Ballet For All as well as coping with injury problems within the Touring Company. But, he remembers, there was always someone who would volunteer to go out. Field's dancers were with him because they wanted to dance, and dance they were going to.

All touring companies tended to be on the road at the same time of the year, and clashes had been a major complaint for years. Now it was decided to turn that into an asset and Bristol in the spring of 1965 was selected for a pilot season in which the Royal Ballet, Sadler's Wells Opera and the National Theatre ran their seasons consecutively, producing a kind of mini-festival. If this could be developed, it was hoped that the companies could play more than one week, thus enjoying more settled conditions, and hopefully build up an audience for a wider repertory than usual. The experiment was deemed to be enough of a success for a similar season to be arranged in Manchester the following year.

It had been felt for some time that standards could not be maintained under the system of one-week stands. These were wasteful both in time and the wear and tear on materials and dancers and it was not long enough to present a sufficiently varied repertory to sustain and build public interest. There was no core of regular balletomanes at each performance, as in London. The company's extrovert style was partly due to the fact that they had no time to 'grow into' a date – they had to make an immediate impact. There was just time to get into a theatre, perform as best they could, and by the time they had settled in and got used to the stage, it was time to move on. Field was quite clear on the matter. 'I think that touring as we do it now is completely obsolete and I am sure we work endless hours quite unnecessarily'.[11] Ideally each theatre and each audience needed different ballets, and sometimes the company was changing repertory every week. The Covent Garden Board would have liked to see at least four week seasons in major centres.

What the repertory needed was a strong narrative ballet to balance out the triple bills and give *The Rake's Progress*, *The Invitation* and *Blood Wedding* a rest. Thus they commissioned a ballet from Norman Morrice, dancer and choreographer with Ballet Rambert, who had established a reputation for creating dramatic ballets in contemporary settings. He found the company helpful and willing but after twelve weeks on tour he had only worked out eight minutes of the ballet because of the demands of rehearsing the standard repertory as injury and illness took their winter toll.

The Tribute, premièred on 5 February 1965 at the Royal Shakespeare Theatre, Stratford-upon-Avon, was the first and only time in the 1960s that the Touring Company appeared in modern dress – mini skirts, heeled shoes and suits. It was in the style of ballets with contemporary settings such as were being produced by Western Theatre Ballet or in various workshop performances. The theme, however, was universal – the fertility rites, with the death of the old king and the taking by the earth goddess of a new mate. Three women represented 'woman' as birth, love and battle, and death and resurrection. The setting was a carnival, in which the rites still lived on, if unperceived. The carnival characters acted out the ritual, watched by a group of tourists, who became caught up in the action; a married couple became involved with a strange young man, leading to the exchange of partners and the death of the hero, thus providing the necessary blood sacrifice.

Morrice relied upon the dancers' abilities to create character, especially Ruanne as the birth figure, and Wall as the Stranger both creating their first major roles. He mixed dance hall steps, modern dance and classical ballet, although they never quite blended into a coherent style. It was an undeniably theatrical piece, if not particularly distinguished choreographically, but it would not replace any of the accepted dramatic ballets.

The company arrived in London for their annual Opera House season to face rehearsals for a revised version of Ashton's *Sylvia* and a new production of *Swan Lake*. By the opening night not one healthy Colas was left standing in England, and even Gable, flown back from America, was not fit to dance on arrival. The company therefore had to put out an SOS to the Royal Danish Ballet, who loaned them Jorn Madsen to partner Nerina.

Field planned the Covent Garden seasons very carefully. They were the reward for the company's hard work throughout the rest of the year, and he was determined that the dancers would be seen at their best in what was, after all, the national showcase for the national ballet. He tried to cast well in advance, so that he had twelve weeks to tune his performers to the highest pitch possible. Thus a dancer scheduled to do Lise or Odette-Odile in London would concentrate on that role on tour.

The Tribute. Deirdre O'Conaire as The Lady in White, Patricia Ruanne as The Lady in Red, Elizabeth Anderton as The Lady in Black and David Wall as The Stranger.

Photograph by Anthony Crickmay.

Similarly he paced his dancers' careers. If a girl was felt to be ready for *Swan Lake*, he would first cast her in *Les Sylphides*, so that she had a good grounding in lyrical *pas de deux*, then he would put her into the *fouetté* girl in *Les Patineurs*, and so on, so that the technical foundations were well laid before she tackled *Swan Lake* itself.

The Paris Opera star Attilio Labis partnered Nerina in the new production of *Swan Lake*. The pretence of interchangeable repertories, even in the classics, had by now been abandoned. The Resident Company had mounted a new version of *Swan Lake* at Covent Garden in 1963, produced by Robert Helpmann, for which Ashton had made considerable revisions to both storyline and choreography and also created a new last act. The Touring Company had been guardians of the original Sergeyev version, which had been one of the glories of the repertory since its first production in 1934. Now Ashton revised the choreography, not as drastically as the 1963 Covent Garden version (and

leaving Act IV intact), but just enough to take the ballet another step away from Sergeyev, and it retained all the implausibilities of that version, without choreographic or dramatic gain. For the 1960s it all seemed rather old-fashioned.

It was this season that finally established the Touring Company as a group with its own clear identity with nothing to fear from comparisons with the sister company, and hailed by audiences and critics alike. Even the Opera House authorities could not deny that 'they brought an extraordinary vitality and zest to their performances and displayed a sheer delight in dancing which provided immense pleasure throughout the season'.[12] Although Fonteyn, Nerina and Labis were dancing, the main achievement of the season belonged to the company's own dancers, Wells, Grahame, Anderton, Last, Farley, Emblen, Mosaval and Wall.

During the season it was announced that Kenneth MacMillan was to leave The Royal Ballet to become Director of the Deutsche Oper Ballet in Berlin, and that Seymour would go with him. Nerina was also leaving. She had been an indispensable member of the Royal Ballet since her early years with the Theatre Ballet. In the 1960s she had been a frequent guest with the Touring Company on the road, and many a provincial audience had made their acquaintance with the great classical roles in her sensitive, strong interpretations, and those fortunate enough to have seen her Lise have never forgotten her sparkling strength and vitality. It was as Lise that she took her farewell on the last night of the season, the audience cheering her and Field in equal proportions.

(*Opposite*) On tour in Leeds, 1966.

Photograph by Richard Farley.

Chapter XIII

The Royal Opera House might praise the Touring Company achievements, but its attitude was thoroughly ambivalent whenever finances were under discussion, when its work seemed to be regarded as almost extraneous to the main business of the House. The company which had been welcomed less than a decade before as an instant means of touring the Royal Ballet, was now being seen as a drain upon resources. In the Annual Report for 1964–65, the Opera House could actually say, 'Touring at home is an activity which is to be regarded as a discharge of duties laid upon the House by deliberate Arts Council policy'. It was a grudging acceptance of the company's achievements in taking the Royal Ballet's name to the country which, after all, supported the Opera House through its taxes. The Report also pointed out that if there was no touring in England and the 'establishment' were reduced accordingly, the deficit under which the Opera House laboured would be substantially less.

After the relatively hectic 1964–65 season, with its three new works and a major new production, 1965–66 was their most unproductive year on record. The company never seemed able to get the balance quite right, either there were no new works, or two or three in preparation at once. The reception of the new *Swan Lake* on tour varied from the ecstatic to the *Guardian*'s criticism of the company for retaining their 'fundamentally undramatic and unsatisfactory production' instead of presenting the 'enterprising' 1963 version.[1] London Festival Ballet had just mounted its first full-length *Swan Lake* in the spring of 1965, but Clement Crisp in the *New Statesman* pointed out that 'only the Royal Ballet can meet the requirement of well presented and danced classics on tour' and marvelled that Field could maintain these standards.[2]

Coppélia was revived for the spring tour of 1966, and, as ever, the company produced an excellent crop of lively Swanildas (Wells, Grahame, Last and Anderton) and personable Franzes (Wall, Kenneth Mason and Kerrison Cooke) – 'I cannot remember when I saw a performance more spirited, nor with the classical and character dancing better matched',[3] wrote John Percival. Wells and Wall were ideally cast, and increasingly suited to each other as partners. Also making his debut as Franz was the very young Paul Clarke – who attracted attention from his first day with the company by his uncanny resemblance to Gable – with a sunny smile, enthusiasm and attack that almost made up for his as yet rather slapdash presentation. The pushing of dancers as young as Clarke (he was only eighteen), was due to a seasonal crop of injuries, giving rise to the usual fears of young dancers burning themselves out with overwork. Brenda Last echoed the feelings of many when she said, 'I would rather wear myself out dancing too much than in frustration at not dancing enough',[4] but there must have been a happy medium somewhere.

To students at this time, the Touring Company was a remote body, seen only occasionally around the School at Baron's Court. Gail Thomas, who joined the Touring section in 1964, remembered them as 'the more friendly and less stereotyped part of the Royal Ballet ... When in London they spent a good deal of their time in rented rehearsal rooms, barracks and the like, which was rather adding insult to injury as they had enough of draughty halls when on tour'.[5] Both companies were dependent upon the training from the School, which produced dancers of high standard with a grounding in the basic repertory that enabled them to be absorbed into either company at a moment's notice without disruption.

Occasionally, however, the need for a principal dancer could not be met from within the organization. In autumn 1966, therefore, the company was joined by Lucette Aldous, former ballerina of Ballet Rambert, who would take some of the pressure off Wells. Royal Ballet School-trained, Aldous had been rejected by both companies as being too small, but within Ballet Rambert's classics she had developed into a tiny powerhouse of a dancer, her strength softened by lyrical charm. At first sight she seemed a soubrette, but she also possessed true classical qualities. Within a few weeks of joining she had made her debut in *The Two Pigeons*, *Giselle* and *Swan Lake*, bringing to them all her charm and wonderful breadth of movement that belied her small stature.

Wells was consolidating her reputation as the darling of the provinces – their own ballerina whom they had followed and encouraged from her early days with the company. She was a beautiful stylist, with lovely line and breadth of movement, strong but not aggressive technique, natural glamour and chic, and audiences adored her. When paired with the equally good-looking and talented Wall the combination was irresistible, and they were courted by the provincial and then the national media, rivalling the partnership of Sibley and Dowell at Covent Garden.

It was Wells and Wall who took the leads when the company mounted Ashton's *The Dream*, his enchanting version of *A Midsummer Night's Dream*, created for the Shakespeare Quatercentenary in 1964. In December 1966 the Touring Company got its own specially designed production, and took to the ballet as if it had been made for them. They performed with love and gusto and many expressed a preference for their production and performances. No one was going to match Sibley and Dowell on whom it had been set, but Wall was an imperious, subtle Oberon, and Wells a spirited, if not particularly fey, Titania. David Morse, who had danced in the ballet at Covent Garden, was outstanding as Puck, as was Mosaval – darting, mischievous, quicksilver figures – and Emblen was an appealing Bottom. Peter Farmer produced a much admired shimmering Victorian wood, although there was some doubt as to how the provinces would react to Oberon's open-chested tunic.

Ashton continued to work with the company, creating for them an abstract ballet *Sinfonietta*, which was premièred at the Royal Shakespeare Theatre in February 1967. Many of the younger dancers were unused to working with choreographers. Wall, working with Ashton for the first time, found it exhausting; Ashton liked a creative input from his cast, and Wall found 'when you're as tired as dancers are when they're on tour ... you're just not capable of making the creative effort needed on top of everything else'.[6]

Sinfonietta was in three sections, an intricate double *pas de deux* for Last and Cooke, Anderton and Farley, the dreamlike Elegy with Wells, and a cheerful Tarantella to show off Wall. Most successful was the beautiful central elegy, which grew out of the 'floating' sequence in *Ondine*, and the purity of *Monotones*; supported by five men, Wells was manipulated, glided and revolved, never touching the ground, like some remote heavenly body. As always Ashton found inspiration in his dancers – Wells' almost too perfect line, Wall's swift strength, and he brought out in Last's virtuosity a hitherto unsuspected softness.

Unfortunately the outer movements reflected only too clearly the restlessness of Malcolm Williamson's score, and Peter Rice's startling fluorescent striped costumes and a distracting set made up of ever changing lights, devised by the Hornsey College of Art Light/Sound Workshop, did not help matters.

During their Covent Garden season, on 26 May, the company acquired another abstract ballet, MacMillan's *Concerto*, set to Shostakovich's Second Piano Concerto, which had been created for the Deutsche Oper, Berlin in 1966. A ballet of pure dancing, *Concerto*, like *Sinfonietta*, was in the form of a lyrical second section, flanked by two allegro movements. It was not major MacMillan, but has proved popular over the years, mainly due to the central *pas de deux*. Inspired by the sight of Seymour doing stretching exercises at the barre, it translated these basic movements into an elegiac *pas de deux* with the ballerina using her partner for support. The original cast served MacMillan well; Anderton and Wall bounced cheerfully through the first movement, Wells, partnered by Farley, serenely glided through the second and the tall Jane Landon joyously cleaved the air with her long legs in the last.

There was continued cause for worry, however, about the repertory. Concentration on the classics over the years had diminished the number of new works, and none of those produced over the last few years had proved to have much staying power. The staples of the one-act repertory were those inherited from the 1930s and the 1950s – *Les Rendezvous*, *Blood Wedding*, *Les Patineurs*, *Solitaire*, *The Rake's Progress*, *Pineapple Poll*, *Danses Concertantes*, *The Invitation* and *Les Sylphides*. Only in *The Dream*, *Concerto* and *Raymonda Act III* did the company have for the first time in years, valuable additions to the touring repertory which would stand the test of time and cast changes, and establish themselves as public favourites.

The dearth of new choreographers was beginning to worry everybody. The growth in the number of ballet companies over the last decade had not seen a corresponding flowering of choreographic talent, and no choreographer had emerged from the Royal Ballet since MacMillan a decade before. Thus the launching of the Royal Ballet Choreographic Group under Leslie Edwards, and with backing from the Friends of Covent Garden, had considerable significance. The group was founded to provide a showcase for the work of new choreographers, very much as the Sadler's Wells Choreographic Group had been during the 1950s. It gave its first performance in December 1967, and was still doing sterling work twenty years later.

Field was aware that the company was not producing as much new

Doreen Wells as Raymonda and David Wall as Jean de Brienne in *Raymonda Act III*.

Photograph by Zoe Dominic.

work as it might, but he felt strongly that people should only be encouraged to choreograph if they felt a desperate need to do so – he was never in favour of just anyone being allowed to 'have a go'. Also, until the company had reached a certain standard in the classics, he was unwilling to divert their energies. Everyone admired how he and his staff retained a standard worthy of the Royal Ballet. As *The Times* remarked: 'Simply to maintain a decent standard in the hazards of touring conditions ... would be impressive. To bring on, in addition, so many dancers of talent and promise ought to earn for the company's director, Mr John Field, and his ballet master, Mr Henry Legerton, astonishment and admiration in roughly equal proportions'.[7] Performances might sometimes be uneven, but they were never dull. Official approval of the work of the last decade came with the award to John Field of the CBE in the Birthday Honours' list in June 1966 – a richly deserved honour for him and his company.

Chapter XIV

The success of the pilot combined seasons by drama, opera and dance companies in Bristol in 1965 and Manchester in 1966 had led to the setting up of DALTA – the Dramatic and Lyric Theatres Association – and the first major DALTA seasons were arranged for Glasgow and Manchester during the autumn tour of 1967. The other companies involved were the Royal Shakespeare Company, the Sadler's Wells Opera and, in Glasgow only, Western Theatre Ballet; the Touring Company would play a four week season in each town. The season was billed as an 'immediate and exciting demonstration of the benefits of this powerful association of theatres ... a theatrical feat which could not have been envisaged under former touring arrangements ... an unprecedented opportunity for discriminatory and selective theatre-going, hitherto impossible outside London'.

It was not easy for an audience, used to one week a year, to adjust to planning, not just for a four week ballet season, but the opera and drama as well, and it remained to be seen whether it would be possible to find enough interest to last the four weeks, or whether the weekly audience would simply stretch over the longer time. It was demanding both in money and time, and audiences stood in danger of severe theatrical indigestion for a short period, and then nothing of note for the rest of the year. Certain aspects of the season were not well handled. Casting was usually available in advance, but here booking had to open so far ahead that no details could be given except for Fonteyn performances, which had to be at higher prices. Then after casting was announced, people turned up for the performance to find yet different dancers were actually performing that night, and the changes had been made without explanation or announcement.

Fonteyn came to both Glasgow and Manchester, dancing *Swan Lake* with Wall, she, as always, rising to the challenge of a new partner, he matching her well, physically and emotionally. For towns that had not seen her since the touring days of the Sadler's Wells Ballet she was a revelation. 'The theatrical experience of a lifetime', exclaimed Paul Foster in the *Glasgow Evening Times*. 'She is incomparable. The glorious control of her warm, fluid line, the glowing vibrance of her steps, and the ineffable tenderness of the softly-flowing arm movements are magical'.[1] She was an inspiration to the company, both in her performing and her behaviour on and off stage.

The outcome was predictable, not only for the Royal Ballet, but the other companies as well. The classics drew the largest audiences, *La Fille mal gardée* and *The Two Pigeons* well below them, and then the triple bills. It was the same pattern for opera – with the modern works doing badly, and though the RSC's most 'modern' offering was Ibsen, it was well down in the ratings.

Audience appetite for the classics was seemingly insatiable. Their popularity lay partly in familiarity at least of the music, partly in the idea purveyed by the media during the ballet-boom that ballet was a fairytale world of glamour and beauty. The harder, sophisticated audiences of the 1930s had been replaced by a more general, less discriminating audience, who saw only superficial prettiness and visual splendour, and did not see the works often enough to begin to appreciate the finer points – the very points that made them endlessly fascinating to the balletomane. But part of the problem lay in insufficient publicity and promotion. A full evening work on its own was no guarantee of a full house, as *La Fille mal gardée* originally proved, yet until the 1970s there was no attempt to give details about the individual ballets on the throwaways. The classics were obviously going to go on playing a significant part in the dance life of the nation.

DALTA seasons were established in one or two towns during the autumn season, and the rest of the year was given back to the week-long dates. Wells and Wall were occupied for part of the spring tour learning the leads in Nureyev's new production of *The Nutcracker* at the Opera House. Despite the importance of their partnership to the Touring Company, the Covent Garden Board were anxious that Wall should transfer to the Resident Company. He, however, resisted, feeling that he would benefit by remaining on the road.

Brenda Last and Johaar Mosaval as the Can-Can Dancers in *La Boutique fantasque*.

Photograph by Anthony Crickmay.

During the winter tour of 1968 the Touring Company acquired two Massine ballets, from the Resident Company repertory, *La Boutique fantasque* and *Mam'zelle Angot*, mounted for them by the master himself. Massine had not had a particularly good time with the Royal Ballet in the 1960s. *Le Tricorne* and *Donald of the Burthens* had dropped out of the Resident Company repertory; *Le Bal des Voleurs* and a revival of

Mam'zelle Angot. Lucette Aldous as Mam'zelle Angot, Paul Clarke as the Caricaturist and Ronald Emblen as The Barber.

Photograph by Zoe Dominic.

The Good-Humoured Ladies for Covent Garden had left him with a somewhat tarnished reputation among younger balletgoers, who could not begin to understand the magic he held for audiences in the 1930s. Performers had changed, and it was not easy to find character dancers with the necessary sensitivity to period and style, or the theatricality to enliven his rich, character cameos, expressed in wildly ingenious movements.

Massine, however, suited a company familiar with de Valois' ballets (she was a great admirer of his work), and *La Boutique fantasque* still exercised its irresistible charm. It was a perfect example of narrative dance, with all the character and action expressed through movement alone. If the company could not grasp all the subtleties of the Massine style, they caught the necessary gusto. Wells missed the naughty charm of the Can-can Dancer, but Emblen, though lacking Massine's magnetic personality, had a good shot at the role of the male Can-can Dancer. Last and Mosaval were later an excellent team. Despite sometimes indifferent performances, *Boutique* has remained a stubborn stayer over the years and a popular favourite with audiences whenever it is revived.

Mam'zelle Angot fared even better, because it had been extensively reworked for the Resident Company when Massine revived it for them in 1947. It concerned the little Barber, who loved Mam'zelle Angot, who loved the Caricaturist, who loved an Aristocrat. It was a curate's egg of a ballet, with a brilliant first scene, full of wildly inventive Massinian characters, but declining slowly into one of those endless finales which he never could work out how to finish. Aldous was suitably vivacious and assertive in the title role, and Grahame was a beautifully elegant Aristocrat; Wall had all the smooth charm for the Caricaturist and Emblen triumphed over a domineering wig as the downtrodden little Barber. Holden was borrowed from Covent Garden to recreate his Chief of Police – 'a seedy, would-be Scarpia, whose constant discomfiture is unerringly ludicrous'.[2]

The ballets had been well prepared before Massine's arrival, and he was more than pleased. He later paid tribute to the company:

> To obtain such results as this was only possible because of the Company's attitude in regard to what they had to accomplish, as the preparation time was extremely short. In spite of the eight weekly performances and perfection of their current repertory these artists worked with me practically in all their free time, not only without ever saying they were tired, but asking me to do some rehearsing on Sundays. Such devotion I have hardly ever witnessed since Diaghilev days.[3]

Also during the tour, the company returned to a well tried practice for breaking young dancers into *Swan Lake* – sharing the roles of Odette and Odile. In the 1930s Fonteyn's first Odette had been to Ruth French's Odile, and later Mary Honer's. Now Sandra Conley and Alfreda Thorogood split the roles between them, one dancing Odette, the other Odile and then vice versa.

Doreen Wells as Giselle and David Wall as Albrecht.

The 1968 Opera House season brought a new *Giselle* produced by Peter Wright. He had been very influenced by Ulanova's performance in the Bolshoi production, when he realised that the story could actually relate to and move a contemporary audience. 'I think you have to create your own Romantic style and I think it has to relate to the way we move today without looking modern ... I never set myself up as the creator of these ballets. I am not. I regard myself as a caretaker. I like to keep them alive and kicking and accessible to the public of today'.[4]

Wright stripped away all the 'traditions' that had accrued over the years and looked at the characters, and their motivations afresh. He respected the choreography and period style while applying logic and common sense to the production detail and relationships, trying to give it a theatrical relevance without making it seem a musty period piece. The gestures were not stylised but arose naturally out of the situation. Characters were established quickly and economically, and there was a continuous choreographic and dramatic flow. So that the Peasant *pas de deux* did not distract attention from the principals, Wright expanded it into a *pas de six* (or a *pas de quatre* on tour if the stage space was limited), using the original steps but duplicating them in multiple form.

Peter Farmer created sets sensitively designed for both the Opera House and for touring, on the simple principle that if you design the backcloth right then the wings can sit at any point without destroying the proportions. Autumn colour predominated in the first act, and the white Wilis of the second had their costumes streaked with green, like lichen.

The production saw many admirable performances. The first Giselle was Wells, a little uninvolved in Act I, but light and ethereal in Act II. Anderton, a truly demure Victorian maiden, with her soft rounded line and movements, gave a great performance that married drama and dance to sensitive feeling for period style. Wall was Albrecht to both – a heedless youth in the first scene, growing to a noble maturity in the second. However, when Aldous was unable to appear the management decided to try two *corps de ballet* dancers in the leads, and Margaret Barbieri and Nicholas Johnson became the sensation of the season. She not only looked like everyone's idea of a Romantic ballerina, with large dark eyes, oval face and dark hair, but also had a fine sense of nineteenth-century Romantic style without mannerism. Johnson was boyish and dashing, with outstandingly clean and clear dancing. Extremely touching in their youthfulness, they were encouraging signs for the future. The lack of new works went almost unnoticed, when a new generation of young dancers brought such freshness and vigour to the familiar repertory.

Such opportunities for very young and inexperienced dancers were, in fact, few and far between. Dancers might sometimes be thrown on at the last minute on tour but on the whole a hierarchy was maintained, and dancers worked their way up gradually through the ranks, feeling honoured and privileged as new roles came their way. Thus Barbieri was a seasoned *corps de ballet* dancer of three years' standing; but at that time such quick promotion to principal roles was unusual.

The company was very close, and the principals are remembered for being friendly, approachable, welcoming to newcomers and helpful to the younger dancers. Before her first Gypsy Girl in *The Two Pigeons* with the company, Barbieri was helped by Anderton, and Wells advised her upon her make up. The principals were looked up to by the younger dancers, not with unapproachable awe, but as an example to aspire to, and their help was greatly valued and appreciated. It was the soloists, Marion Tait remembers, who kept the *corps de ballet* in their place and maintained the necessary hierarchical structure of the company. According to Stephen Jefferies 'There was none of this diplomatic "Would you move off the barre, there's a principal hanging onto the scenery" – it was off by the scruff of the neck'.[5]

During the season came the announcement that Ashton would retire from the Royal Ballet in 1970, to be replaced by a 'joint directorship' of Field and MacMillan. It was unusual to make such an announcement so far in advance, but rumours had been running through the company for some time, and the Board felt that these must be allayed. The Opera House Annual Report for 1968–69 stressed MacMillan's gifts as choreographer and his talent for stretching his dancers, while the Touring Company 'proves the fitness of John Field to complement Kenneth MacMillan in directing and running the large and complex organization that the Royal Ballet has become'.

The announcement was favourably received; it was felt that the two men had complementary qualities – MacMillan the creator, and Field the administrator – but what that would mean in practice no one knew. The Board expressed the hope that Hart and Somes would continue to be associated with the Royal Ballet,[6] but it did not seem that there was any clear plan as to how they would fit into the new regime.

Meanwhile the company set out upon its 1968 European tour – the most gruelling to date. Organized by Julian Braunsweg, former Director of London Festival Ballet, it was a ten-week journey through the European Festivals, taking in Portugal, Spain, Italy, France and Switzerland. Fonteyn and Nureyev were guest artists – indeed many foreign managements would not take the Touring Company without them and the company often must have felt that it was little more than wallpaper. Fonteyn and Nureyev appeared in two-thirds of the scheduled performances, and some posters advertised them in enormous letters and 'The Royal Ballet' in tiny type beneath. The venues were varied – open air arenas, parks, a palace courtyard, a skating rink and even a bullring – and the conditions such that the company must sometimes have thought nostalgically of even the worst provincial theatre back home.

The tour was due to open in Bordeaux in May 1968. Despite student unrest in France the company had been assured that there was no trouble in the town, but they arrived to find the airport under military control. They were actually rehearsing in the Grand Théâtre when the students broke in and took over the building, and they had to be escorted back to their hotel by the police. The dancers had a wonderful few days of freedom before the French part of the tour was cancelled, and they moved on briefly to Germany. Here the accommodation left a lot to be desired, and in Wiesbaden the beds seemed to be being slept in about three times a day – and not by the dancers. It was in Wiesbaden that Meryl Chapell, invited to a lunch reception, found that a place had been thoughtfully laid for Delibes. The company then returned to London before setting out for Portugal and the 'Festival' leg of the tour.

In Lisbon the girls were a sensation in their mini-skirts, a fashion which had not yet reached Salazar's Portugal. The 1,200 seats of the San Carlos theatre were not enough to satisfy public demand, and so performances were transferred to a vast music hall seating some 6,000. A huge crowd milled around in the orchestra stalls, with lots of changing seats, the mêlée punctuated by cries of 'thief' directed at the organizer by those seated behind pillars. As Fonteyn began the mad scene in *Giselle*, the heavens opened, and the orchestra was drowned out by the rattle of the rain on the tin dome of the theatre.

Blood Wedding did not prove popular in Lisbon, and Braunsweg tried to withdraw it from the repertory before Spain, but Granada had been promised *Blood Wedding* and *Blood Wedding* it wanted. Braunsweg craftily got round the problem by pretending that the scenery had been damaged in a lorry accident (the accident was actually genuine), and managed to get *Concerto* substituted instead.

There were endless problems with the repertory. Partly because of the difficulty of transporting scenery over long distances overnight, and partly because many of the venues were not proper theatres, most scenery had been dispensed with, although in that case it was perhaps unwise to include ballets like *The Dream*, and *Giselle*. *Marguerite and Armand* had to be cancelled in several places because Fonteyn thought, rightly, that it was unsuitable for open air performance. Festival audiences usually liked fireworks, and a repertory of fireworks the company did not have.

Travel was a nightmare. The journey from Oporto began at 4.30 in the morning and when the plane arrived its cargo had to be unloaded before the seats could be put in; unfortunately they were not bolted down properly, and slid about during the journey. It was hardly surprising that, before long, half the company was off with travel sickness. The heat was overpowering, and the girls began to need larger pointe shoes because their feet were swelling all the time.

Fonteyn at this stage in her career was concerned about unauthorized and unflattering photographs appearing in the press. In Granada she refused to allow photographers into the dress rehearsal for *Giselle*, and Braunsweg claims he could only placate them by allowing them to photograph during the performance – an extraordinary and unheard of measure. The performance went on in the presence of Juan Carlos, Pretender to the Spanish Throne, the British Ambassador and the Spanish nobility, punctuated by the clicking of dozens of shutters. Half way through the first act Nureyev came down to the footlights and shook his head at the photographers, to warn them to stop, but to no avail, and Fonteyn eventually walked off the stage followed by Nureyev, who was heard to remark to the conductor that they would have it faster next time. The rest of the cast followed, and the photographers had to be removed before the performance could continue. There was, not surprisingly, a terrific row, and Field had to call a press conference at which Fonteyn tried, but failed, to smooth over the incident by explaining her misgivings.

Fonteyn and Nureyev, with their performances geared to the more stylized, consciously Romantic Covent Garden production, did not fit easily into the new *Giselle*. It was however, greeted with acclaim everywhere, even if in some places the scenery was reduced to basic flats for Giselle's cottage, and Albrecht's hovel could not even boast a door, but had to make do with a piece of sacking. It was hardly a satisfactory way to show a major British ballet company abroad, and another indication that the festivals and audiences were less concerned with the company than with the stars.

Fonteyn danced part of the tour with an injured knee, sustained during a rehearsal. She and Nureyev were greeted with hysteria everywhere, although it was noted that it was the partnership that brought in the crowds – Nureyev on his own did not guarantee a full house. During the tour he made his debut as Oberon, a fascinating, arrogant interpretation, danced to Aldous' Titania.

The company on the whole enjoyed the sunshine and what little sightseeing they could cram into the hectic schedule. The strains of the tour were such that Braunsweg started out booking twenty-nine double rooms and fifteen singles but by the end it was seventeen doubles and twenty-seven singles.

From the heat of Spain and France, the company travelled up to the cooler Netherlands, and then to the chill of Switzerland before returning to Spain. Conditions were often extremely bad, culminating in the débâcle of Barcelona, where the company had been booked to appear in the gardens of the Cascade del Parque de la Ciudadela. The authorities, however, changed the venue to the local bullring, which lacked the most basic amenities for a large touring company, and all the men were crammed into tiny dressing-rooms under the stage with only just enough room to stand. The place was filthy. There had been no attempt at publicity, and the arena, seating 25,000 was hardly full. Next day Nureyev pushed a too persistent photographer out of his path, an incident that was photographed by another photographer, and the resulting publicity ensured a packed bullring for the rest of the visit.

It was an exhausting and dispiriting tour, with long journeys and no time to settle into each venue. But as the company got exhausted and more jaded, Fonteyn got better and better until she was in what Legerton described as 'startling form'. Her knee recovered and she was marvellous and we were all getting tireder and tireder. That was very Fonteyn'.[7]

Covent Garden might berate provincial theatres for their conditions, but seemed quite willing to subject the company to this kind of junket in the name of international prestige, but many began to wonder who was benefiting and if whatever prestige the company got outweighed lowering their standards in this way.

Chapter XV

After the conditions endured in Europe, even the familiar dis-
comforts of the provinces seemed welcome. The demanding
summer tour had meant a shorter holiday than usual, and the 1968
autumn tour was marked by one of the worst outbreaks of sickness the
company had known. At one point a quarter of the dancers were off,
including most of the principals, and the company had three new
Albrechts in just over twenty-four hours – Robert Mead, Piers Beaumont
and Paul Clarke.

Another result was the postponement of the first night of Antony
Tudor's new ballet *Knight Errant*, created for David Wall. Wall, having
been off with an injury for several months, now sprained his ankle only
a few days before the première, and when finally the ballet went on on
25 November 1968 in Manchester, it was with Hendrik Davel in the
leading role. Tudor based the scenario on Pierre Choderlos de Laclos'
Les Liaisons Dangereuses – that amoral little work set in a decadent
society where style and manners are more important than morals.
Tudor's libretto was a complicated comedy of manners, in which the
Chevalier d'Amour seduces three women at the home of a Lady of
Consequence. He makes assignations with each of them for that night,
but entices their regular lovers to take his place. However, the Knight
is himself exposed for what he is by the Lady of Consequence and is
left at the end alone and humiliated.

As it was almost impossible to follow the intricate plottings and
relationships, much of the fun came from the excellent characterizations
of the three seduced women – Thorogood, her demureness hiding a

true wanton, Barbieri, wildly operatic and Anderton nymphomaniacally predatory. Davel did what he could with the leading role, but it was not until Wall took over that his magnetism and subtle characterization gave the ballet the focus that it needed, as he undertook each different seduction with amused detachment. At the end, betrayed by his paramour, stripped of all pretensions (and his clothes) he made the final gesture of the ballet – a shrug of acceptance and defiance that perfectly summed up the amoral tone of the original story. It seemed as though Tudor wanted to make a hard, satirical comment on contemporary morals, but it was lost in the complexities of the action and a clutter of period detail. The Richard Strauss score (*Le Bourgeois Gentilhomme*) was suitably sensual, and the settings, by Stefanos Lazaridis, ingenious – a series of L shapes, manipulated by the supporting cast of lackeys and servants, into doors, windows, beds, coaches.

If some complained that ballet was becoming fossilized in its own past, there were signs of regeneration and renewal outside the Royal Ballet. In 1966, Ballet Rambert was transformed into Britain's first contemporary dance company. In 1969, Robin Howard signed a lease on a former drill hall in London, to be known as The Place, where he created a home for his dance group, London Contemporary Dance Theatre. In the same year, Western Theatre Ballet was transformed into Scottish Ballet, based in Glasgow, under the direction of former Sadler's Wells Theatre Ballet dancer Peter Darrell. At the same time Laverne Meyer proposed Northern Dance Theatre based in Manchester. It had been suggested for some time that one of the answers to ballet in the regions (as the Arts Council now preferred to call the provinces) lay not in large touring companies but in locally based ballet companies, although to establish groups of as high a standard as existing companies would obviously take many years.

The late 1960s were not good years for classical companies, and people were beginning to ask if they could maintain their relative artistic isolation in a rapidly changing world. There were, not surprisingly, signs of weariness in the classics, and their familiarity began to tell on company and press, if not on audiences. There were calls for the Royal Ballet to be more adventurous and experimental, or at least to search out a new generation of choreographers – 'a matter of selection and finding out where the dance can be extended into new areas of vision and thought'.[1]

Thus 1969 saw the first moves to build a repertory of new works for the Touring Company by young choreographers, starting on 17 January 1969 with works by David Drew and Geoffrey Cauley, both of whom had been working with the Royal Ballet Choreographic Group.

Drew's *Intrusion* was a reworking of a ballet he had made for the Choreographic Group and which had been danced subsequently by the Royal Ballet School; he now expanded and made the choreography more difficult for the Touring Company. It had a slight theme of a love affair disrupted by outside influences, and if deficient in construction and emotion, it showed that Drew had a certain facility for putting steps together.

Cauley's ballet was more substantial and showed a completely idiosyncratic style. *In the Beginning* was set in the Garden of Eden, a cool, remote world of clear geometric shapes and colours by Peter Unsworth that perfectly matched the period feel of two Poulenc sonatas which formed the score. The theme was the temptation and the fall of man, leaving the Adam and Eve figures chained together – summed up by Cauley as 'man and woman, having made their mistakes, should be forced to live with them'.[2]

It was a work of great elegance, with a sophisticated coolness which reminded many of the 1920s (Cauley had been very influenced by Bronislava Nijinska's *Les Biches* which she had revived at Covent Garden in 1964). The style was characterized by the powerful use of moments of stillness, sculptural groupings of great simplicity and beauty. It was an extremely interesting first professional ballet, but it remained to see how expressive the style could be. The dancers all looked ravishing – Wall and Thorogood as the Adam and Eve figures, with Davel as an ambiguous Deity-cum-Adam's alter ego-cum-tempter and Aldous as the temptress – but later cast changes brought doubts as to how much of the ballet's quality lay in its choreography and how much in its performers.

Fonteyn gave some performances in *Swan Lake*, partnered by Richard Cragun from Stuttgart, who whipped up the audience to screaming pitch with his triple *tours en l'air* in Act III. Fonteyn could make up in artistry for her now waning technique, and she was a matchless Odette and a magical seductress in Act III, hypnotizing with her expressive eyes Prince and audience alike.

Both companies were beginning to wonder what the future held in store for them after Ashton's retirement. Field was quoted as saying that he would like all Royal Ballet dancers to do a spell with the Touring Company, to learn 'the hard facts of theatrical life before coming in to the more cloistered world of Covent Garden'.[3] And MacMillan publicly voiced his concern about The Royal Ballet's current standard of male dancing, saying that he would like to import foreign male dancers to bridge the gap until a new generation could be produced, an idea that had also been discussed by the Board.

The opening of Ashton's last season as Director in autumn 1969 found the Touring Company in Cairo as part of the city's celebrations of its millennium. The company left for Egypt amid increasing fears of war between the Arab states and Israel. The situation was tense, but nothing could detract from the beauty of the setting, a stage built in front of the Temple of Chephren, near the Great Pyramid. There was a national guerrilla congress in progress, and delegates were allowed to attend performances, so long as they didn't wear uniforms and left their guns behind. *Swan Lake* attracted a huge uninvited audience of Bedouins and villagers, who materialized out of the desert on their camels and donkeys, and watched from the sand dunes. Bats from the tombs of Gizeh fluttered around the lights, and from the stage the dancers could see the moonlight glinting on the machine guns.

As the decade drew to a close it seemed that the company too was reaching the end of a road. Every year the injuries and illnesses seemed to increase. Wall was to be off with a fatigue fracture for the whole year and many other dancers were temporarily incapacitated. The pushing of sometimes absurdly young dancers under these conditions was inevitable, but Field was certainly taking a chance in putting Stephen Jefferies, after less than three months with the company, to partner Barbieri in her début in *The Sleeping Beauty*. That he survived was due to an extraordinarily instinctive performing sense that compensated for the still rough technique. As with all young dancers there was concern that this kind of forcing would prevent technique from developing as it should.

In the absence of Wall, the proposed new Cauley ballet had to be cancelled, and in its place, for the economical sum of £390, the company acquired one of his first ballets, made for a Choreographic Group performance. Set to Ernest Bloch's *Voices in the Wilderness*, *Lazarus* was an impressive work, based on Nikos Kazantzakis' *The Last Temptation of Christ*. It showed the struggle between Jesus and his conscience as to whether He should bring Lazarus back to life and Cauley now added a *pas de deux* for Christ and Mary Magdalene. Cauley consciously reacted against ballets in which 'you're not given enough time to assimilate what has been expressed',[4] and like *In The Beginning*, *Lazarus* was notable for a dreamlike emotional detachment, and the frozen beauty of its groupings, although the linking passages were of less originality.

Change was in the air. No sooner had the new decade dawned than a bombshell fell. The whole Royal Ballet was summoned to a meeting and told that at the end of the season, in July 1970, the Touring Company in its old form would be disbanded and the dancers merged with the Covent Garden company. Twenty-six dancers would then be cut, leaving a single company of about 125. From September 1970 touring would be split between the whole Royal Ballet presenting the classics in the largest of the regional theatres during the summer,[5] and 'a smaller group of twenty-five dancers, each one independently interchangeable with the larger group ... concentrating on the development of repertory to be specially prepared for small numbers of dancers'. This group would undertake two six-week tours in autumn and winter and have a London season. The combined company would provide the dancers for the opera ballets at Covent Garden, and Ballet For All.

It is believed that this reorganization, with considerably greater flexibility than is provided by the present arrangement of two separate companies, will give dancers greater opportunities for performance in a more varied repertory; and because of the change of scale it will be capable of speedier development.[6]

The Opera House had been operating under a deficit throughout the 1960s, and the Board could not see any way of making sufficient economies to eradicate that shortfall. The grant to Covent Garden of course took into account the sum needed to keep a touring company in operation, but as early as 1966 it had been pointed out to the Arts Council, who controlled the subsidy to the Royal Opera House, that the liquidation of the Touring Company would mean a large saving. The same solution was mentioned again in 1968, when the financial situation was exacerbated by gross overspending on a new production of *Aida* and the mounting of Nureyev's *The Nutcracker* on the Resident Company. The public appetite for spectacle had increased, and the lavishness of the productions accordingly, with painted cloths giving way to three-dimensional textured sets and an increase in the use of embroidery and appliqué on costumes. It is hard not to feel that the Board was using the Touring Company as a pawn in their battle with the Arts Council for increased grants before, in November 1969, the decision was taken to abandon the Touring Company in its existing form.

Lord Drogheda, Chairman of the Board, insisted to the press that the decision had been made on artistic grounds, claiming that the classics could no longer be presented fittingly in existing regional theatres, although he did admit that there were also some financial advantages. Indeed, the Touring Company productions were by this time in need of drastic and expensive overhaul. It was generally felt that standards had declined over the last two years, the dancers were certainly tired and injuries and illness had increased. But it did not go unnoticed that the abandonment of the company would save about £100,000 a year, and that there was no mention of economies being made by the opera company; it was generally felt that once again the ballet was being sacrificed to keep the opera in the manner to which it had become accustomed.

For some the reorganisation would be the end, for redundancies would be inevitable. These were to be on a last in, first out basis, and so would mainly affect the *corps de ballet*, but there was considerable resentment that, in the end, almost all the dancers shed came from the Touring Company – effectively the management simply axed its *corps de ballet*. In an effort to protect the most promising of the recent intake, Field made sure that they danced at least one solo role in those final months of the company's life, so that he could argue for their retention on the grounds of exceptional talent.

The idea of one large interchangeable company had a familiar ring, but the dancers initially found the idea of the smaller group exciting and challenging. At the meeting, the company was told that on the notice board was the list of the twenty-five dancers selected for the first of the tours. Tait and Barbieri remember that, when they saw their names as part of the list headed by Sibley and Dowell they felt like the company élite. If your name was not on that list, they remember, then you felt you were nowhere, and for the few it looked like a new beginning.

The changes came as almost as much of a surprise to Field and MacMillan as anybody. They, Hart and Somes had hardly been consulted in the discussions about the future of the company, and were pretty much presented with a fait accompli. Also a little nonplussed was Peter Wright, brought in to take over the Touring Company when Field moved to Covent Garden in September 1970, who suddenly found himself faced with a very different company indeed.

Field, however, believed that the new policy could be made to work, and made it clear that, in his opinion, old-style touring was no longer possible – 'In this form we've achieved all we are going to achieve. Demands from the public are greater, and rightly so; standards must be higher', and he added, 'I think the public in the provinces are getting a little bit tired of the classics.'[7]

The provincial press rose up as a body and their full wrath fell upon the Opera House. They ignored the promise to tour the Covent Garden company – it was *their* company that was being axed, and they showed no appreciation of the promised smaller group. They saw the plan as part of a growing centralization, depriving taxpayers of their right to see what they had come to accept as their own company. 'Of course', wrote the *Northern Echo*, 'you can see what could possibly happen as a result. After a year or two of poor receptions for their team of twenty-five pioneers, the Royal Ballet pundits will probably get their wise heads together and decide that this proved they were right in cutting back provincial touring. In the end they might feel justified in ending touring altogether.'[8] The Opera House reckoned that there would only be a week or two reduction in touring throughout the year, since the major centres would be served by the Covent Garden company's summer tour, but the regions showed remarkably little faith in their arithmetic.

Shocked and stunned, the Touring Company set out upon its winter tour. There was to be no relaxation in their schedule, and they had to continue new casts and ballets as planned. Fonteyn was dancing with them again, partnered by Cragun, and in Sunderland people slept outside the theatre for nights to see her – 'They didn't even do that for the Beatles,' said the manager Reginald Birks, who had been leading the regional campaign against the Royal Ballet touring cuts.

The winter tour got under way with David Drew's *From Waking Sleep*, premièred on 30 January 1970 at the Royal Shakespeare Theatre in Stratford-upon-Avon. The title referred to 'that state of mind in which according to Buddhist belief we normally exist', and from the names given the various characters it seemed that The Favoured was in search of spiritual regeneration – His Awakening Self. Drew could, and did, verbally explain in fascinating detail his intentions beyond this, but they never became clear in the choreography and the ballet descended into almost total obscurity. It was a pity, for it was not without interest, and there was a beautiful *pas de deux* for Johnson, as The Favoured, and Barbieri as His Awakening Self. Johnson's strong personality held the ballet together, with his 'dare-devil impetuosity and manly fire'.[9]

With Wall's continued absence, there was a desperate shortage of male dancers, and Field began to look around for reinforcements. He found Desmond Kelly. Born in Southern Rhodesia, Kelly had come to London at the age of seventeen to join London Festival Ballet. After six years he went to New Zealand Ballet, where he became Ballet Master, and he had also worked in Zurich and with Frederic Franklin in the National Ballet of Washington. He was handsome, a strong technician and partner, with virile strength and natural nobility. For him, to work with the Royal Ballet was a dream come true – it still represented the Mecca for many dancers throughout the world.

During the Opera House season, Geoffrey Cauley made his first narrative ballet, *La Symphonie Pastorale*. Based on a story by André Gide, it told of the rescue of a young blind girl by a clergyman. He falls in love with her, causing estrangement with his wife and the jealousy of his son. On regaining her sight the girl realises that the love she feels is for the son, and seeing the havoc her presence has caused she drowns herself. Cauley had obviously felt the inadequacy of his choreographic vocabulary, for much of the narrative was spoken over loudspeakers, and the action was reduced to a series of illustrative *tableaux vivants*. Stunning performances from Thorogood as the Girl and Adrian Grater as the Pastor gave the ballet whatever validity it possessed. Thorogood was also a striking and very individual Giselle during the season.

The success of a rather low key season was the revival of de Valois' masterpiece *Job*. At its last revival by the Resident Company eleven years before, the 'Masque for Dancing' had begun to look old-fashioned, but, in the way of all fashion, its time had come round again. De Valois' affinities with the Central European school of the 1930s was clear in the choreography, and to the eyes of the 1960s the ballet now had a very 'modern' feel. The presence of Adrian Boult on the rostrum ensured the necessary high musical standard. As Noël Goodwin wrote about the score, which applied equally to the choreography, 'The poetry and the harmony of *Job* is peculiar to itself, and an enrichment of experience that can still penetrate the spirit.'[10] The role of Satan was hallowed for ever in Dolin's proud fallen angel and Helpmann's study in malevolent evil, and it would be impossible for any of the three Touring Company dancers to reach those heights, but Cooke was a physically impressive figure, although Davel lacked forcefulness. Most promising, if most tentative, was Jefferies, with a complete understanding of the strength and pride of the role, if as yet too inexperienced to put it fully into effect. Johnson was a radiantly serene Elihu.

Field was unwell that spring, so the 1970 European tour took place under the wing of Peter Wright. Foreign touring was now becoming extremely expensive, and many managements would consider the company only if Fonteyn and Nureyev were guest artists. The highspot of the tour was in Bonn where they premièred the last of Ashton's works as Director, *The Creatures of Prometheus*, presented as part of the celebrations of the bicentenary of Beethoven's birth. Beethoven had written *The Creatures of Prometheus* for Salvatore Viganò in 1801, at a time when gods and muses still reigned supreme on the ballet stage. Prometheus creates two human figures and displays them before the Gods. They are brought to life and given emotions by Apollo's music, and then educated by the muses in the pains and pleasures of living.

Ashton presented a light-hearted view of the story, set in the period when the ballet was originally written – so that Apollo looked like Beau Brummell, Mars like Napoleon and Prometheus like the young Beethoven. As a short, witty ballet it might have stood a chance, but there was nothing short or witty about Beethoven's score, and after a while the jokes wore thin. Best off, choreographically, were Conley as a mournful Melpomene, Thorogood as Thalia, muse of Comedy and Last as an stern ballet-mistress Terpsichore. The designs by Ottowerner Meyer added to the general blandness that permeated set and choreography alike.

Back in England the company had a fortnight of life left, to be spent in Oxford and Wimbledon. Even now young dancers were making their débuts – and the neat, crisp style of Marion Tait, was seen to advantage in the *pas de trois* in *Swan Lake*.

On 25 July 1970, in Wimbledon, in the presence of Ashton and de Valois and the whole London ballet audience, the company danced their hearts out in *Swan Lake* led by Wells and Kelly. A real lake could have been formed by the tears that were shed that night. At the end, amid cheers and tears, Ashton, de Valois, Field, Legerton and the injured Wall joined the company on stage. Typically, in her speech, de Valois did not dwell on the past, but looked to the future and thanked the company for 'fulfilling what was a wild dream of mine forty years ago'.

Somehow it seemed right that the last appearance of the Touring Company should be at a small suburban theatre, unsuited to large-scale productions and with no pretensions to grandeur – typical of those they had served over the years. Right, as James Kennedy put it, that 'the Royal Ballet's second company should go out neither with a bang nor

Doreen Wells as Odette in *Swan Lake*.

Photograph by Anthony Crickmay.

with a whimper but with an unrelenting, unfussy devotion to the task which it was set when, twelve years ago, it took up the assignment of touring Britain with the best and biggest that the Royal Ballet could offer'.[11] 'Royal Ballet II has been the finest advocate for our national ballet's importance,' wrote Clement Crisp. 'Splendid artists, splendid troupers, they have all earned our respect and admiration and, yes, love.'[12]

But the critics could afford to take the wider view, and for the company it was a bitter time indeed. 'It's the only thing I have any sad memories about', said Legerton, 'that at the end it just petered out ...'[13]

Part 3

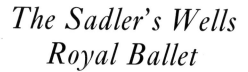

The Sadler's Wells
Royal Ballet

Chapter XVI

'I think we are the luckiest people who ever ran a ballet company'[1] Field was reported as saying soon after he took over the Royal Ballet with MacMillan in the autumn of 1970. Indeed, on paper the future looked bright indeed, with a strong company, rich in principal dancers, a new group to bring on young talent under the direction of Peter Wright, and an exciting new policy for the regions. It was a period of all change at the Opera House too, for David Webster had retired that summer, and the new General Administrator was his former assistant, John Tooley. Far from being listed as joint directors of The Royal Ballet, however, MacMillan and Field were named as Artistic Director and Administrative Director respectively, which is what many had assumed would be the distribution of duties. But Field had been much more than an administrator, and, having had artistic control of a company for so long and a proven ability for rehearsing and bringing on new dancers, he was unlikely to want to submit to mere paperwork while artistic decisions were made elsewhere. The question of the roles of Hart and Somes under the new regime had been resolved when Hart had resigned, feeling that there was no job for him in the reorganised Royal Ballet, and Somes was designated Senior Répétiteur with particular care of the Ashton repertory.

In fact it was all an unsatisfactory muddle. When Ashton had been appointed as Director in 1963, Webster had told Field that he would be the next in line.[2] According to Edward Thorpe's biography of Kenneth MacMillan,[3] Webster offered MacMillan the Directorship on the opening night of *Concerto* in Berlin in 1966, and only just before Ashton retired had John Tooley asked MacMillan if he would accept Field as co-Administrative Director. MacMillan agreed, having no desire to be desk-bound, and only later discovered that Field had been given the impression that they would share the artistic direction. There had been a total lack of communication and it seems that no one had actually defined their respective duties. It was not an auspicious beginning.

Peter Wright had accepted the job of running the Touring Company before the new policy had been announced, but, feeling that the project had possibilities agreed to stay on with the title of Associate to the Directors to oversee the new touring group. He thought that touring copies of the Covent Garden classics had become unviable, and that the Royal Ballet had reached a watershed in its development; for many years it had been held up as the great example of a ballet company in the classical tradition, and had perhaps become a little oblivious of developments taking place outside.

The combined company was 120 strong, of which a third were listed principals, and juggling so many dancers into three performances a week at the Opera House was going to be a headache all its own. Standards varied widely – principals in the Touring Company had tended to be much younger and less polished than those in the Resident Company, because of the conditions under which they worked. The number of principals would certainly prove a bar to promotion, but there was a relative lack of good dancers at soloist and coryphée level. A certain resentment was inevitable. There had always been too few performances for the Resident Company, and now they had to be shared among even more dancers than before. There must have been considerable apprehension among all the dancers. Having been away for four years, MacMillan was an unknown quantity to many of them; the Resident Company knew nothing of Field, and must have felt that his dancers would get preferential treatment. In fact Touring Company principals got only occasional performances, and only Wells and Wall were used to any extent; Grahame and Aldous had already left, the former joining London Festival Ballet, the latter Australian Ballet. At lower levels there were mixed casts of Friends in *La Fille mal gardée* and Townspeople in *Romeo and Juliet*. But dancers who had been used to performing regularly were frustrated and dissatisfied. 'I'd been used to dancing eight times a week', recalls Desmond Kelly, 'and not a couple of times a month. My house looked wonderful, my garden was tended, but I was not happy. It was not what I had come to do.'[4]

The devising of a touring repertory for the new company of twenty-five was not easy. It had been assumed that the group would devote itself to new works, and the word 'experimental' had been bandied about a great deal. Field believes it was assumed that MacMillan would provide most of the new repertory. Two new works were in preparation, one by MacMillan and the other by the American Glen Tetley. It was obviously impossible to produce an entirely new repertory overnight, and of necessity there would be a reliance on existing one-act ballets. By drawing on those of the Resident Company, a number of works unfamiliar to the regions were in the repertory when the first group went out on the road for a five week tour opening on 9 November in Nottingham. Nottingham had always been one of the old Touring Company's best dates, but even they had never responded in large numbers to the triple bills, and from the advance bookings it did not look as though the new programmes would alter this resistance.

The first of the new programmes opened with the world première of Glen Tetley's *Field Figures* – the flagship of the new era. However, as the Nottingham press pointed out, Tetley was hardly new and exciting to them, for they were quite familiar with his work from Ballet Rambert's visits. The question was whether the Royal Ballet's audience, (not necessarily the same audience as for Ballet Rambert), with its classically oriented expectations would accept the new image.

Tetley was familiar with both classical and modern dance technique, but his career had mainly been with modern dance companies, including Martha Graham. For *Field Figures*, however, he selected the most elegant and classical dancers in the Royal Ballet – Deanne Bergsma, Vergie Derman, Kelly and Johnson. They found the new style invigorating, and enjoyed the experience of stretching and extending (literally and metaphorically) their capabilities, and Tetley's own contemporary style took from them something of their academic classicism. The ballet was built around the relationship of the central couple, Bergsma and Kelly, their isolation in relation to each other and the other dancers, expressed with cool unemotionalism underlaid by an unstressed eroticism that was Tetley's trademark. The stage space was defined by beautiful Nadine Baylis-designed screens of vertically suspended metal bars.

The dancers rose magnificently to the challenge. Despite the initial agony of using unfamiliar muscles as they settled into a new style, they enjoyed working for Tetley, feeling that he made them look at their best. The ballet was modern enough to be hailed by younger members of the audience as indicative of a new direction, but others had strong reservations, and no inhibitions about expressing them, so performances

Deanne Bergsma, Desmond Kelly and Nicholas Johnson in *Field Figures*.

Photograph by Zoe Dominic.

were punctuated by the sound of upturning seats as they walked out. Doubtless part of their antipathy was to the Stockhausen score – in fact much of the regional aversion to modern dance came more from a dislike of the music than antagonism to the movement itself, for traditional audiences were being asked to accept music that even to the musical fraternity was of limited appeal.

The rest of the programme was made up of two masterpieces rarely seen outside London, Ashton's *Symphonic Variations*, and Balanchine's *Apollo*. *Apollo* had a lacklustre performance and not until Kelly took over in the lead did the ballet come to life. Looking every inch a Greek god, he understood, and made manifest, the meaning behind the steps, as the young god explores his world and then grows into his maturity as leader of the Muses, expressing the development in a flowing, masculine style.

Sibley and Dowell were the central couple in *Symphonic Variations* on the opening night in Nottingham. During the five week tour, mainly due to injury and illness, there were an extraordinary number of changes in a ballet that had always been very carefully cast at Covent Garden. It was however a strange choice. If, as had been asserted, the old policy had been abandoned partly because the classics could not be seen to advantage on the smaller regional stages, how could they now present the one ballet in the repertory built expressly for the spaces of Covent Garden, however small its cast?

For the rest of the repertory *Danses Concertantes* and Tudor's *Lilac Garden* looked under-rehearsed – rumour had it that Tudor could only spare three days to prepare two new casts for *Lilac Garden* and it had also acquired a hideous new set. Only *The Rake's Progress* seemed in relatively good shape, fielding two good Rakes, Morse and Cooke, and one potentially excellent one in Jefferies.

Above all, it had been stressed that the new arrangement would lead to higher standards, with adequate rehearsal time and coaching. In fact the general standard seemed lower than before, despite the presence of Covent Garden stars, like Sibley and Dowell, and Beriosova and MacLeary. MacMillan believed that it was only courteous to allow visiting choreographers, like Jerome Robbins (mounting *Dances at a Gathering* at Covent Garden), Tetley and Joe Layton, now working for the touring group, to take their pick of the Royal Ballet dancers. Thus although there was a large body of principals at Covent Garden, everyone tended to use the same ones for both new works and the regular repertory. So Sibley and Dowell were scheduled to appear at Covent Garden in *Romeo and Juliet* and *The Dream* and Robbins also chose them for *Dances at a Gathering*. At the same time they were supposed to be out on tour from time to time in *Symphonic Variations*. Bergsma too was needed by both companies, and travel for these dancers was as bad, if not worse, than anything experienced in the 1960s. It was not only a matter of travelling up and down the country, but also between London rehearsal rooms, for the Royal Ballet studios at Baron's Court were full of Resident Company dancers, and the new group was rehearsing at Donmar studios in central London. Scheduling was a nightmare. An impossible situation developed, with half the Royal Ballet being on three times a week and the other half hardly performing at all. On tour, star names were not evenly distributed over the five week tour, and some towns got all the star names and others none. The initial euphoria that the dancers had felt in being one of the 'chosen' for the small group quickly evaporated in the face of reality.

Who were the star names the regions had been promised? Beriosova and MacLeary were familiar from their performances in the provinces throughout the 1960s; Sibley and Dowell, like most of the Covent Garden principals, were known only to the balletomane, and were totally unknown to the general public. To the regions stars now meant Wells and Wall – Field's policy of developing his own dancers had been all too successful.

The audiences could not be blamed. For twenty years they had been conditioned to expect a particular repertory and presentation from a company bearing the name of the Royal Ballet. The change had not even been gradual. It might have been argued that Ballet Rambert had done the same when it had been transformed into a modern dance company in the mid 1960s, but they had realised that they must build a new audience and play different theatres. The Royal Ballet still wanted to play the number one touring dates and to the same audiences as before.

MacMillan's first creation for the Royal Ballet in six years, *Checkpoint*, was premièred on 27 November in Manchester. On the opening night a scheduled thirty minute interval, needed to set up the complicated set and film projector, stretched to over fifty as the stage staff strove to rewind the film, which had been accidentally dropped. Thus the audience was not in an entirely receptive mood when the curtain finally rose on some Orwellian future state where Big Brother has forbidden love. Trying to evade the watching cameras, two lovers meet up against a wall, and as they try to climb it to freedom they are discovered and eliminated by being absorbed into the wall. Unfortunately the projectors, which transmitted the all seeing eye and flashed alarming messages onto the back wall, failed after a few seconds and the climb and absorption of the lovers into the wall were only too clearly assisted by hands behind the elasticated fabric. Elisabeth Dalton's battery of lights, TV screens and surveillance cameras was suitably threatening, but there was nothing of menace or emotion in the choreography. MacMillan seemed to be using awkward movements for their own sake, and even succeeded in making Beriosova look ungainly in the leading role. It was a mistake to mount such a complicated piece for touring. Besides the complexities of the set, the score, Roberto Gerhard's *Collages*, had had to be prerecorded, so that music and projections could be synchronized, thus incurring large fees, for the musicians had to be paid both for the recording and for a full evening's work whenever the ballet was given. On the spring tour they demanded even higher payments for not playing, which the management refused to meet, and the ballet was hardly seen again. Unfortunately, it was by far the most expensive new work of the year, costing over £12,500. At this rate the small new touring group was hardly going to be more economical than the large old one.

Things came to a head after only three months. On 23 December, the Royal Opera House issued a statement:

> The Royal Opera House, Covent Garden, announces with regret the resignation of Mr. John Field, who has decided that the time has come for him to follow his career in other directions.
>
> Mr. Peter Wright, in his capacity as Associate to the Director, Mr. Kenneth MacMillan, will now be responsible for the administration of the Royal Ballet.

There had been difficulties from the beginning. Field had believed his job was to be 'the backbone of the direction'[5] thus leaving MacMillan free to concentrate on the creative side, but his positive assertiveness obviously clashed badly with MacMillan's introverted nature, and matters could not have been helped by the fact that MacMillan had hit an uncreative patch in his choreographic career. Field was also unhappy about the attitudes of Resident Company dancers and staff towards former Touring Company dancers – there had always been antipathy to the company and resentment of its success in some quarters. He left unhappily, with only the grateful thanks of the Board to show for his thirty-five years with the organisation, and no public expression of gratitude. His subsequent career took him to La Scala, to London Festival Ballet, the Royal Academy of Dancing and then to the British Ballet Organisation, but he still looks back on his time as director of the Touring Company as the high point of his career.

The Royal Ballet had lost the one person with long experience of running a ballet company and with extensive knowledge of touring. The announcement implied that Wright would now assume Field's responsibilities without his status; his main energies would be deflected from the group, and there was no director announced to replace him.

The management turned to John Auld, whose varied theatrical experience had included a period as Assistant Artistic Director of London

Festival Ballet and, since 1964 Ballet Master of the Gulbenkian Ballet in Portugal. He accepted the position of Company Manager of the touring group but as he was unfamiliar with the dancers and repertory it would obviously take him time to adjust. Most experienced of the staff was Peter Clegg, former soloist with the Resident Company, who came from the Royal Ballet School to be Ballet Master. But Wright was still in overall charge, and his new position at the Opera House meant that the group had a director *in absentia* and felt leaderless. It was hardly surprising if they made comparisons with the old Touring Company, where they felt Field was always there to fight for them.

Some stability was imperative, both for the dancers, and for audiences, if touring was to be in the hands of anything more than an ad hoc group. It would also ease the problems at Covent Garden if a regular group could be designated for touring and, except for some principals, be treated as a separate entity. Already it had been realised that an integrated company would not work. It all sounded very familiar, and the business of rebuilding a company and a repertory began all over again. In the attempt to save money and to establish a new type of company, the dancers in the group had been cut off from their classical roots, and it is not surprising if the ensuing years saw them wandering in the wilderness in search of an identity.

The dancers seconded to the group were mainly those who had been with the Touring Company – Last, Ruanne, Mosaval, Clarke, Cooke, Barbieri, Johnson, and some of the more promising of the *corps de ballet*, like Tait and Jefferies. The repertory for the spring tour also had a very familiar look for few ballets were carried over from the autumn; *Symphonic Variations* returned to the Royal Opera House, and, as *Field Figures* had been mounted using several Resident Company dancers, they eventually appropriated it as well. Instead there were revivals of *Beauty and the Beast*, *Pineapple Poll* and *Les Patineurs*. In place of *Checkpoint*, the company briefly performed one of MacMillan's best abstract ballets *Diversions*, but shorn of its set of architectural fragments by Philip Prowse, so that the overall stage picture was lost. Two new ballets, albeit one of them short, were in rehearsal.

The new company, once again, lacked a distinguishing name, and performed under the title of The Royal Ballet, thus reviving audiences' expectations of full length classics. It would take many years to break these expectations down, and until then the company faced another period of resentment and criticism. Several names were suggested over the years, including the unfortunate 'splinter group' but in the end the simple factual description 'New Group' was settled on; although the company was never actually billed as such, the term was used in the rest of its publicity.

Also familiar was the itinerary for the tours. The autumn had taken them to Nottingham, Leeds, Manchester, Glasgow and Edinburgh, the spring added Norwich, Stratford, Bournemouth, Oxford, Cardiff and Liverpool, with the small Theatre Royal in York the only new date. Thus the company was playing a one-act repertory in the very theatres familiar with their old policy – theatres which were also those designated as suitable for the Covent Garden company tours.

However much official reports tried to make out that audiences were welcoming and enthusiastic, the reality was different. Triple bills had never sold well, and did not now, even when nothing else was available. Reports of 'good' houses can be looked at in two ways, depending on whether a theatre is seen to be half full or half empty; previously good dates continued to be relatively good, and not so good dates relatively bad, but whichever way one looked at it, audiences were down.

The two new ballets for the winter tour of 1971 were in the hands of American choreographer Joe Layton. Layton had trained as a classical dancer, but most of his experience had been in musicals, as both choreographer and director. He had directed Rodgers and Hammerstein's *The Sound of Music* and Noël Coward's *Sail Away* and was working in London with Carol Channing when he heard about the new Royal Ballet policy. He approached MacMillan with several ideas, and MacMillan, obviously thankful to find a new choreographer, had within twenty-four hours commissioned him to do a ballet to music by Noël Coward and a short curtain raiser to Leonard Bernstein's *Candide* overture. 'I think the main reason my contract with the Royal Ballet was settled in a day', Layton said later, 'was that I said I would like to do something light for them. I got the feeling that they were in dire need of something light.'[6]

The premières were in Norwich during the winter tour. The first, *Overture*, was a bright little curtain raiser. The dancers dressed up from a property basket and then introduced the names of the ballets for the evening with banners and a great deal of cheerfulness.

The Grand Tour, first seen on 10 February 1971, was an immediate hit. With all the publicity threatening change and experiment, audiences seemed relieved to find that new works could be enjoyable. If *The Grand Tour* did not set out to do more than amuse, in that it certainly succeeded. Its setting was a ravishing pink and silver Art Deco ship by John

The Grand Tour. Vyvyan Lorrayne as the American Lady, Gary Sherwood as Noël Coward, David Drew as G.B. Shaw, Doreen Wells as Mary Pickford. Paul Clarke as Douglas Fairbanks, (Back) Nicholas Johnston as Gertrude Stein.

Photograph by Zoe Dominic.

Conklin – a cruise, peopled by as diverse a group of celebrities as never came together in one place, including Douglas Fairbanks and Mary Pickford, Theda Bara, George Bernard Shaw, Noël Coward, Gertrude Lawrence, Gertrude Stein and Alice B. Toklas. The odd character out was a frumpish, middle-aged American tourist, scorned by the celebrities, but at the ship's dance befriended by a young steward, who shamed the celebrities into accepting her.

Layton cast the ballet beautifully. Deirdre O'Conaire and later Ruanne and Barbieri were ravishingly elegant as Gertrude Lawrence, Clarke was a dashing Fairbanks, Wells delightfully fluffy as Mary Pickford and Sherwood marvellously smooth as Coward, miming with great conviction to a recording of the Master himself singing 'Half Caste Woman'. Especial fun were Johnson as a dour well-upholstered Gertrude Stein aided and abetted by a wide-eyed Jeanetta Lawrence as Alice B. That none of them really resembled the originals did not matter much, audiences being more than willing to do half the work of impersonators for them; Layton produced his cast meticulously and much of the choreography was amusing in its own right.

Most of all the ballet belonged to Lorrayne and Jefferies as the American tourist and the steward. Lorrayne had moved over from Covent Garden, where her career had been in a rut. She was well proportioned, with a lovely arabesque and her particular qualities had been discerned by Ashton, who enshrined her beauty of line in *Monotones No 2* and her warm femininity as Isobel Fitton in *Enigma Variations*. Layton now cast her against type as the dowdy, gauche spinster, and she performed a character that became touching in its lack of sophistication. In the charming and amusing *pas de deux* with the steward, each of her clumsy movements saved by him from disaster, she had an awkward naivety, which brought the character to life. As the steward, Jefferies performed with miraculous finesse, revealing his great gifts of timing, and ability to create real people on stage. Layton gave him only one direction, 'smile', confident that his instinctive performing talents would do the rest; the result was a smile that was at once charming, disarming, amused, sympathetic and reassuring. Both roles could easily have slipped into sticky sentimentality, but performed as they were with delicate tact, the whole episode became dignified and touching. It was all good fun and was to remain so over several seasons.

By the end of March 1971 the company was back in London, and it was the turn of the Covent Garden company to take to the road. With a repertory of *Swan Lake*, *La Fille mal gardée*, *The Two Pigeons*, *Raymonda Act III* and *Giselle* they set out on a seven week tour to five venues, two of which, Leeds and Manchester, had already had a visit from the smaller group. It was the first regional tour by the company for fifteen years and was hardly an unqualified success, audiences in Bristol especially being alarmingly bad, with only Fonteyn nights sold out. The management were bemused. Audiences wanted the classics, and now they were getting them by the major classical company in Britain. Audiences had clamoured for Covent Garden stars, and now they were getting them. What went wrong?

The fact was that the company were presenting exactly the same repertory as the former Touring Company, but a new generation of

Resident Company dancers were unknown outside London. There was sometimes more than a touch of condescension about the Opera House's dealings with the regions, expecting to be welcomed with open arms, and bemused when they did not get the instant results that they expected for having consented to tour at all. The regions would need time to adjust to the new names, and ballets new to them, like *Romeo and Juliet*, might have helped.

Meanwhile the Group was preparing for its first London season in May and June 1971. The theatre selected was Sadler's Wells – the first Royal Ballet appearance there since Field had taken his company to Covent Garden in 1957. As the opening ballet was *Danses Concertantes*, and the repertory included several other old friends from the 1950s, it was hardly surprising if many drew a parallel between the company and the Theatre Ballet. All the ballets that had been performed on tour were given, and Coward, in London for his seventieth birthday celebrations, was in the audience to see Sherwood impersonate him in *The Grand Tour*. Additions to the repertory for the season were MacMillan's *Las Hermanas* and new ballets from David Drew and Geoffrey Cauley.

Las Hermanas had been created for Stuttgart in 1963, and was Mac-Millan's melodramatic retelling of Lorca's play *The House of Bernarda Alba*. Five sisters are ruled by their domineering mother. The repressed eldest daughter is to be married, but the youngest sister seduces her fiancé, and when discovered hangs herself. For the first performance the ballet used an all star cast from Covent Garden, including Seymour and Monica Mason, with only Barbieri representing the Group. Seymour produced a moving study in inhibited frustration as the Eldest Sister, and Barbieri was suitably spiteful as the Youngest Sister. Dominating the ballet was Sherwood as The Man, like a young bull in his prime, self-satisfied, animalistic, confident in his masculinity and his devastating effect upon the all female household.

Drew was scheduled to produce two works for the season. However, the major one, *Impressionist*, based on the life of Monet, was finished but withdrawn only four days before its intended première. The other, *St Thomas' Wake*, had already been seen at a Choreographic Group performance. It conjured up the world of the 1920s in puppet-like dance of the period, until an assemblage of rubbish amassed by Peter Logan was blown over the stage, presumably symbolising the end of the era. It was, however, no repertory piece.

Cauley's offering was the equally short-lived *Ante Room*, its characters waiting in some kind of limbo. As much of his work, he had stripped the movements to the bare bones, and the beautiful sense of sculptural form was there, but it was cool and remote to the point of non-involvement.

What particularly hurt the Group's younger dancers was that Resident Company dancers were brought into London performances to take over roles they had not danced on tour. It hardly bred a sense of confidence and company spirit, and strengthened the feelings of being second-class citizens.

The Opera House *Annual Report* expressed itself well satisfied with the progress over the year, although the statement that the Group had fulfilled the hopes as a vehicle for experiment and younger choreographers was hardly well founded, for audiences had been sparse and unenthusiastic. Tetley had certainly produced a ballet outside the norm for the Royal Ballet, but hardly 'experimental' while Layton's was in an established tradition. But there was not much that could develop and feed the future of either company, nor build a new basic repertory.

Chapter XVII

It was four months before the Group set out again. The autumn of 1971 saw the companies divided more firmly than ever. Wright was appointed Associate Director to MacMillan and Auld moved up to take over as Assistant to the Directors, with special responsibility for touring, but Wright was still in overall control. There were no creations scheduled and the only additions to the repertory were two ballets by American choreographer Herbert Ross – *Caprichos* and *The Maids*. Both dating from the 1950s, neither ranked as experimental, nor, despite their undeniable qualities, major additions to the repertory. They were given their first performances at the Wimbledon Theatre in October 1971 as the company embarked upon its autumn tour.

Caprichos, inspired by four of Goya's commentaries to his etchings of the same name, displayed man's callousness to man, but the performance lacked the necessary viciousness and bite. Only Tait as the dead girl in the Tantalus episode made any impression.

However, *The Maids*, based on Jean Genet's play, was extremely well cast, with Cooke and Johnson as the two maids who re-enact their relationship with their mistress, until pretence becomes reality and the 'maid' murders the 'mistress'. In accordance with Genet's wishes the two maids were played by men, and Cooke and Johnson admirably avoided all suggestion of camp, Johnson especially conveying an androgynous sense without effeminacy. It was an effective piece of dance theatre, played with a nice sense of menace and sadism.

Without settled conditions it was going to be difficult to produce new works or even adequately rehearse the repertory. The Resident Company's studios at the Royal Ballet School were in full time use, and the group desperately needed a London base. It was therefore good for them to return to Sadler's Wells in the new year of 1972, where at least there was a proper rehearsal room.

Sadler's Wells was undergoing another of its periodic financial crises, and had just launched an appeal for £300,000, accompanied by the uncompromising statement that the theatre would have to close unless the money was forthcoming. The Group responded by organising an 'instant' midnight matinée gala for the penultimate night of the season which Princess Margaret agreed to attend. Fonteyn danced *Le Spectre de la rose* with Anthony Dowell, Nureyev appeared in *Les Rendezvous*, Merle Park and Kelly danced the lyrically acrobatic *pas de deux* from Peter Wright's *The Mirror Walkers* (which was later to become a popular repertory piece on tour) and the Group appeared in *The Grand Tour*. With additional help from the Arts Council and the London boroughs, the appeal raised sufficient funds to enable the theatre to stay open for another two years.

The only creation of the Wells season was another ballet from Joe Layton – *O.W.*, based on the life of Oscar Wilde. A first scene presented the public view of Wilde as a high camp aesthete, the trial reduced to a boxing match between Wilde and the Marquess of Queensberry, with Wilde answering the Marquess' parries and jabs with the flick of a sunflower. This was contrasted with the imprisoned Wilde of the *De Profundis*, extracts from which were taped by John Gielgud. It was an almost impossible subject balletically, since it was difficult to convey in movement Wilde's wit and charm, which lay almost entirely in the spoken word. The young Wilde was played by Paul Clarke, and the older Wilde by Michael Somes, who brought great poignancy to the figure of the ageing writer, accepting his fate with dignity and resignation. Johnson was an attractive, arrogant and self-absorbed Bosie.

Audiences might be forgiven for making comparisons between the Sadler's Wells Theatre Ballet and the New Group, with their predominantly young dancers, similar repertory, half of which dated back to the 1950s, and policy of producing new works. But times had changed. The new works were by choreographers from outside the company, and few were creations. A company that had always been self-sufficient in its creativity was now having to look outside itself for inspiration.

People were still confused about the company and its purpose. If insisted upon, it was described as 'a separate contingent of the Royal Ballet, in no way a reserve branch or junior team, but a separate, autonomous company', whereas the Theatre Ballet's role as a 'graduate' company was always stressed. The Group had more experienced dancers at the top, including Last, Mosaval, Johnson, Cooke, Barbieri and Ruanne, than ever the Theatre Ballet had at its disposal, besides a lively group of young dancers like Tait, Jefferies and Lois Strike.

As in the early days of the Theatre Ballet, the spring tour saw classical excerpts introduced into the repertory, although now dancers were often seconded from Covent Garden to perform the *pas de deux* from Act II or Act III of *Swan Lake*, a sign that the Group's dancers were not felt to be technically strong enough, but also an attempt to add some 'star' names to the casting. However, the result was to make the programmes seem fragmentary and insubstantial. Visits from the Resident Company dancers were fleeting and sometimes, regrettably, condescending, and confirmed with some members of the Group a sense of inferiority. There was also the inescapable criticism of those who objected to ballets like *The Maids* or *O.W.* which were not suitable for children.

Meanwhile, arrangements were under way for the Covent Garden company's 1972 visit to New York, and Sol Hurok was demanding a world première to give focus to the season. MacMillan therefore choreographed a short *pas de deux* to Stravinsky's *Circus Polka* for Seymour and Nureyev. It was decided to give it a try out before New York, and so performances were arranged for the last day of the Group's visit to Liverpool on 1 April 1972. Liverpool became very excited, for this would be the first time that Nureyev had ever danced in the city, but in the event, the audience might have been forgiven for thinking that an April Fool had been played upon them. Instead of Nureyev of the fabulous technique and unerring stage sense, they were faced with him and Seymour in a jokey, but not very funny, take off of an acrobatic circus act. As Bill Harpe wrote in the *Guardian*, 'The deepest insults are often unspoken, often even unrecognised or uncomprehended by their authors. This *pas de deux* and its performance was just such an insult.'[1] It was a most unfortunate episode, and showed yet again how little understanding the Covent Garden management sometimes had of the regions, and it did nothing to help the image of The Royal Ballet or the New Group out of London.

On the night that The Royal Ballet opened at the Metropolitan Opera House in New York, the Group was appearing in a vast and highly unsuitable cinema in the London suburb of Golders Green. The twenty-five dancers had now risen to thirty-six, and in addition to rehearsing a

Grosse Fuge. Carole Hill, Stephen Jefferies, Margaret Barbieri, Kerrison Cooke
and Paul Clarke.

Photograph by Anthony Crickmay.

new ballet by MacMillan, they mounted the *pas de six* from *Laurentia*,
and Hans van Manen's *Grosse Fuge*.

On 29 April, at a typical Saturday matinée, with excited children
predominating, the company gave van Manen's *Grosse Fuge*, his first
work to be performed by a British company. A founder member of
Nederlands Dans Theater in 1960, van Manen had become their leading
choreographer and then artistic director, bringing the company to the
forefront of the European modern dance movement. His personal style,
however, had its roots deep within the classical tradition, and so made
it particularly suitable for the New Group.

To Beethoven's *Grosse Fuge* four couples danced out a mating ritual.
The men dominated at first, their aggressive fluid movements accented

by voluminous full length skirts; the women in contrast had a lyrical confidence, and they came together in a series of flowing solos and *pas de deux*. To the Cavatina from the B Flat Quartet, the skirts were cast away, and the couples became more intimate. Movements now centered around the men's heavy leather belts, by which the girls were pulled, supported and lifted. A cool eroticism permeated the whole ballet.

Many objected to the music being used at all, but van Manen created movements that had their own validity and achieved something of the passionate austerity of the music. It was the first of the 'modern' ballets for the company that established itself in popular favour, and proved an excellent gentle way to overcome any prejudices against 'modern' dance, for dancers and audience. The work was full of van Manen's characteristic earthbound supple flow and beautiful precise construction, which David Morse described as like 'a Swiss Watch, all put together so immaculately'.[2] The cast of eight thoroughly enjoyed performing it and all danced with assurance and commitment – Ruanne, Barbieri, Strike and Carole Hill partnered by Clarke, Cooke, Johnson and Jefferies.

On the following two month tour of Portugal, France and Switzerland it was the old story – advertised as The Royal Ballet, that was what people expected, classics and all. Disappointment was thus unavoidable. The group was headed by Beriosova and MacLeary and Fonteyn made some appearances, dancing various *pas de deux* with Attilio Labis.

MacMillan created *Ballade* for the tour, a slight work for four dancers, which was premièred on 19 May in Lisbon. It was short and the relationships between the three men and Lorrayne as the only woman did not develop any particular shape or point and the whole work was dismissed by John Percival as a 'kind of choreographic doodling'.[3] They also inherited from the Resident Company MacMillan's *Triad*, but neither ballet lasted long in the repertory.

The tour was not without incident. Between Portugal and Bordeaux the scenery trucks were held at the Spanish–French border until some official paperwork could be cleared. 'The resultant Monsieur Hulot-type farce involved British Consuls dragged out of bed before dawn, the complications attending a Spanish holiday during which nothing moves, especially the telephone, and culminating in a dramatic dash from the Spanish–French border complete with siren-screeching police escort to Bordeaux.'[4] They were, however, too late for the opening night, and there was a frantic scramble to put together replacement sets and costumes. Peter Clegg was given 2,000 francs and bought tights, shoes, and tunics; six plastic garden beds took the place of the elegant deck chairs in *The Grand Tour*, costumes were improvised from the Bordeaux Opera House wardrobe, and Barbieri cut the back from one of her own dresses to wear as Gertrude Lawrence.

In an effort to keep the public informed, and to answer some of its critics, the Opera House called a press conference for both Royal Ballets – the first for some years. Wright did most of the talking. He admitted that the difficulties attendant upon the amalgamation had affected the standards of both groups. The aim for the group, he announced, was to 'build up a repertory of new works so that it can have its own repertory' and preserve certain ballets 'which are important to the Royal Ballet and without the New Group would probably vanish altogether'. The search was still on for new, home-grown choreographers. Rehearsal time would be available to those who wanted to try and the more promising results could be given on tour. He also confirmed that the idea of a single company was now officially buried.

At the Maltings, Snape, on 28 July, Ashton created *Siesta*, his first work since retiring as Director. Described as a short 'birthday card for Willie Walton' to celebrate the composer's seventieth birthday, it featured Lorrayne and Barry McGrath, who rolled and entwined upon a large, foam-rubber mattress. At the same performance *Façade* was given a rarely performed version with a narrator, Peter Pears, speaking the Edith Sitwell poems to accompany the dances.

Few of the ballets, except *The Grand Tour* and *Grosse Fuge*, would establish themselves in the repertory, and the dancers seemed to spend an inordinate amount of time in rehearsal for short-lived works. Admittedly it is difficult to estimate the success of a ballet before it is created, but there seemed to be no clear guidance for the building of a repertory, which now had a distinctly second-hand and insubstantial look about it. There was no sign of a new choreographer emerging within the company. Wright came out on tour as much as he could but the dancers felt very isolated, and that no one really cared about them or their development at all. It was difficult not to feel that the company was being run down to a point where it could be disbanded.

The Group, 'brimful of that second-line talent in which the Royal Ballet enviably and, perhaps wastefully, abounds',[5] opened the 1972–73 season at the Royal Opera House with three performances, but they really had neither the repertory nor the numbers to fill the larger stage. Then, before setting out on the road, they moved to Sadler's Wells, a much more suitable London venue for them (they eventually had two seasons a year there, in the autumn and winter). Here they presented two new ballets, *The Poltroon* with choreography by MacMillan, and *In a Summer Garden* by Ronald Hynd.

The Poltroon was an intentionally unpleasant little ballet showing the nastier side of the traditional *commedia dell'arte* figures. Pierrot, the Poltroon of the title, the much put-upon butt of the other characters, eventually turns upon his tormentors and massacres them. MacLeary had a fine cold frenzy in the title role and Last was flamboyantly free with her favours as Columbine, but whatever distinction the ballet had lay in the wonderfully tawdry glitter of Thomas O'Neill's designs. However, everyone got a good deal of fun out of speculating whether the subject was really MacMillan revenging himself upon his critics.

In contrast, Hynd's *In a Summer Garden* was a dreamy, impression-istic romantic encounter on the river between an Edwardian lady and a young man. Set to Delius, it captured all the sensuality and period atmosphere of the music, Peter Docherty's gauzy settings were extra-ordinarily pretty, and the whole effect was of a perfect harmony of the parts. Lorrayne was excellent as the lady whose desires overcome her repressions, and McGrath was a suitably sympathetic seducer.

In the spring of 1973 came the confirmation of what everyone had suspected – that the Covent Garden company would not tour the regions again. The management, while 'not attempting to deny our responsibilities toward the Regions' were not convinced that the best interests of either company or audience was served by touring 'in the manner so often demanded by those living out of London ... we believe that the degree of compromise in presenting (the ballets) is such that we should not attempt to show them out of London until such a time as theatres are built which will enable us to perform them in the way it was intended'.[6] The fact that the regions might be willing to put up with less than the best rather than with nothing was an idea abhorrent to the Opera House; compromise (or reality depending on how you look at it) was a word that was not in their vocabulary. As Merete Bates wrote in the *Guardian*, 'It is as if neurotic perfectionism is fossilizing a medium that should be as adaptable as it is natural.'[7] Laudable though their attitude might be in a perfect world, by the terms of their argument, the management should never have allowed the Bolshoi Ballet to appear at the Opera House, as its stage was so much smaller than that of the Bolshoi itself.

The changes that had been announced in 1970 had now all gone by the board – the exciting experimental repertory had not materialized, and the excerpts from the abandoned classics often showed only too clearly that adequate rehearsal time had not materialized either; Covent Garden dancers were sometimes shuttling up and down the country just to perform a *pas de deux*, and now the promised touring of the classics by the Covent Garden company to fill the gap left by the disbanding of the Touring Company was to be axed. Much of the blame was laid on MacMillan. It might not have mattered so much if he had been on a choreographic winning streak, but beset with company problems, and his new ballets for the Resident Company subjected to vicious criticism, it was not surprising if his creativity was at a low ebb. Ashton had had a more stable company and three Assistant Directors, but even so he had found it impossible to create as fluently in his early years as Director as he had before. Equally worrying were the accounts for the fourteen weeks of touring by the Group in 1971–72, showing expenses of £309,700 and receipts of only £92,200. Already the New Group was costing more to run than the company axed to save the Opera House £100,000.

The Group's ensuing tour was overshadowed by the coverage given in the regional press to the Opera House announcement. One press agency put out that all touring by The Royal Ballet would cease and the resultant outcry by the regional press eclipsed the whole of the tour, and the regions might have been forgiven if they therefore saw the Group as a mere sop. It was very confusing for the public – one week the headlines announcing no more touring, then a small band of dancers with a relatively unheard of repertory and no known names.

It was a very low period indeed. The company had to bear the brunt of the adverse reaction. Audiences were small and there was no air of excitement or expectancy at performances. The repertory looked tired – what else could be expected of *Façade*, *Les Rendezvous*, *Pineapple Poll*, *The Lady and the Fool* and *Solitaire* after so many years – and much of the remainder, apart from *Grosse Fuge*, *The Grand Tour* and *In a Summer Garden* seemed universally grey, both visually and spiritually. None of the other new ballets were to prove popular. The old pattern of overwork and overperforming seemed to be repeating itself – McGrath reckoned he appeared in eighty ballets in the eight week tour and Barbieri remembers it as the most hectic time in her career; besides appearing in two or three ballets a night, there were sometimes rehearsals or costume fittings on Sundays. There had been no alteration in the company classes to take account of the modern ballets in the repertory, and there were already reports of strains and injuries, especially to backs, due to more difficult and unusual lifts. It was not surprising that from this time the company toured its own physiotherapist, yet another person to fit into the already overcrowded theatres, but a much needed addition to the staff. No longer would it be necessary to seek out the local football team's physiotherapist on tour.

To give the dancers more technically demanding works, Balanchine's *Allegro Brillante* was brought into the repertory. It certainly provided a challenge for the dancers, but it was an unrewarding work for the general audience, with a great deal of extremely hard dancing for remarkably little effect. Balanchine insisted on the original unflattering designs being used – the girls dressed in wispy pastel chiffons, and the men in the most unfortunate tunics, grey, very short, with puffed sleeves and lacing across the wide, deep V necks.

It had been hoped that van Manen would create a work especially for the company, but instead he mounted for them one of his most effective works, *Twilight*, set to John Cage's *Perilous Night*. Ruanne and Clarke never looked better than as the sparring couple, dancing out their sexual contest before Jean-Paul Vroom's curiously beautiful power station backcloth. Van Manen had been attracted by the difficulty of a girl dancing in high heels, and the contrast between those movements and similar ones performed barefoot. Thus Ruanne stalked the stage with tigerish tension in the first part, while Clarke watched warily, and then, with her shoes off, they danced a *pas de deux* full of nervous aggression and sexual tension. What audiences there were much enjoyed the ballet, and were fascinated by Cage's score for 'prepared piano', which demanded pieces of plastic, screws, rubber washers, a wooden block wrapped in a handkerchief and other objects fitted between the strings.

The most successful of Drew's ballets was *Sacred Circles*, set to Shostakovich's Piano Quintet, which was premièred in Stratford on 2 March 1973. The 'sacred circles' of the title were wedding rings, and the ballet began with two couples each encircled in large hoops. With these removed by the ambiguous figure of the Ringmaster, the couples were seemingly offered freedom, and they mixed and swopped partners, but at the end they were just as bound as the hoops descended, trapping them again. The symbolism was fairly obvious and did not obscure some of Drew's most inventive choreography to date, notably for Johnson as the Ringmaster, with his bright, bounding solos, and the *pas de deux* for Lorrayne and Cooke as the exchanged couple.

Van Manen's *Tilt* was built upon a typically off-beat concept. Stravinsky's Concerto in D for Strings was played twice, each time with the same choreography but distributed among different dancers, so that the perception of the steps changed according to their context. The ballet proved equally well liked in its first performances at the Wells in May and on the subsequent tour, audiences responding to the commitment and energy that characterized van Manen's work, and the good performances that he coaxed from the dancers.

After the depression of the year, it was uplifting for company morale to be hailed as a major attraction of the Israel Festival when the Group gave a week of performances in August 1973 as part of the celebrations of twenty-five years of an Israeli state. A great deal of the attention centred upon Nureyev's guest appearances – characteristically he arrived with no razor or toothpaste, but had thoughtfully remembered several striking outfits for the battery of photographers who followed him wherever he went. Seymour and MacLeary were also with them, as was Wells – her first appearance with the Group since her marriage to the Marquess of Londonderry and the birth of a son the previous year. Mrs Golda Meir came to see them in Jerusalem, accompanied by eight cabinet ministers (the first time so many had appeared together in public since the Six Day War in 1967), and numerous army, police and security men. She enjoyed herself so much that she attended another performance, this time in the Roman amphitheatre at Caesarea, where two hundred seats had to be found for her secret service men. Nureyev also needed a bodyguard, albeit smaller, when he decided to go sightseeing in Jerusalem.

The press received the Group favourably – 'a fine well-trained company, every dancer conforming to a standard of professional excellence in a wide stylistic spectrum', wrote the *Jerusalem Post*.[8] The dancers were constantly stopped in the street by people who complimented their work and thanked them for coming. They also gave a much appreciated extra performance for charity and there were free seats for Israeli dancers and teachers who had not been able to get into the other sold-out performances. What was not appreciated, however, was the orchestra – the Haifa Symphony Orchestra had to be augmented by players drafted in from the army bands, who kept disappearing according to their military duties. Matters were not helped in Tel Aviv where concrete pillars in the pit prevented many of the orchestra from seeing conductor David Taylor at all.

In Israel the company gave their first performance of Balanchine's *Prodigal Son* with Nureyev in the title role, Lynn Seymour as the Siren and John Auld as a powerful and moving Father. As usual, it was insisted that Nureyev dance as much as possible, and at one performance he knocked off *Les Rendezvous, Le Corsair pas de deux* and *Apollo*. Despite his heavy schedule, he still found time to coach Last and Johnson in the *Flower Festival at Genzano pas de deux* – although Johnson subsequently pointed out that he had now learnt five different versions of the *pas de deux*, all from people who had learnt it from Erik Bruhn.

The whole ballet world had been shocked in June by the untimely death of John Cranko, and during their Sadler's Wells season, on 3 October, the Group mounted a gala in the presence of Princess Margaret to raise funds to found a scholarship in his name. The programme was made up of *The Lady and the Fool, Pineapple Poll* and *Card Game*.

Stravinsky had been commissioned to write *Card Game* for Balanchine's American Ballet in 1937, which he must have enjoyed, for he was a fanatical poker player. Cranko's ballet had been created for Stuttgart in 1965, but had failed to establish itself in the Resident Company repertory when he mounted it for them in 1966.

Although centred around the intricacies of poker, the action was quite easy for the uninitiated to follow – each movement took the form of a 'deal' and the influence of the Joker upon each. In the first deal Lorrayne was delightfully dejected as the unnecessary Queen of Hearts, ruthlessly dispensed with by the Joker, and Barbieri was a wonderfully daffy Two of Diamonds in the third, although the group was hard put to find five men who could cope with the solos for a straight flush of Hearts in the second movement.

Dominating the ballet with devastating roguish impudence was Jefferies as the Joker. Up to the dress rehearsal he had found no particular character, but by the first night had had a perceptive flash of inspiration. He developed a loose-limbed, doggedly determined style of moving, based upon the walk of comedian Norman Wisdom, that was at once wildly funny and immensely appealing, and an immediate hit with audiences, especially on tour.

Less of a hit was what proved to be Drew's last ballet for the Group, *Sword of Alsace*. He had obviously taken to heart criticisms of obscurity in his previous works, and he now turned in a narrative ballet, set at the time of the Franco-Prussian War. Mouchette (Barbieri) scorns her pacifist fiancé, Etienne (Jefferies), flirts with his soldier brother (Clarke) and offers kisses to those men who will enlist. After one of the longest and most unrewarding *pas de deux* on record, Mouchette and Etienne fall asleep and dream – she of having sent men to their deaths, he, in patriotic guilt, of committing suicide on the spike of a regimental banner.

Stephen Jefferies as the Joker in *Card Game*.

Photograph by Anthony Crickmay.

The immense detail of the first scene overbalanced the rest of the ballet and though the large cast coped bravely with their characters, including the Blacksmith's ex-fiancée (a designation that defied all mime), they were indistinguishable and the whole effect was extraordinarily old fashioned and prosaic.

Part way through the season, and with the casting already announced for the forthcoming tour, Ruanne, Cooke and Clarke made the devastating announcement that they were leaving the company to join

London Festival Ballet and in one blow the company lost three of its most experienced principals. Ruanne and Clarke both missed the old Touring Company; at the time of the reorganisation she had just been about to step into the classical ballerina roles, and she now knew that she would never get the chance at Covent Garden. She felt the Group could not offer her the same performing satisfaction, and London Festival Ballet was now the only large company touring a classical repertory in Britain. Like all the dancers, she had found the New Group schedule a terrible strain – 'Coming on three times a night as three different people and trying to convince the audience that you're not anything to do with the last ballet,'[9] – and felt that after that to perform a single role an evening, even a strenuous classical one, would be something of a rest. The traffic was not, however, one way. Alain Dubreuil had joined the Group at the beginning of the season from London Festival Ballet, and had already made his mark as the most successful of the Hearts in the second deal of *Card Game*. A totally reliable and professional performer, with an easy, likeable stage manner, he added much needed weight and experience to the now depleted ranks of the male dancers.

Slowly the company was growing, mainly to ease the schedule for many of the dancers, but also so that there would be an increased number of ballets from which to select the repertory. Thus by the autumn of 1973 the company was large enough for Wright to stage a revival of *Les Sylphides*, although with a *corps de ballet* of sixteen, instead of twenty. Even so, four senior students had to be brought in from the School on nights when it was performed. The ballet was moderately well danced, but improved dramatically after Wright started making unannounced visits to see the company out on tour in addition to his regular weekly visits. It was performed with *Prodigal Son* and *Card Game*, an excellent programme, strong choreographically, musically and design-wise, and an audience drawn in by the happily familiar *Les Sylphides* found themselves equally enjoying the drama of the one and the humour of the other.

Prodigal Son was to become one of the company's most popular dramatic works. Looking as fresh as the day of the Diaghilev Ballet première in 1929, it produced an excellent number of profligate sons from among the Royal Ballet – notably Kelly, Wall and Dubreuil. Most successful was Jefferies, unerringly tracing the Prodigal's downfall and redemption, from his fretful frustration with the home of his youth, greeting each new experience with naïve enthusiasm and his sexual initiation with a mixture of innocence and guilt, until the final humiliation and the fearful return to his father. It was an extraordinary evocation of the journey from youth to maturity.

The last of van Manen's works to be mounted for the company was *Septet Extra* on 12 February at Sadler's Wells, a cheerful, quirky little work, set to Saint-Saëns, and danced against Jean-Paul Vroom's gigantic crossword puzzle backcloth. Van Manen mocked the conventions of classical ballet with affection and humour, amusingly resolving conventional steps in an unexpected way and the company responded with slick good humour. Out on the road audiences, partly unused to laughing at non-narrative ballet, and partly unacquainted with the minutiae of classical ballet, missed the more subtle jokes, although they enjoyed the general non-dance comedy of the finale.

Much as he liked working with the company and admired many of the dancers, van Manen was never to create a ballet for them. When the chance came, it was Covent Garden and the formidable talents of Anthony Dowell that claimed him and his only original work for The Royal Ballet was to be *Four Schumann Pieces* in 1975. As Tetley's second creation for the Royal Ballet, *Laborintus*, had also been for the Resident Company, the Group might have been forgiven for sometimes feeling like a mere stepping-stone.

By early 1974 the company had lost another male principal, Barry McGrath. Much of the repertory had devolved upon Jefferies, and it looked as though Dubreuil had arrived just in time. The company could occasionally call upon dancers from the Resident Company where the repertory was shared, but it was not always satisfactory. Desmond Kelly, however, frustrated by not dancing much at Covent Garden, began to tour more often. But scheduling left a lot to be desired, and he would find himself returning to London and being faced with a performance of, say, *Romeo and Juliet*, with insufficient time to readjust.

Local interest always helped a ballet on tour, and so it was Bradford, with its proximity to the Yorkshire moors and Haworth, that was chosen for the première of Ronald Hynd's *Charlotte Brontë*. In trying to put into balletic terms the undramatic life of the Yorkshire novelist and her literary siblings, Hynd had chosen an intractable subject. The ballet certainly had sincerity, and committed performances from its cast, with Barbieri (substituting for Lynn Seymour) as a suffering Charlotte, Lorrayne as a frenzied Emily, Jeanetta Lawrence as a wan Anne, and Morse as a suitably debauched Branwell.

The Brontë Society was out in force for the première (and Brontë biscuits were on sale in the foyer), and gave their seal of approval, but the critics withheld theirs, putting it down as a muddled and gloomy, if honourable, failure. The Bradford audience, however, gave it a rousing reception, especially Douglas Young's harsh, atmospheric score, which they felt conveyed all the bleakness of the moors. The orchestra was playing particularly well under a new conductor, Barry Wordsworth.

The search for new choreographers was still on, and during the May season at Sadler's Wells the company presented *The Entertainers* by soloist Ashley Killar. Killar had already had one short work, *Migration*, tried out for a couple of performances on tour, and *The Entertainers* was his chance to produce a ballet for the repertory. It was a pleasantly elegant if slight work, set among the Italian comedians of the French court immortalized by Watteau and Fragonard, and was particularly well danced by Lorrayne and Barbieri as court ladies, with Peter O'Brien and a promising young soloist, Kim Reeder, as the comedians.

During the season the company took part in a programme to celebrate the centenary of the birth of Lilian Baylis, for which they performed for the first time Ashton's 1937 ballet *A Wedding Bouquet*, in which Dubreuil proved a wonderfully harassed Bridegroom and Tait a simperingly innocent Bride. The programme also included the de Valois-Ashton collaboration *Harlequinade* from Ballet For All's *The World of Harlequin*. Ballet For All was continuing its work in the smaller venues, although its programming was becoming ever more ambitious – too ambitious perhaps for the young inexperienced dancers to cope with and still maintain Royal Ballet standards. It began to assume the status of a small company in its own right, performing cut-down versions of Covent Garden works like *Romeo and Juliet* in the name of education, a situation which was obviously good neither for the inexperienced performers nor the company in whose name they appeared. Thus in 1978 funding was withdrawn from Ballet For All and it ceased to function.

Chapter XVIII

The touring group was developing fast, and not before time. The desperate need to do something to ensure its validity was shown by the box office figures, which in the course of the 1973–74 season ranged from ninety seven percent in Leicester (a not surprisingly good response as the company were the first to play in the new Haymarket Theatre) and over eighty percent in traditional strongholds like Brighton and Newcastle, which used to yield averages in the high ninety percent, to a disheartening twenty six percent in Coventry.

Plans for the next season showed even more clearly that it had been accepted that the policy must change. Both *Giselle* and *Coppélia* were announced, and the company was further increased to cope with them. As a final severing of links with the unsuccessful past, the company was now referred to as The Royal Ballet on Tour.

The company had also acquired a new chief conductor, Barry Wordsworth. Under his leadership, the orchestra was welded into a semi-permanent group that could accept work outside the company during foreign tours or holidays. This offered the musicians a much better deal than before, and had the advantage of building up a more stable orchestra, thus obviating the worst aspects of the previous system, although the musicians retained their freelance status.

The 1974 autumn season opened at Sadler's Wells on 2 October with *Unfamiliar Playground*, the first ballet created for the company by Christopher Bruce, the brilliant dancer and choreographer developed by Ballet Rambert. Whether because of a fundamental misunderstanding, or insufficient time for dancers and choreographer to adjust to each other's styles, the ballet was not one of Bruce's more inspired works, and lacked his usual strong choreographic invention and sense of construction. The work was mainly notable for its masterly delineation of space by Nadine Baylis, and for a raptly performed sinuous solo by a young recruit from the Resident Company, June Highwood. The score by Brian Hodgson and Anthony Hymas, was the first electronic score commissioned by The Royal Ballet, and was described by them as 'Dankhausen', a cross between Johnny Dankworth and Stockhausen.

The revival of *Giselle*, however, bore out Wright's belief that The Royal Ballet was fundamentally a classical company and that, as such, had to perform the classics – both for the sake of audiences and dancers. Indeed, there had been a noticeable falling off in technical standards among the New Group dancers and it would take several years before they were back at full strength. Last was appointed Ballet Mistress in addition to her performing duties, and Ronald Plaisted transferred from Covent Garden to become Ballet Master.

Giselle was still the basic production that Wright had mounted for the Touring Company in 1968, but scaled down for the smaller *corps de ballet*, which had the effect of throwing even more focus onto the principal roles. It was not surprising if the first performances were tentative, and the company had lost the sense of style and the experience in mime roles. The first Giselle and Albrecht were Barbieri and Dubreuil, she with a sweet innocence and soft Romanticism, he charming, welcomely intelligent and an excellent foil. Lorrayne, partnered by the noble Kelly, looked too mature for the role, and Tait and Jefferies made their debuts, both giving well thought out and personal interpretations, if neither was, as yet, in full technical command of the roles. As Myrtha, Kathryn Wade was frighteningly authoritative and icily brilliant. As in the past, the Resident Company began to use the company as a try-out for some of its own principals, and both Lesley Collier and Monica Mason came to make their debuts as Giselle.

Although *Giselle* was never regarded as a great crowd puller, audiences reacted with relief to the signs of a return to the old policies, and responded in gratifyingly better numbers. The production was to provide a high proportion of acceptable Giselles, including a charmingly period interpretation from Anya Evans, remarkably successful in both

---

Margaret Barbieri as Giselle and Desmond Kelly as Albrecht.

acts, and a highly idiosyncratic interpretation from Seymour, including a shatteringly moving mad scene. Slowly the *corps de ballet* began to weld itself into an ensemble once more.

The autumn tour was one of the best for years, and the company even broke box office records in Manchester, where there were demands for more than a one week visit. Throughout the year, audiences rarely fell below seventy percent, encouraging for dancers and audiences alike, for there is nothing more dispiriting than performing to, or being part of, a small, scattered audience. The new repertory was vital if theatre managers were to go on booking the company, which despite its unpopular repertory, had continued to charge a high guarantee, so that the theatres could make nothing but a loss. 'They have got to produce new ballets, which appeal to the true balletomane,' admitted Sam Bell, Entertainments Manager of Bournemouth Catering and Entertainments Committee, 'but these have a limited audience and we have to provide entertainment at the Pavilion with the widest appeal.'[1]

The end of the autumn tour saw Johaar Mosaval's last performance with the company. For more than twenty years he had brought distinction to a very particular part of the repertory, and his waif-like personality that could be pathetic without sentimentality would be much missed in the roles that he had made his own, like Jasper in *Pineapple Poll* and Bootface in *The Lady and the Fool*.

Both the Arts Council and the various Boards and Sub-Committees were keeping a close eye on the standards of both the Group and the Resident Company. The decline in their technical and performing standards had been giving rise for concern, although in the touring company this could largely be attributed to overwork and the misguided 'experimental' policy that had cut them off from their classical roots. Since Field's departure, MacMillan had been in an impossible position, asked to be administrator, artistic director and principal choreographer. Depression and disillusion had not only been prevalent among the dancers on tour. Wright began to spend more time out on the road with the company.

The policy of bringing back tested favourites continued into the winter tour of 1975, as *The Dream* was revived. Because the repertory lacked classically based 'tutu' ballets, Wright expanded his ballet *Arpège*, originally created for the Royal Ballet School. It was an agreeable if not particularly distinguished work, but its main purpose was to break the dancers into more classical choreography than the current repertory provided. Like *Allegro Brillante* it was a step along the way to the formation of a different type of company.

Jack Carter's *Shukumei*, in contrast, was a strongly dramatic visual spectacle of the kind that regional audiences had always enjoyed. Carter, who had worked extensively in Japan and had at his fingertips the essentials of Japanese theatre, drew upon the more obvious traits of Kabuki drama – the screens, Kurago stage hands, the visual splendour – which he translated into effective balletic form. A Bride becomes a Samurai warrior to revenge the killing of her Bridegroom, then commits ritual suicide. The score was by the popular Japanese-cum-rock composer Stomu Yamash'ta, and it admirably complemented and heightened the drama. It was not intended to be an authentic reconstruction, and music, choreography and design all had the same striking and forceful style.

As the Bride, Tait despatched the three killer brothers, Kelly, Dubreuil and Jefferies, with style and a passionate intensity drawing upon the then hugely popular kung-fu, and garrotting one of them with her hair. The whole work depended upon effect rather than deep emotional involvement, but it was highly enjoyable and 'suggests both the ferocity and the ritual dignity that we associate with Japanese theatre'.[2]

In the spring the company returned to the Opera House, and revived *Coppélia*. It was not a completely new production, the economic situation precluded that, but had its roots in the admirable 1954 Resident Company production and still used the pretty Osbert Lancaster designs. Wright made some alterations, including the addition of a new solo for Franz in the sequence for Swanilda and her friends in Act I, which had the unfortunate effect of breaking up that charming sequence, and a revision of the dances in Act III. The *corps de ballet* was improving rapidly, and 'the zest and technical skill with which, under (Wright's) direction, the second company has infused the actual performance, are quite remarkable ... a delight'.[3] The number of principals that the company could produce for the ballet was, as always, astonishing. Last, 'a flawless soubrette and proud of it',[4] was the first of the Swanildas with Dubreuil. Barbieri was a more romantic heroine, and Tait and Johnson, a 'delightful and formidably inventive partnership'.[5] Jefferies was Dr Coppélius, an amiable eccentric, if for him curiously superficial, and he also danced Franz – a brashly witty interpretation, which revived memories of David Blair.

In June the company joined the Resident Company in a season under canvas in Battersea Park in London. The season was originally to be at

Brenda Last as Swanilda and Alain Dubreuil as Franz in *Coppélia*.

Photograph by Leslie Spatt.

the London Coliseum, but the exorbitant demands of the Coliseum
stage crew for 'get out' payment decided the Opera House management
to call their bluff and transfer the season to the Big Top which the
Resident Company had used for the first time the previous summer in
Plymouth. The tent was an attempt by the Opera House to find a
suitable touring venue, with a large enough stage for the Resident
Company out of London. It was felt that this structure would enable
the company to tour without compromising standards – although
compromise was inevitable as there was no provision for scenery (because
there was no height to fly it) and the dressing-room accommodation was

228

a series of Portakabins. The audience suffered most, for the sightlines from at least a third of the house were, and remained, appalling. The tent was subject to the vagaries of the English climate, and the atmosphere was most unsuitable for a major classical company.

The touring company left before the end of the season for the warmth of Greece, where they danced in the Herodes Atticus in Athens. Fonteyn and Seymour were guests; all performances were sold out, and, gratifyingly, the company was invited back.

The greater success of the company during 1975 was due in no small part to Peter Wright, who over the previous few years had been severing the links that bound him to the Resident Company, and concentrating on the touring group – the job he had been engaged to do five years before. His constant presence helped to raise company morale and his strict eye did much to lift standards. With Auld as his second-in-command, the outlook was certainly brighter. The more popular repertory was reflected in better audience response at the Box Office, but the company was finding the balance that it needed without too much compromise. The ballets represented both the Royal Ballet heritage and the classics, rebuilding at the same time the confidence of audiences and the dancers' techniques.

It was evident that the company now had a planning, forward thinking Director and there was no longer a feeling of living from season to season. As it grew in confidence, it built up a new personality with principals who had a definite style of their own, and they began to recover the lost impact-making vitality which had so characterized the touring dancers since the very foundation of the Theatre Ballet.

As the company began to regain an identity and public favour, its existence was once again put in jeopardy. Again economic factors were to the fore. It must have been obvious at the time of the change-over in 1970 that the new policy was unlikely to be profitable, and that the Board might not be willing to continue to support a company operating at a certain loss. By the beginning of 1975 its future was again under discussion. Also in trouble was Manchester-based Northern Dance Theatre. The Arts Council did not have sufficient funds to support both companies and felt that a merger into a company based in Manchester would be a 'sensible rationalization of dance resources'.[6]

Unbeknownst to the dancers, discussions began in July 1975. While the Group was on holiday, an article appeared in the *Guardian*, from which the dancers of both companies learned of the proposals for the first time. The Opera House management hastened to assure their dancers that there was no commitment to the move and there would not be until they were convinced of its desirability and practicability, but insecurity was naturally rife in both companies.

Meanwhile, the company opened the 1975–76 season at the Edinburgh Festival. The Festival organisers had agreed to take the company only if Nureyev were guest artist, and they insisted on him appearing every night. Seymour came up to dance with him in *Giselle*, *Apollo*, *Prodigal Son*, and a revival of *Raymonda Act III*, while Tait was Titania to his Oberon in *The Dream*. While it was good for the dancers to work alongside an artist of Nureyev's calibre, it was hurtful to feel that they were good enough for routine performances but not for prestigious occasions.

Raymonda was just what the company needed to stretch it technically, but it also showed just how much ground had been lost in the last five years. The first performances were given with all the solos, but the dancers were simply not up to the demands of the choreography, and the solos were all cut, save one. They were not restored until 1983.

Wright created a new work for the Festival, *El Amor Brujo*, to Manuel de Falla's magnificent score. The story told of Candelas, whose lover dies; she takes a new man, but the ghost of her former love tries to separate them. Her sister Lucia tries to exorcise the ghost by fire (the celebrated Ritual Fire Dance), but only succeeds when she and Candelas exchange shawls, so that the ghost follows her and thus Candelas is set free. The story was extremely difficult to express in dance terms, the musical climaxes were not matched choreographically, and although Wright reworked the Ritual Fire Dance several times it was never satisfactory. The dancers did what they could with the characters; Jefferies was a chillingly vengeful ghost, and Lorrayne a frantically tormented Candelas, but the choreography was not strong enough to establish its own validity over the score. Most distinguished was Stefanos Lazaridis' set – matted strings and rags, merging into the roots of a huge tree, which dominated the action.

Johnson left just before the following Sadler's Wells season, depleting the ranks of the male dancers still further, but the girls were strengthened by the presence of Maina Gielgud as guest artist. She was a dancer who had never settled long with any company, and her varied background ranged from Béjart to London Festival Ballet. She was to appear with the Royal Ballet over the next few years, proving one of the best Sirens in *Prodigal Son*, her cold eroticism, long legs and angularity admirably suiting Balanchine's choreography; she was also an angry and bitter

Myrtha and an excellent Black Queen in *Checkmate*.

The first performance of the revival of *Checkmate* that season was dedicated to the memory of Arthur Bliss, who had died earlier in the year. Natalia Makarova was the Black Queen with Dubreuil a sturdy Red Knight and Leslie Edwards as the Red King. *Checkmate* had now come back into its own after a sticky period during the 1960s when it was regarded by many as an old-fashioned Expressionist bore. The whole Sadler's Wells season was highly successful, and people were willing to overlook deficiencies in technique in view of the enjoyment and liveliness that the company brought to every role.

The season was dominated by Jefferies, especially as the Joker in *Card Game*, a role that he had now made completely his own, a comically resourceful Captain Belaye and above all the Prodigal Son. His expressive powers were coming to maturity, and what Clement Crisp wrote about his Prodigal Son had become true of all his work – '(his) vivid dramatic response to a situation springs from within the dance: the whole body is involved – eyes, hands, the turn of the head, are part of a uniquely communicative procedure which speaks with tremendous intensity'.[7]

By January 1976 the question of the possible move to Manchester had become urgent and an exploratory meeting was held at which it was agreed to set up a Working Party to explore the desirability of an amalgamation between the Royal Ballet touring company and Northern Dance Theatre. But further considerations would have to wait until the Greater Manchester Council, on whom the scheme depended for financial support, had fixed its general level of rates for 1976–77. In the meantime discussions about the pros and cons of a merger went on within the Royal Opera House.

Politically it was advantageous for the Opera House to be seen to be supporting the regions in such a practical way. But it was felt that there should be some guarantee that the company would maintain standards worthy of The Royal Ballet. If standards dropped to an unacceptable level the company could not continue to carry that name, and Covent Garden would again be under pressure to tour the Resident Company. Also, as the company would still be part of The Royal Ballet organisation control would still have to be in the hands of The Royal Ballet and the Opera House in London, which might cause friction with the Greater Manchester Council, who would now be partly supporting the company. There was not much financial gain to the Opera House – there might be an immediate saving, but nothing in the long term, and indeed the

Opera House grant might be cut if they were no longer the sole supporter of the second company. An incalculable benefit, however, would be that the company would gain a much-needed home base.

There was naturally disquiet within both the Royal Ballet's touring section and Northern Dance Theatre. As the proposed company was only to be forty-five there would have to be redundancies, and Northern Dance Theatre was afraid that preference would be given to the more highly trained and experienced Royal Ballet dancers. But not all of the touring group principals were willing to move to Manchester, and without them all the company would be seriously weakened and probably not strong enough to be the kind of regional company envisaged by the Manchester Council and the Opera House.

In the event the merger came to nothing when it became clear that the funds would not be forthcoming from the Greater Manchester Council for the coming year, and it became imperative to make plans for the touring company in that period. The idea died.

It was with relief that the group set out upon its winter tour. A preponderance of new works had always been presented at Stratford, partly because of its adequate rehearsal facilities, and the offering for January 1976 was *Pandora* by David Morse. Morse had been producing works for the Choreographic Group for some time, but this would be his first professional work. He made some of the elementary mistakes of the young choreographer, especially in trying to take in too much of the Pandora myth, from the stealing of fire from heaven by Prometheus to the release of troubles into the world by Pandora. His choice of the Roberto Gerhard score was excellent and he showed himself a musical and fluent choreographer with a command of classical movements, if not particularly expressive of character.

Another link with the past was the revival of *La Fille mal gardée* in Norwich in March 1976. Last was now the only experienced Lise, and she repeated her romantically crisp performance, full of lovingly observed details. Her Colas was Jefferies, as yet unable to cope fully with the technical demands of the role, but already with a delightfully rounded characterization. The company was not short of young lovers – there were also Tait, Dubreuil, Barbieri and Kelly. At first Shaw and Emblen came from London to perform Simone, but it became clear that Morse and later David Bintley were going to give them a run for their money, and that the company would soon be self-supporting once again.

It seemed as if nothing could stop the growing success of the company and, as always, success bred confidence. For their spring season at

Sadler's Wells the demand for tickets meant that an extra five performances had to be added. The liveliness and variety of the programmes was much appreciated by audiences, especially at a time when programming at Covent Garden was becoming more and more restricted.

Following the success of *Shukumei*, Jack Carter was invited to produce a new ballet for the Sadler's Wells season. *Lulu*, premièred on 2 June, used a Darius Milhaud score and was strikingly designed by Carter's regular collaborator, Norman McDowell. If the choreography was somewhat thin, there was a good deal of action. It was a breathless scamper through the seamier of Lulu's experiences – the young girl who innocently wreaks havoc upon every man who comes within her orbit, before coming to a grisly end at the hands of Jack the Ripper. Merle Park, outside her usual run of roles with the Resident Company, was a stylish Lulu.

Park joined the company for the subsequent three week European tour, during which she and Kelly danced the first performance of *Aurora's Wedding*, produced by Wright. He used the traditional formula of presenting Act III of Petipa's *The Sleeping Beauty* with the addition of the Fairy variations from the Prologue (four were used), and he also included the Hop o'My Thumb solo choreographed by MacMillan for the 1973 Covent Garden production. The production was more important for its potential than actual achievement – a sign of the way Wright saw the company developing.

For the 1976–77 season David Ashmole and Carl Myers transferred from the Resident Company replacing Jefferies, who had been granted a two-year leave of absence. As Kelly had also decided to throw in his lot with the company, and even though Dubreuil had temporarily returned to London Festival Ballet, the male side had never looked stronger. Both Ashmole and Myers had seemed inhibited at Covent Garden, but on tour they blossomed from being eternally promising dancers into fully rounded performers. The company's vitality was infectious and both benefited enormously from the change. Kelly too was expanding into unfamiliar territory; at the Opera House he had been seen almost entirely as a *danseur noble*, but now he had much more variety and challenge. Wright also began to encourage him, and on his return Dubreuil, to teach and coach. His company was beginning to develop its own traditions.

The new confidence permeating the company and its successes were entirely due to Wright. His dancers and staff are unanimous – he pulled the company back from the brink. It had been an impossible situation in the early 1970s, when he had been trying to deal with both companies – neither had his undivided attention. As Field had done, Wright grew with the company, learning diplomatic and public skills that he had never needed as a ballet master. He had to learn these in public, whereas Field had had the advantage of acquiring them in a relatively uncontroversial period, and it was notable from year to year at the annual press conferences how quickly Wright learned.

Whereas Field in the 1960s had always been 'Mr Field', a distant figure to most of the company, with his own group of friends, Wright in the more casual 1970s and 1980s was 'Peter' and more accessible. This did not imply any lack of respect – the company knew too well how much he had done for them, and gave him their backing and loyalty. He was a lower-key figure than Field, who had been blustering, outgoing, jovial and gregarious, and less dictatorial, as the company now needed. Each had been the ideal director for the company at a particular stage in its development.

Chapter XIX

With the failure of the Manchester plans, it became increasingly important to find a home base for the company. Naturally and inevitably, it seemed, it was decided that Sadler's Wells should be their home, and from April 1977, they would take on a new name, the Sadler's Wells Royal Ballet, while remaining under the management of the Royal Opera House. The Sadler's Wells Foundation undertook to make improvements to the theatre, including a new rehearsal room, a large wardrobe, administrative offices and a music library. Ironically the Wells was smaller than many of the regional theatres in which the company appeared, and some ballets looked even more cramped in London than on the road. It was, however, familiar ground, and well loved, and would provide them with much needed stability. Now they had an assured future and the chance for expansion without insecurity.

In view of the announcement, the 1976 autumn season at the Wells was seen as a homecoming. There was a gala on 29 September in aid of the Appeal Fund set up to finance the alterations and the new studio. As a tribute to the Royal Ballet's first Musical Director, Constant Lambert, who had died twenty-five years before, the programme included *Les Patineurs*, for which he had made the arrangement of the Meyerbeer score. £10,000 was raised, to which were added the proceeds of the 1973 Cranko gala.

It was an extraordinarily busy season, with twenty-eight performances of eight different programmes in the four weeks. There was a whole new generation of dancers to break into the repertory, and yet there was time to rehearse two new ballets and Balanchine's *The Four Temperaments* – an excellent exercise, if as yet the true Balanchine style was alien to them.

The first of the new ballets was *Summertide*, choreographed by Wright to Mendelssohn's Second Piano Concerto. It was his most successful work for the company, a romantic, dreamy reverie, danced in a pretty gauzy poppy field created by Elisabeth Dalton. Wright had never used his dancers better; Barbieri and Ashmole had a warm flow in their *pas de deux*, he revealing a hitherto unexpected radiance. Particularly heartening was the use of the younger talents in the company, including Kim Reeder and the bright freshness of young Nicola Katrak.

The second ballet was Seymour's *Rashomon* to a score by Bob Downes, set in a beautiful forest of white strips created by Pamela Marr. Based upon the famous Japanese film, the ballet foundered partly because it was so difficult to make clear that the action – the rape of a wife and the death of her husband at the hands of a bandit – was the same episode seen through the eyes of the three protagonists. Robert North came from Ballet Rambert to dance the Bandit and Kelly was a dignified husband, but the ballet belonged to June Highwood as the Wife, her flexible strength coping admirably with the athletic rape to which she was subjected. Although it was impossible to deny its theatricality, the choreographic interest was slight, and it was not a long stayer for the repertory.

The company set out upon its spring tour, the last under its old name. There were an exceptional number of debuts, and with *The Two Pigeons* restored to the repertory, and *La Fille mal gardée*, *Coppélia* and *Aurora's Wedding* also on offer there were plenty of opportunities for all the dancers. Following the breakup of the New London Ballet, the company she had formed with André Prokovsky, Galina Samsova joined the company as guest artist to dance Lise in *La Fille mal gardée*, which she performed with gay humour and delicate sweetness. Among the young notables were Sherilyn Kennedy and a young man in his first season who had been catching the eye of many by his at times too enthusiastic characterisation in the *corps de ballet* – David Bintley; before the tour was out he was dancing Widow Simone as well as a fussily suspicious Dr Coppélius.

Amid all this activity the company found time to mount two more new ballets, David Morse's short-lived *Birdscape*, with its bird motifs drawing on the qualities of the individual dancers, and Lynn Seymour's *The Court of Love* first seen in Bournemouth on 21 April.

The Court of Love, produced as part of the celebrations for the Queen's Silver Jubilee, was little more than a *divertissement*, held together by the theme of Queen Eleanor of Aquitaine's court at Poitiers, where judgement was pronounced upon the rituals of courtly love. Most distressing was the work's lack of shape, but Seymour made good use of some of the younger dancers, notably Susan Fitzgerald (later to change her name to Siobhan Stanley) as the Enchantress and Susan Lucas as a Maiden. Lorrayne presided as Queen Eleanor with her customary grace.

Both new ballets were on offer during the Jubilee season at Sadler's Wells in the spring of 1977. There was a large repertory, but only one new work, the briefly acquired *Gemini* by Glen Tetley. The ballet had been much admired when the Australian Ballet, for whom it was created, performed it in London, but it never sat happily upon the very different bodies of the Sadler's Wells Royal Ballet dancers, and it did not establish itself in the repertory.

The highlight of the season was the appearance of Robert Helpmann in two of his most celebrated roles – the Red King in *Checkmate* and Dr Coppélius. Helpmann was now performing to a whole new generation of audience and dancers. The definitive Red King, his presence in *Checkmate* inspired a fine performance from Maina Gielgud as the Black Queen and a magnificent one from Ashmole, proving himself to be one of the best Red Knights ever, strong and chivalrous and pacing beautifully the tricky Mazurka solo. As Coppélius, Helpmann repeated his famous richly comic performance, reminding everyone that there is nothing wrong with the oldest jokes if performed by a comic genius.

The season was tinged with sadness, for on the last night Last took her farewell of London as Lise. She had served the company loyally for over fourteen years, and her quicksilver brightness had won her countless admirers in London and on tour. She was the ideal repertory dancer, so characteristic of the Royal Ballet, and the ultimate professional, versatile, dependable and able to cope with any emergency. As Ballet Mistress she had done much to improve standards. She left to become Director of the Norwegian Ballet, but she was to return to the Sadler's Wells Royal Ballet from time to time as guest artist.

The company had already gone off on holiday when the next bombshell struck. The strains on MacMillan at Covent Garden had not lessened, nor had he learned to cope with the day-to-day running of a company, and he felt that his choreography was suffering. With Wright's time now taken up with the touring company, MacMillan found the pressures on him unbearable, and repertory and dancers were suffering from the lack of strong direction. He therefore decided to resign as Director of The Royal Ballet and the Board looked around for a replacement to revitalize the flagging reputation of the Royal Ballet and halt the deteriorating standards at Covent Garden. Their choice fell upon Norman Morrice, former Director of Ballet Rambert, probably because he had been instrumental in the successful revitalization of that company when it had been transformed into Britain's first contemporary dance company. MacMillan remained with the Royal Ballet as Principal Choreographer.

The Sadler's Wells Royal Ballet dancers had already broken up for the summer and learnt about the changeover by letter or from their newspapers. The Resident Company were only told a short while before the changes were announced to the press, although many of them had already heard the news from their colleagues in London Festival Ballet.

With Wright virtually in complete control of touring, the Sadler's Wells Royal Ballet embarked upon the 1977–78 season by taking the Big Top to Cambridge. This was the first, but not the last time that they would use the tent for visits to towns like Exeter, Milton Keynes and Sheffield that no longer had suitable theatres for their productions. The links with Cambridge went back to the very beginnings of the Vic-Wells Ballet, but the tiny stage of the Arts Theatre had been too small for anything much larger than a chamber ballet. Now audiences could see full-scale ballets for the first time. Here Patricia Neary mounted Balanchine's *Concerto Barocco*. The choreography suited them rather better than *The Four Temperaments*, but with a somewhat lethargic tempo the ballet lacked attack and crispness and looked blurred. Balanchine's choreography would never sit happily upon the less streamlined bodies of the company, and only Tait had the necessary clarity of line and movement.

It was an odd Sadler's Wells season that autumn, with no less than four Balanchine works on view (*Prodigal Son*, *Apollo*, *Concerto Barocco* and *The Four Temperaments*) against only one Ashton (*The Two Pigeons*) and one MacMillan (*Concerto*). It was ironic to hear some critics asking if it was fair to *Coppélia*, *The Two Pigeons* and even *Concerto* to show them in the cramped conditions of the Wells, but for many there was a nostalgic delight in the reforging of old links between the Wells and The Royal Ballet. Backstage all was activity and on 22 September Princess Margaret opened the new rehearsal studio, named in memory of John Cranko. Gradually the company and staff began to fit themselves into the many nooks and crannies that proliferated in their new home.

David Ashmole as the Red Knight in *Checkmate*.

Improvements were not only being made to their London base. Slowly the pattern of regional theatre was changing. The majority of the larger theatres were owned by either Howard and Wyndhams or Moss Empires, but over the last decade most had been running at a loss and the owners had begun to sell them off. Several local authorities stepped in and, with help from the Arts Council, acquired their local theatre, and programmes of improvements both backstage and front of house were now being carried out. Sometimes, as in Manchester or Liverpool, this meant choosing between two theatres, but one medium sized theatre in major cities was needed for the touring of opera and ballet and the large musicals. Any theatre building since the war had concentrated on stages for drama. No one was likely to build large theatres in England again, so it was vital to establish a chain of existing theatres if the lyric arts were to survive outside London.

An old master, Leonide Massine, came to oversee the revival of *La Boutique fantasque*. Like many choreographers, he could never resist making changes to his ballets, which was often confusing for young dancers who might even find themselves learning two versions simultaneously. Massine was unrepentant claiming '(revival) involves looking at the thing from a different point of view ... I have tried to apply logically what I know now, which is more than I used to know at the time of its production ... *Boutique fantasque* ... will be 1978.' He wanted to see ballet return to the Diaghilev ideal of a fusion of the arts, of which *La Boutique fantasque* was a magnificent example. 'Virtuosity by itself is sterile,' he told the *Birmingham Post*. 'It is time that we brought the aesthetic and harmony back to the torso. The legs must serve the torso.'[2]

The company also mounted MacMillan's delightful *Elite Syncopations*, originally created for the Resident Company in 1974. Set to the infectious ragtime compositions of Scott Joplin and with inventive and often wittily painted all-over tights by Ian Spurling, it was a bright, cheerful series of solos and *pas de deux* in dizzy and often dazzling form. It was the light-hearted kind of ballet that the repertory needed, and was an immediate hit with audiences and dancers alike. Tait and Kelly were the stylish top-hatted leading dancers and Christine Aitken and Myers were shyly tongue in cheek for the Golden Hours *pas de deux*. It was a huge success.

Even more heartening was the emergence of a new choreographer from within the company. From his earliest days in the *corps de ballet*, David Bintley had attracted attention as an inventive performer whose

Marion Tait, Nicola Katrak and Jennifer Mills in *Elite Syncopations.*

Photograph by Graham Brandon. From the collections of the Theatre Museum. Reproduced by courtesy of the Board of Trustees of the Victoria and Albert Museum.

interpretations sometimes verged on scene stealing – his miserly, sly Dr Coppélius had been particularly admired. He had been choreographing from his student days, and his first professional commission was *The Outsider*, premièred on 16 March 1978 in Birmingham, with a scenario taken from two Camus novels – *The Outsider* and *A Happy Death*. Mersault, detached from the life around him, experiences life through his three faceless 'other selves'; he becomes involved with a whore, and eventually murders her. In true Royal Ballet tradition, Bintley created a highly theatrical work expressed through classical technique, although the theatricality was at this stage more obvious than the choreography. The ballet had a curiously old-fashioned feel about it, harking back to the realistic ballets of the 1960s as produced by Western Theatre Ballet, or even, as many critics pointed out, to ballets like Helpmann's *Miracle in the Gorbals* from the 1940s. *The Outsider* was an intelligent and effective work, with a sensitive choice of composer – Josef Boháč's Suite Drammatica for tympani and strings and, as designer, another talented newcomer, Mike Beckett. The ballet made good use of both established members of the company, like Strike and Morse as the Prostitute and the Pimp, and younger dancers, like the intelligent Stephen Wicks as Mersault.

Back in London for the spring season at the Wells there was no let-up in the revival of old works and the production of new ones. *Solitaire* was revived with new designs by Barry Kay that virtually transformed it into a different ballet. The stage was dominated by a beautiful transparent tree made of inflated plastic, and the dancers were all dressed in fantastical pierrot and pierrette costumes, with high spiked wigs, except the Girl, who was dressed like the Degas sculpture of a little dancer in the Tate Gallery. It was a beautifully designed world of total fantasy, but unfortunately it swamped the essential simplicity of the choreography. Seymour was delightful and wistful in the lead, but the rest of the cast were so depersonalized that it became difficult for her to establish any relationship with them at all.

The company also acquired Cranko's ballet *Brouillards*, a series of solos and small scale sequences set to Debussy's music of the same name. It had been created for the Stuttgart Ballet in 1970, and Marcia Haydée came to mount the revival. It was a variable, fragmentary work, taking its choreographic character from the musical pieces, and the choreography was often quirky without being witty or inventive. Tait and Bernd Berg came off best in the 'Voiles' sequence and Lorrayne with Kelly and Derek Purnell in 'Footsteps in the Snow'.

The season's new ballet was Jonathan Thorpe's *Game Piano*, premièred on 12 May. Thorpe had been principal choreographer for Northern Dance Theatre for some years, but this was to be his only work for the Sadler's Wells Royal Ballet. Kelly was revealed trapped in the entrails of a grand piano, with Barbieri seated at the keyboard, presumably seeking inspiration. In the end she and Kelly had changed places. The programme suggested that the action was a fantasy, based on 'contrasting elements in Prokofiev's concerto; the mechanical drive of virtuoso piano in the enclosing movements, romanticism in the second'. Others saw the theme as the creative artist's struggle for expression. Thorpe requested that the ballet should not be taken too seriously, and indeed it was not and remained only a short time in the repertory.

June 1978 saw the eightieth birthday of de Valois, but it was not until 26 September during their autumn season at Sadler's Wells that the company could pay its tribute; they mounted a gala in her honour consisting of *The Rake's Progress*, *Les Patineurs* and two special birthday pieces – *Take Five* from David Bintley and *6.6.78* from MacMillan. *Take Five* was a last minute addition, a 'token of esteem' from Bintley to de Valois, danced by Seymour dressed in trilby, black tights, high heels and gents' evening dress, like Judy Garland in the film *Summer Stock*. It was an inventive entertaining cabaret-style number which Seymour and her four attendant males performed with relish. *6.6.78* MacMillan described as 'just a soufflé, and I hope it will make her laugh'.[3] Interspersed with 'quotes' from various de Valois ballets, it was an intentionally chaotic view of the signs of the zodiac, who were eventually organised by the Gemini – de Valois' birth sign – and the result was nothing more than the one-off piece it was intended to be.

Dancers from the Resident Company came to the Wells during the season to perform a ballet by Michael Corder, one of their soloists. *Rhyme nor Reason* was set to Stravinsky's *Dumbarton Oaks*, and was a well made workshop piece, which showed a certain facility, even if the choreography could not match the dry style of the music. Steps were bright and spirited with unexpected resolutions of line and movement and the ballet was effective enough to be redressed and taken into the touring repertory.

Seymour also created a new work for the season, *Intimate Letters*, seen on 10 October. At a gathering in an artist's studio, a married woman is confronted by 'the men who affect her life'.[4] Her husband and a man who loves her come to blows, and when they leave the wife consoles herself with her host. The ballet foundered partly on the old problem of expressing relationships in ballet and relied heavily upon the programme note. The choreography was not particularly interesting, and the ballet was memorable only for the luminosity and intensity of Samsova as the woman and Georgiadis' wonderfully cluttered bohemian environment.

Nothing it seemed could stop the growing success and popularity of the Sadler's Wells Royal Ballet. During the winter tour of 1979 the demand for tickets in Sunderland was such that a Sunday telephone booking service had to be set up. Liverpool estimated that it would cost them about £23,000 to bring the company for a week, but by the time the dancers arrived the box office had already reached a record £36,000. In Manchester they took more money than any company in the history of the Opera House and even standing room was sold out in advance. In Bournemouth, where theatregoing had always been erratic, the council decided that it would now only be economic to open the Pavilion for profitmaking productions like the annual summer show, the pantomime and the Sadler's Wells Royal Ballet.

Certainly a major factor in the company's success was the restoration of the classics. By 1979 *Coppélia* had been performed so much that it was almost falling to pieces. The production was twenty-five years old and had been inherited from the Resident Company, and the time had come to replace it. Wright set about a new production, which was first seen in February 1979 at the Royal Shakespeare Theatre in Stratford-upon-Avon. The last act became the Festival of the Bell with a Masque of the Hours – Dawn dispersed by the Sun, the arrival of Night and the marking of the day by the bell, calling villagers to work, betrothal, war and peace. The production had Wright's customary dramatic logic and flow, although the charm and freshness of the dancers were almost swamped by Peter Snow's fussy and highly coloured designs, based on Bavarian folk art.

As always the ballet brought out the best in the company, and especially showed off the lively and good-looking *corps de ballet* and a succession of delightful Friends for Swanilda, among them Karen Donovan, who was later to be an outstandingly witty and stylish Swanilda herself. By the time production reached London, the worst excesses of the designs had been ironed out, production details had been worked upon and a serviceable production had emerged. Touring meant plenty of performances to work upon details, a luxury often to the Resident Company, with its fewer performances and less stage time.

Wright brought to his productions of the classics all his theatrical instinct and his ballet master's skill. Field had been a producer in the theatrical sense, while Wright added to that an understanding that came from his choreographic ventures. Morse summed up the difference between them – 'Field liked to have ideas about production and rearrange the whole thing, but Peter got down to putting in numbers from top to bottom. Peter's influence went far deeper into the company . . . he works from the steps, though his productions bear a master plan as well.'[5] With his dancers he would take them through the choreography from basic principles; he was a dancer's teacher and the whole company enjoyed his rehearsals. They discussed with him their interpretations and feelings about a role and how it would work within the whole.

Bintley's next ballet, *Meadow of Proverbs*, was seen towards the end of the winter tour in Birmingham on 16 March. It was loosely based on Goya's black paintings and the etched series 'Los Proverbios', but Bintley rather took his inspiration from the score, Darius Milhaud's *Carnival d'Aix*, and presented each episode in the manner of the Commedia dell'Arte. The stark setting represented battlement-like structures against a dark blue backcloth. There was no lack of variety or ideas, indeed there were, as in most of Bintley's work too many, but each character was sharply drawn and the episodes well contrasted, even if the whole did not add up to a coherent vision. Notable were Tait and Dubreuil in the *Pas de guitare*, Myers as a drunken officer, with his faceless troops dying around him, a splendid solo for Morse and a mourning sequence, at the end of which the corpse gets up and runs away. 'The harsh implications the choreographer has imposed on it work against the grain,' wrote John Percival, 'and that adds depth and darkness to bright, attractive but superficial music.'[6]

For once during the spring season at Sadler's Wells there were no new works, but the repertory showed the importance of the company in keeping alive the Royal Ballet heritage. Barbara Fewster came to rehearse the revival of *La Fête étrange* and that stalwart of the repertory *Les Rendezvous* was overhauled by Ashton; Markova coached Tait in the lead, and injected into her performance something of her own wit and style. Wright felt it vital that, whenever possible, these ballets should be properly staged by the people who knew them when they were first mounted on the company, so that the style and detailing could be kept as authentic as possible. The company took its responsibilities as the guardians of the historical repertory very seriously, keeping the ballets alive, relevant and as fresh as ever.

Chapter XX

The 1979–80 season began at the Edinburgh Festival, where the company was now deemed able to stand on its own, without guest artists. The Festival that year was dedicated to Diaghilev in the fiftieth year since his death, and the Sadler's Wells Royal Ballet offering was a triple bill of *Les Sylphides*, *Prodigal Son* and a new ballet by Bintley using the score composed by Lord Berners for Balanchine's *The Triumph of Neptune* in 1926. *Punch and the Street Party* showed just what could happen if Bintley allowed his ideas to run away with him. The plot was amazingly complicated and as Clement Crisp observed he 'has opted for unrelenting vivacity as an alternative to characterization or dramatic development'.[1] As with Cranko at the beginning of his career, the time had now come for more guidance and direction.

On August 24 there was an all-MacMillan evening in honour of the choreographer's Scottish birth, consisting of *Concerto*, *Elite Syncopations* and a new work *Playground*. In Yolanda Sonnabend's realistic setting of a wire-enclosed urban playground, the inmates of a mental hospital acted out their psychological inadequacies. It was one of MacMillan's sparest and most powerful psychological studies; he adopted a very narrow vocabulary of movement rather than 'choreography' and the seemingly naturalistic movements were in reality cunningly contrived. It drew intense performances from the dancers, especially Kelly as the young man from 'outside' who becomes involved with one of the girls and in the end becomes one of the inmates. The ballet was dominated by Tait as a girl obsessed with the make-up that provides her for the short recreation period with an identity – a role she performed with unforgettable pathos. 'It offers distress and violence of spirit', wrote

Marion Tait as The Girl With Make-Up in *Playground*.

Clement Crisp, 'yet because it treats of a human condition without romanticising or fudging its subject, it also achieves a harsh uncompromising beauty. The classic dance is taken a further step along a path of truthful precision in revealing depths of feeling and suffering.'[2] It would never be a popular ballet, and only had a short performing life. As many of MacMillan's ballets, it was a shock to the general audience, although they responded to its power and compassion.

Less successful was the redressing of *Danses Concertantes*, which was redesigned in 1920s German cabaret style, with black slicked back hair, sleek red, black and yellow costumes and a sleazy room of red armchairs and black hanging lightshades. Why it was felt necessary to redesign the ballet remained a mystery as the originals had caught so well the particular quality of the score, and, like *Solitaire*, the new set and costumes all but ruined the atmosphere, making explicit what had been ambiguous before.

The company entered upon a series of anniversary celebrations; following those for de Valois and Diaghilev, the next Wells season contained their tribute to Ashton on his seventy-fifth birthday – a double bill of *Les Rendezvous* and *The Two Pigeons*. Lorrayne took her farewell of the company during the season as the Bride in *La Fête étrange*. Her warm maturity would be missed, but there was a host of young soloists who held hope for the future, notably Sherilyn Kennedy, who was beginning to take over leading roles, her clean, careful precision and bright smile holding more hope for the future than might at first have been suspected.

Wright, however, was never one to underestimate either the importance of experience, or the talents outside the Royal Ballet. In 1979 to replace Last as Ballet Mistress, he brought in Anita Landa, former principal dancer with London Festival Ballet and subsequently ballet mistress to various companies. In January 1980 Galina Samsova became Principal Teacher, her duties taking in both Royal Ballet companies and some teaching at the School. Her early training in Kiev had given her all the amplitude, fluency and gracious style of the Russian school, allied to a sweet simplicity in her acting. By teaching and by example she was to have a great influence upon the company and continued the Royal Ballet's Russian associations, which stretched back to Lydia Lopokova in the early Vic-Wells Ballet days, through Violetta Elvin, Beriosova and Nureyev, besides guests like Danilova and Massine.

The company was tackling more new work than ever, and within the two weeks of their autumn season they presented one full length ballet,

Ronald Hynd's *Papillon*, a new creation by Bintley, *Homage to Chopin*, and briefly adopted MacMillan's showpiece *pas de deux*, *Pavane*, originally created for Sibley and Dowell.

Papillon was set to Jacques Offenbach's only ballet score, written for the Paris Opera in 1860. Hynd's ballet had been created for Houston Ballet in 1979, and had also been performed by PACT Ballet in South Africa.

A jealous witch, Hamza, transforms the heroine, Papillon, into a butterfly; Hamza believes a kiss will make her beautiful, which it does until the Shah who has implanted it marries her, when she returns to hag state. Papillon and her lover Bijahn, are finally consumed by fire. Hynd managed to make the impossible scenario clear on stage, but at the cost of reducing the ballet's charm to a rather jokey spectacle. There were some attractive pastiche ensembles for the *corps de ballet*, and the dancers entered into the spirit of the work and provided much of the characterization lacking in the choreography. Barbieri, looking every inch a nineteenth-century ballerina, fluttered sympathetically as Papillon, and Dubreuil and later Wicks did all they could to evoke sympathy for the travesty role of Hamza. Borrowed from the Resident Company and dominating the ballet was Jefferies as the Shah, with his innate sense of comic timing and performing and the effective solos, full of unexpected twists and comic effects, with humour and panache. Peter Docherty produced designs with the necessary glittery pseudo-oriental prettiness.

The first performance on 7 February 1980 was at the charmingly restored Grand Theatre in Leeds, a sensitive example of a Victorian theatre being remodelled for twentieth century use. Reaction to the ballet was split between those who found it all unbearably vulgar and those who found it a pleasant way of passing an evening. If the poetry and charm got submerged in the comedy, that was probably the only way to present such a subject for the general public on whom the company depended for most of their audience, and they also much enjoyed the clever transformation scenes and technical stage effects, which they had little chance to see elsewhere in contemporary theatre.

Bintley followed the excesses of *Punch and the Street Party* with the more disciplined pure dance work *Homage to Chopin* first seen in Stratford on 22 February. Set to music by Andrezej Panufnik, it was a lyrical pure dance work, for one man and six women, it matched the shape and moods of the score, with its Polish folk dance overtones. Ashmole had a quiet controlled authority in the central role, and the ballet certainly showed good use of the classical vocabulary, if not as yet used in a highly personal or original manner. The structure and mood were Bintley's homage to *Les Sylphides*, and the ballet was refreshingly unfussy and economical in its effects. It was, however, short and by the end of the year Bintley had choreographed a companion piece, the less successful *Polonia* – a more robust view of Polish dance, but the two ballets made uneasy bedfellows.

Bintley was not the only young choreographer being given chances. Michael Corder's first work for the company and his first professional commission, was *Day Into Night*, which showed the contrasting effects of sun and moon on the earth's daily cycle. The elaborate costumes by Lazaro Prince and the theme itself rather overwhelmed the apprentice choreography but the ballet was later improved by new and simpler costumes and the elimination of the allegorical overtones.

Wright was preoccupied with raising the company's classical technique. Samsova's presence was undoubtedly the impetus behind the mounting of the *grand pas* from Marius Petipa's *Paquita* in April 1980, a series of variations in his grandest and most demanding manner. She produced a splendid classical display piece for the fast developing technical skills of the soloists and *corps de ballet*, and instilled into them something of her own breadth and sweep of movement and phrasing. As the sole male Ashmole showed himself to be the best *danseur noble* in either Royal Ballet company at that time while Samsova herself danced the lead at the first performance. There were heartening signs of real virtuosity and bravura being developed within the company. It was the first time in years that many of the girls had worn a classical tutu, and Peter Farmer provided them with dull gold costumes and a lushly swagged setting to set off the brilliance of the choreography.

With both the Big Top available and some rebuilt and improved theatres in the regions, it was now felt that the Resident Company could make the occasional foray out of London. While they were in Liverpool in May 1980, the Sadler's Wells Royal Ballet moved into the Opera House for a few performances and it was good to see them expand and grow into the larger stage after the confines of the Wells.

Out on the road, theatres were indeed improving. The Theatre Royal in Norwich had new dressing-rooms and a suspended stage. The Gaumont in Southampton was at last sinking a proper orchestra pit. The Grand in Leeds and the Theatre Royal in Nottingham had both been restored and refurbished in their original Victorian style. The Palace Theatre in Manchester was undergoing dramatic rebuilding, after

Sherilyn Kennedy and Roland Price in *Paquita*.

Photograph by Leslie Spatt.

which it would be large enough to take even the Royal Opera productions. Few, however, were incorporating proper rehearsal facilities; there were still far too many dingy, cold halls, necessitating in winter the importation of industrial heaters, which all added to the escalating costs of touring. There were still the concrete floors on which it was impossible to do more than warm up for fear of injury. And the band rooms in provincial theatres rarely improved, and it was fortunate that the orchestra had to spend relatively little time in the theatres.

It was in the Big Top that Jonathan Burrows created his first work for the company on 20 June 1980. From his student days at the Royal Ballet School, Burrows had been noted for his exceptional response to folk dance, and his first ballet *Catch* was a lighthearted work reflecting his interest in fusing classical and folk dance styles. It remained to be seen how much expression the style could contain.

Despite the company's growing success, the touring outlook remained bleak, for there was no way of operating a large touring company except at a loss. Year by year the gap between expenditure and receipts grew, despite the improving box office returns, larger Arts Council and local authority grants and an ever-growing band of sponsors. Financing foreign tours was also increasingly difficult, for they required special government funding or private sponsorship.

Thus, it was with backing from Barclays Bank International and the British Council that the Sadler's Wells Royal Ballet undertook its first major overseas tour in the autumn of 1980. The most ambitious of the company's tours since the 1960s, it took them to the Far East, including Seoul, Manila, Singapore, Kuala Lumpur, Penang, Bangkok and Hong. Kong. They were given a rousing send-off at a reception by Barclays Bank, and, flaunting their special Barclays T-shirts and travel bags, they left London on 4 September.

The final rehearsals in England had been held in the larger studios of the Royal Ballet School expressedly to accustom them to the larger stages, but the dancers were none the less apprehensive at appearing in the Sejong Cultural Centre in Seoul with its proscenium arch opening of 100 feet. As on all their foreign tours, Wright urged the company to make as much contact as possible with local dancers, many of whom had little chance to see a fully professional company, and he and his ballet staff gave classes to local students. Throughout the tour the company also had the chance to see local dance groups.

Scheduling was tight and, having learnt from past experience, each dancer was told to carry with them between dates black practice dress and shoes, in case there was any hitch in the transport of wardrobe and equipment.

The Koreans were an appreciative but orientally restrained audience, whereas the Philippinos were noisy and enthusiastic and hospitality was overwhelming. The final performance in the Philippines was in the open air Folk Art Theatre, where cheaper seats meant that many of the local population, who had never seen ballet before, could afford to attend. Audiences in Singapore warmed to *Paquita* and *Elite Syncopations* rather than the more delicate charms of *Giselle*. The conventions of *Giselle* were to cause problems for the audience in several places on the tour, and in Kuala Lumpur the action was punctuated by laughter, which proved somewhat disconcerting.

Conditions in theatres varied considerably, from the ultra modern to those with no proper plumbing or hot water. Hong Kong had no theatre large enough to take full scale ballet, so a stage designed to Royal Opera House specifications, similar to that of the Big Top, was built in England and erected in the sports hall of the new Queen Elizabeth Stadium.

The tour made a big impact on Far Eastern audiences. It was the largest ballet company ever seen in many places, and in several the first with a full orchestra. Foreign tours were highly regarded in official circles as cultural diplomacy. They were good for company morale but always hard work, and the dancers often lost all sense of time and place with the constant travelling and battling with unfamiliar conditions in such a short space of time. There were the inevitable crop of injuries and consequent understudy rehearsals, which meant little free time.

There was no time for the dancers to readjust on their return to England, an they set out immediately on their autumn tour, during which they had to rehearse Bintley's *Polonia* and learn Cranko's full length ballet *The Taming of the Shrew*.

The Taming of the Shrew had been premièred in Stuttgart in 1969, and mounted for the Resident Company in 1977. It was a large company ballet with two star roles, Katherina and Petruchio, created for the formidable talents of Marcia Haydée and Richard Cragun. The ballet was built around a series of spectacular knockabout *pas de deux*, expressing the development of their turbulent relationship, from its first meeting to its joyous consummation. Cranko, still sometimes unable to leave well alone, added to the Bianca-Lucentio sub-plot an episode where Lucentio tricks his rivals into marrying whores. It was an extremely episodic work and not particularly distinguished choreographically, except for the inventive *pas de deux* for Katherina and Petruchio. The ballet's weakness lay in Kurt-Heinz Stolze's arrangement of Scarlatti, which had a dreadful sameness, with no proper climaxes or development.

The leading roles called for a mastery of drama and comedy, and might have been made for Tait and Jefferies. She was a spirited shrewish virago, dwindling convincingly into a wife with tenderness and dignity. He, with his god-given comic timing, was a swashbuckling Petruchio, concealing a warm humanity behind the male chauvinism; the choreography made formidable demands upon his technique and showed

Marion Tait as Katherina and Stephen Jefferies as Petruchio in *The Taming of the Shrew*.

how much he had improved in the more settled conditions of the Resident Company. Barbieri was a warm, wide-eyed Bianca, and as her suitors Wicks was an amusing Gremio, coping admirably with some of Cranko's more tiresome jokes, Ashmole an almost too pleasant Lucentio, and Dubreuil a suitably bemused Hortensio. The company worked with a will and their customary ebullience hid some of the repetitiveness of the often thin choreography. It was to be a popular ballet, and there were a considerable number of satisfactory cast changes, an encouraging sign of their growing strength.

Such strength and confidence were heartening signs for a healthy future as The Royal Ballet entered its fiftieth year, for the Resident Company had hit probably the most unproductive and uninspired period in its existence. But in the Sadler's Wells Royal Ballet, as Tait, Barbieri, Ashmole and Myers came to their maturity, a new generation of young talent was following in their wake – Kennedy, Katrak, Susan Lucas, Karen Donovan, Sandra Madgwick, Iain Webb, Roland Price – and it was good to see a new generation of young choreographers using them in their ballets.

6 January 1981 was the fiftieth anniversary of the reopening of Sadler's Wells, and was celebrated by a midnight gala combining past and present members of the ballet and opera companies. Led by Tait and Ashmole, the Sadler's Wells Royal Ballet contributed an excerpt from *Les Rendezvous*, knowing that they were watched by the eagle eyes of Markova and others who had danced in the première of the ballet in 1933. Tait then teamed up with Auld to give her own special version of 'A Couple of Swells' – 'Sadler's Swells'. Wright staged the orgy scene from *The Rake's Progress* with Jefferies as the Rake, and using as many former members of the Vic-Wells Ballet and Sadler's Wells Theatre Ballet as possible, including June Brae, Pamela May, Michael Somes and Stella Claire.

The accent in the early part of 1981 was very much on the future, with Kennedy giving her first British Giselle – an unfussy performance of gentle, sweet clarity. *Three Pictures*, a new Michael Corder ballet had its première in Glasgow on 27 February. Described in the programme as a 'continuing cycle from mourning and death, which journeys through to the celebration of a new life', it was a not entirely satisfactory work that still left in doubt the extent of Corder's choreographic talent.

Back at Sadler's Wells in the spring, the repertory was both a homage to the past and a sanguine guide to the future. The past was represented by *Danses Concertantes*, *The Rake's Progress* and *Pineapple Poll*. Wells made a welcome return as a sweet and touching Betrayed Girl and Last was guest artist in *Pineapple Poll*. Two evenings were devoted to new works from dancers from both Royal Ballet companies – Bintley, Burrows, Corder, Jennifer Jackson and Derek Deane.

Most substantial of the new works was Bintley's *Night Moves* to Benjamin Britten's *Variations on a Theme of Frank Bridge*, seen on 7 April. The programme quoted from a poem by Anna Akhmatova – 'But in the room of the banished poet/Fear and the Muse stand watch by turn, and the night falls/without the hope of dawn' – and Bintley found a talented new designer, Terry Bartlett, who produced a crumbling, colonnaded courtyard encircled in swirls of white barbed wire, above which arms reached to grasp stars. The dances reflected the music, and the hopelessness implied in the programme note rested in the set rather than in the choreography, but the episodes were well crafted and varied, and there was an effective solo for Reeder, lashing out with a towel in frustrated anger. Like Cranko before him, Bintley was calculatingly trying out different styles and forms in his ballets, almost flexing his choreographic muscles, but it remained to be seen if from this would develop a truly personal means of expression. At this stage, ideas predominated over the dance interest, and most of his works seemed to come from the head rather than from the heart. As in his performing, he sometimes seemed unable to know when to remain still, emotionally and physically, which could make him a very restless performer and choreographer.

On tour a closer relationship was being forged between the company and the Hippodrome in Birmingham as extensive renovations, costing £2.2m, made it possible for the company to make it their second home. The stage had been refloored and flattened although not enlarged, a stage lift installed and the sound and lighting systems overhauled. The proscenium arch had been widened to give better sightlines and there was a new seventy foot fly tower. There was a new dressing-room block, and internal communication system. The auditorium too had been refurbished and redecorated. It was all part of the Arts Council's new policy of establishing spheres of influence for national companies outside London and it was the first time that such a close relationship between the company and a theatre in the regions had been officially acknowledged. Local fans responded by organising the Friends of the Sadler's Wells Royal Ballet in the West Midlands; and before long souvenirs, including dusters and aprons were circulating in the area, along with a magazine called *Entre-Chat*.

May 5, the fiftieth anniversary of the first full evening of ballet by the Vic-Wells Ballet, saw simultaneous gala celebrations by the Resident Company in London and by the Sadler's Wells Royal Ballet in Bristol. Between those stalwarts of the repertory, *The Rake's Progress* and *Façade*, was sandwiched a pot-pourri of gala *divertissements*, including that favourite from the early days of the Theatre Ballet *Tritsch-Tratsch*, danced by Kennedy, Morse and Denis Bonner. At the end of the performance the company ceremoniously cut a birthday cake on the stage.

At the end of May, the company combined with the Resident Company to give three performances marking the fiftieth anniversary of The Royal Ballet, made up from excerpts from ballets that showed the breadth of the repertory. Sadler's Wells Royal Ballet contributed examples of many of the early ballets that were still the foundation of their own programmes, including *Les Rendezvous*, *The Rake's Progress*, *Les Patineurs* and *Checkmate*, as well as ballets made especially for the second company, like *Danses Concertantes*, *Pineapple Poll*, *The Invitation* and *The Two Pigeons*. Representing an even newer generation of choreographers was Jonathan Burrows with a short solo, *Song*, danced by one of the youngest dancers in the company, the buoyant Michael O'Hare.

With the Resident Company in New York, June saw the Sadler's Wells Royal Ballet installed at the Royal Opera House for a short season. It was a difficult time, with a fifth of the company injured, which could partly be attributed to the increasingly strenuous demands of modern choreography, combined with a lack of rest. *Sinfonietta* was revived with new innocuous designs by Peter Rice and Wells gave some performances of her original role in the Elegy. The main interest of the season, however, lay in showing how much the company was maturing, growing in confidence and stature at almost every performance. The influence of Samsova on the classical strength of the company was clear and it was almost in better technical shape than it had ever been. 'It was a rewarding season', wrote Mary Clarke, 'not because of anything particularly new, but as affirmation of the excellent work being done under Peter Wright's direction and full of promise for the future.'[3]

That promise was made manifest at the last matinée of the season, when Katrak led a predominantly new cast in *The Two Pigeons*, with Roland Price as the Young Man, reassuringly fluent in his dancing, if as yet less confident in his acting and partnering, and Donovan repeating her graduation school performance of only the year before as a firecracker of a Gypsy Girl.

The future held the company's most ambitious production to date – the mounting of the full-length *Swan Lake* by Wright and Samsova. His master plan was now revealed, for it was clear that he had been carefully working the company back into the classical tradition with a view to restoring the Petipa classics. During the Wells season that autumn, the distinguished Russian teacher Sulamith Messerer was giving class, working particularly on arms and *épaulement*.

The company paid a thirteen day visit to Yugoslavia in October, appearing in Skopje, Belgrade, Novi Sad and Zagreb, accompanied for the first time on a foreign tour by their own orchestra. As so often, the venues varied widely, from Skopje, where the stage was built at one end

Peter Wright rehearsing Sherilyn Kennedy in *Swan Lake*.

Photograph by Leslie E. Spatt.

of a theatre-in-the-round, to Zagreb, with its Austro-Hungarian opera house of yellow stone and traditional colonnaded façade. Coping with often inexperienced stage crews in different types of venue meant headaches for the stage management. The get out in Belgrade was, in fact, nearly done by the dancers, as neither the local stage crew nor the van loaders saw it as their job actually to dismantle the sets. The dancers, including their Director, dashed back to the theatre to help, but luckily the dispute was resolved in time.

Back in England, the company began the autumn tour with a relatively restricted repertory as the rehearsals for *Swan Lake* gathered momentum. With several principals injured, the company was left short of Katherinas for *The Taming of the Shrew*, and so borrowed the Cuban-born Marieilena Mencia from Munich Ballet, a tiny powerhouse of a dancer, who whipped through the ballet like a whirlwind.

The chosen venue for the prestigious first night of *Swan Lake* was the Palace Theatre in Manchester. Like the Birmingham Hippodrome, it had undergone a major rebuilding programme, expanding the stage until it was large enough to take the biggest of the Covent Garden productions, building new dressing-rooms for 150, and an orchestra pit to seat 110. The dressing-rooms, however, were on six floors, and there was only one lift, with barely enough space to take a single large costumed figure.

Although the go-ahead for the production had been given at the beginning of 1981, only nine weeks before the opening night did the company get final approval so that work could begin on sets and costumes – a huge undertaking for the Royal Opera House production departments. The size of the production meant considerable extra funding, which was met by the Royal Opera House Trust and an anonymous donor.

Swan Lake would be a completely new experience for many of the dancers. Although they had all learned the basic *corps* work and solos in repertory class at the School, few of them had appeared in the ballet, and indeed most had hardly seen it since their student days, so hectic were touring and performing commitments. It would make considerable demands on them, but would also provide opportunities for dancers at all levels. Wright was determined that his company should be self-supporting in the principal roles, and he had no less than ten dancers learning Odette-Odile and nine Princes. Although only four or five of the casts were used for the first few seasons, with the number of injuries a company could suffer on tour it was imperative to have as many covers as possible. Even during the pre-première tour several dancers were off, by which time the tenth Odette had become sixth.

Wright believed 'that a classical ballet company without the great Russian ballets is like a drama company without Shakespeare. He feels that these old ballets provide the measure against which dancers can test themselves. And he feels that a regional audience has the right to expect such traditional works from a touring Royal Ballet company.'[4]

Samsova went back to Kiev to study their Gorsky production, parts of which were then incorporated into the basic Sergeyev version, originally mounted for the Vic-Wells Ballet in 1934. Wright provided new choreography where the original was in doubt. He re-examined and rethought every detail to establish a dramatic logic and validity that would make the work live not only for the regular audience, but for those who had never seen the ballet. He worked closely with Barry

Wordsworth, who scrutinized and revised the score in accordance with Tchaikovsky's original.

The first night on 27 November 1981 was a gala night in Manchester. Wright enclosed the action within two images of death. He made clear the tone of the first act by showing, during the overture, the funeral procession of the old king, whose death forces Siegfried into a new responsibility and thus the urgent need for his marriage. The Queen Mother's displeasure at the revelry in Act I was reinforced by the presence of Ambassadors, who brought portraits of their Princesses, from whom the Prince must choose his bride. Throughout, Benno became the close companion of the Prince. Because of the need to get through the ballet in under three hours, thus avoiding the dreaded spectre of overtime, Wright ran Acts I and II without an interval, and so the girls had to leave half way through Act I to change into their swan costumes, leaving the peasant dance to be transformed into a stylish Polacca for the men.

The second act followed Ivanov closely, and here the influence of Samsova and Messerer was seen in the more expansive 'Russian' arms. Von Rothbart wore his visored helmet throughout the ballet, simply donning a cloak over his owl costume and raising his visor for Act III. By such simple logical touches the action was made clear to the most uninitiated audience without resorting to programme notes.

In Act III the *pas de quatre* was replaced by an effective *pas de six* for Benno, three girls and two men. Instead of the dance of the fiancées, Wright created difficult and striking solos for three princesses, Polish, Italian and Russian, each of whom brought with her a group of national dancers. The act ended as Odile and Von Rothbart disappeared amid smoke and flames – made even more exciting on some occasions when the huge costumes of the attendant extras got too close and caught fire; luckily the costumes were so hugely padded that the fire could never get strong hold.

In the last act Wright choreographed a *pas de deux* for Odette and Siegfried before the final battle with Von Rothbart. Odette drowned herself and in the ensuing struggle Siegfried removed Von Rothbart's helmet and with it his power, after which he followed Odette into the

---

Marion Tait as Odette and David Ashmole as Prince Siegfried in *Swan Lake*.

lake. In a final *coup de théâtre*, during the last bars, Benno rushed onto the stage and as the curtain fell he bore from the lake the drowned body of Siegfried while, above his head, appeared a vision of Odette and her Prince. It was a stunning and moving ending which cunningly kept tension right up to the fall of the curtain.

As designer, Wright chose one of the most imaginative and creative designers in Britain – Philip Prowse. The style was Gothic revival, as seen through Russian eyes of 1890. The set was basically six Gothic pillars, which created the courtyard for Act I; festooned with creepers it became the ruined lakeside edifice, beyond which the lake glistened in the moonlight, and draped with banners it became a magnificent ballroom for Act III. It was brilliantly designed for touring, and cut intervals to a minimum – a welcome feature at a time when many ballet programmes seemed to be more interval than performance. The sumptuous costumes, all in Prowse's favourite black, grey, gold and red, were huge – big enough to fill out the largest stage and disguise the relatively small cast with which Wright was working – and encrusted with layer upon layer of gold braids and appliqués to give the impression of great richness. His sense of shape, especially in the male tunics, was impeccable, and they enhanced without hiding the dancers' line. The tutus were the bell shapes of 1890 rather than the 'plate' tutu that had become fashionable in the second half of the twentieth century, although sometimes weighed down with appliqué. The cost was over £150,000, but it was obvious that everything was built to last.

The first night was in the capable hands of Samsova and Ashmole, she was a magnificent example to the company, with her ballerina authority and behaviour. Ashmole was a noble and ardent partner, having now totally overcome the diffidence that had so bedevilled his career in his Covent Garden years. As the Princesses, Kennedy, Barbieri and Petal Miller performed their solos with panache and Kelly was a malevolent and powerful Von Rothbart. Price was a soaring and brilliant Benno, but it was encouraging to see in the *pas de six* young Webb and the even younger Michael O'Hare jumping and turning with equal confidence. Wright brought Landa back to the stage as an authoritative and truly gracious Queen Mother, without the condescension that so often passed for majesty in The Royal Ballet. The whole company rose magnificently to the occasion, especially the *corps de ballet*, looking as though they had been dancing the ballet all their lives, and the round of applause that greeted them as they rose from the mists at the beginning of the last act was well deserved.

The critics were almost unanimous in their praise for the production. 'Wright has also done a great service for the ballet and Tchaikovsky's music by insisting that it is no mere sentimental fairytale but a romantic tragedy of dramatic as well as fantastic character', wrote Noël Goodwin,[5] while Mary Clarke observed, 'A ballet which has become, almost everywhere, victim to the whims of choreographer-producers (often also the principal male dancer), has been given back its true dignity.'[6] 'For Peter Wright,' claimed Clement Crisp, 'it also represents a complete justification of his company's right to dance *Swan Lake* ... (It is) more opulent, more dramatically convincing than that at Covent Garden.'[7] On the other hand, Nicholas Dromgoole found himself 'disenchanted', the new choreography 'largely derivative and rather tiresome' and the whole production 'over-designed and over-dressed'.[8]

Within two days the company presented three different couples as Odette and Siegfried, and there were many changes in lesser roles, thus proving the value of the ballet to the company as a means of building up a new generation of soloists and principals. With Tait injured, Kennedy made her début as Odette-Odile, partnered by Myers, as yet she lacked an individual approach, but showed the benefits of Samsova's coaching in her clean and strong technique, proving an unexpectedly strong Odile. Myers was a more boyish Siegfried than Ashmole's moodier Prince. Barbieri had had the advantage of dancing the dual role before, when she had guested abroad, and she was an intense Odette and a brilliant Odile partnered by the ardent and dramatic Kelly.

The first night, however, was nearly put in jeopardy by the orchestra. The problem was the forthcoming visit to Monte Carlo, which meant that the orchestra would be laid off for seven weeks in all. The musicians were incensed that they would not be taken on the tour, particularly as they had gone to Yugoslavia, and previously the Opera House had paid compensation to keep the orchestra together for long periods when they were not needed by the company. The Opera House could not insist upon its own orchestras being used abroad, especially as the Musicians' Union forced foreign companies to use British orchestras when they visited Britain. None of the players wanted to lose their lucrative freelance status, but they also wanted the benefits of being a full-time company orchestra.

The short Monte Carlo season was sponsored by Barclays Bank International. Barclays had been so encouraged by the response to the previous foreign tours that they had backed, that in September of 1981 they made £500,000 available over four years for foreign tours by both

Royal Ballet companies. As government funding for such tours was only allocated from year to year, this sponsorship meant the companies could now plan ahead with confidence.

The company left for Monte Carlo on 23 December, accompanied by assorted wives, husbands and children. The ornate little Opera House had changed little since Diaghilev had made it his company headquarters in the 1920s, and they rehearsed in the famous studio with its incredibly low ceiling and a piano that sounded as if it had not been tuned since the days of the Ballets Russes. The audience was full of sumptuously dressed society, led by the Monegasque Royal family, who received the company restrainedly, but favourably. It was in Monte Carlo that Tait made her début as Odette-Odile, a performance full of her customary intelligence, musicality and clarity of line.

Meanwhile, talks had been going on between the Opera House and the orchestra. By the time the company returned matters had reached deadlock, and the musicians were on strike. The Musicians' Union made the strike official, so that no other orchestra could be engaged, and the first three weeks of the 1982 winter tour and part of the London season had to be cancelled before the dispute was settled.

Thus 2 March became the opening night of the Sadler's Wells season. At the end of the performance, de Valois presented Peter Wright with the *Evening Standard* award for outstanding achievement in dance in 1981, a tribute not only to his *Swan Lake*, but also a recognition of the transformation he had wrought on the standards of his company. In a moving speech he thanked his company by giving the credit back to them and their teamwork. He stated his intention to continue the traditions of the company, but also begged for more aid to improve the facilities at the Wells; there was a real danger of the company outgrowing its home, and it was unsatisfactory that many ballets could no longer be seen at their best in London. *Swan Lake* could not be given in London until a season at the Royal Opera House, or until the stage at the Wells was enlarged.

It had been hoped that MacMillan would create a new work for the season – *Noctuary*, to a commissioned score from Richard Rodney Bennett – but he felt he needed more time to develop his ideas. Instead he turned to a *pas de deux* set to the first movement of Verdi's String Quartet, which he had made for Peter Schaufuss and Elsabetta Terabust under the title of *Verdi Variations*; this he decided to use as the first movement of a full ballet to be entitled *Quartet*. He choreographed the second movement for the Wells season – a series of shifting relationships between four dancers, Tait, Samsova, Kelly and Myers.

The company also brought forward their first performance of a delightful *pas de six* from Arthur Saint-Leon's *La Vivandière*, reconstructed by dance notation expert Ann Hutchinson Guest from the nineteenth-century choreographer's notes. It was a short virtuoso piece, full of soft, fluent, bouncing choreography that epitomized the French school of the period. Price was the lone male, neat and precise, controlling his long line well in the fleet footwork, and showing off his soaring jump to advantage.

To make up the programme, Sally Gilmour, former ballerina of Ballet Rambert, revived *Confessional*, which had been created for her formidable dramatic talents by Walter Gore in 1941, and which no one but herself had ever danced. Basically a dramatic solo danced to Browning's eponymous spoken poem, interspersed with extracts from Sibelius' *Pelléas and Mélisande*, the movement traced the suffering and despair of a young woman tricked into betraying her revolutionary lover and then herself imprisoned. The dance sequences between the girl and her remembered lover were set against passages of powerful mime and gesture, which Gore wove together in a masterly way, so that words, movement and music interrelated to create images of great strength. Tait, with her intensity and concentrated anguish, was a worthy successor to Gilmour as the Girl. It was an honourable, if short-lived, revival, and showed once again that Wright was willing to take the best for his company, irrespective of its source.

MacMillan completed *Quartet* for the following spring tour, and it was premièred in Bristol on 7 April 1982, at a gala in aid of Wells Cathedral in the presence of Princess Margaret. To the double *pas de deux* of the already seen second movement, MacMillan now added a first movement based upon the original *Verdi Variations*, but with its technical difficulties tailored to the more lyrical talents of Kennedy and Ashmole; the final movement was a scherzo for Madgwick and Price, after which the entire cast repeated the main choreographic themes. The ballet as a whole seemed unfocused, and showed little of the originality that had marked so many of MacMillan's pure dance works in the past.

No new work could compete with the pulling power of the classics. *Swan Lake* was making an impact at a time of great visual poverty in much regional theatre. More than ever it was a guaranteed draw at the box office, and was welcomed back wherever it played. 'Has there ever been', asked the *Bournemouth Evening Echo*, 'such a lavish staging of this or any other ballet for a provincial theatre?'[9] The reassurance that the Sadler's Wells Royal Ballet was back on tried and tested ground was shown in increased attendances at the triple bills, for confidence in one part of the company's activities could not but reflect beneficially upon the rest and audiences for dates on which *Swan Lake* was included were running at over ninety percent.

Back at the Wells for the 1982 spring season, finance was again in everyone's mind as yet another marathon Gala in aid of the building fund was mounted on 20 May. Wright created *Adagio* for Samsova, supported by Ashmole, Dubreuil, Kelly and Myers, while Bintley tossed off a jazz number, *Unsquare Dance*, for Merle Park, Wayne Eagling and four men. Reeder did a tap solo leading into a rousing finale chorus paying tribute to the Wells and to the company's sponsor of many a regional tour – Sainsbury's. As a final *pièce de résistance* the company performed for the first time the *Pas de Légumes* by Ashton, created for the film *Stories from a Flying Trunk* – his tribute to the old fruit and vegetable market in Covent Garden – with ingenious vegetable costumes by Rostislav Doboujinsky.

The dancers themselves were not slow in devising money-raising functions in aid of their London home, and somehow amid all the routine rehearsals and work on new ballets they managed to organise outside performances, craft fairs (at which star buys included pottery made by Peter Wright and his wife, former dancer Sonya Hana), and even fashion shows, raising several useful thousands.

Following the Wells season, the company paid its first visit to Milton Keynes. Like many new towns, a theatre had not been thought a necessary part of civic life, and so the Big Top was once again pressed into service. The tent allowed the company to extend their touring circuit similar to that of the 1960s, a yearly round dominated by Manchester, Liverpool, Birmingham, Hull, Glasgow, Newcastle, Bournemouth, Bristol, Leeds, Southampton, Eastbourne and Oxford.

There were other aspects of touring that had not altered much over the years. Travel was as difficult as ever, for the scheduling never seemed to take British Rail timetables into account; Sunday trains got fewer by the year, only ran between major cities and, as always, were often held up by engineering works. Soon Saturday night sleepers disappeared as well. It was hardly surprising that car ownership increased. Sunday train calls became a thing of the past, and with them went something of the old company 'togetherness' and a new sense of freedom and individuality.

Chapter XXI

For two years Bintley had been planning his most ambitious work to date, and at the age of only twenty-four, he produced his first three-act ballet – *The Swan of Tuonela*. Never one to make things easy for himself, he chose as his subject the massive Finnish epic *Kalevala* (Land of Heroes), published by Dr Elias Lonnrot in 1835. Rather than select one episode, Bintley chose to reflect the epic feel of the whole, with 'the tribal wars, the shamanistic religion, the forging of and battles for the magical sampo. These, plus the story of Lemminkainen's descent into Tuonela, his death and resurrection, became the basis for the ballet.'[1] It was almost inevitable that for the score he turned to the greatest of Finnish composers, Sibelius and his tone poems inspired by the *Kalevala*, and which were full of the grandeur and spirit of his native land. Unfortunately, Sibelius had rarely proved himself a suitable composer for ballet.

The ballet was premièred at the opening of the 1982–83 season on 1 September at Sadler's Wells. The Swan of the title, danced by Highwood, was the magical creature who originally carried dead heroes to heaven, but the demon Tuoni stole her and turned her into an instrument of death. The ballet traced the life of the hero Lemminkainen, his marriage to Rauni and her subsequent slaughter, the reforging of the magic sampo (talisman), and Lemminkainen's death, which releases the Swan from evil. 'I'm trying to make it say something quite deep about all myths and the basic truths they contain,' Bintley told the *Manchester Evening News*.[2]

To evoke characters and situations of such legendary proportions was no easy task, and Bintley did not succeed in creating a heroic

Marion Tait as Rauni and David Ashmole as Lemminkainen with Ian Webb and Michael O'Hare in *The Swan of Tuonela*.

Photograph by Leslie E. Spatt.

choregraphic style to match the characters' epic qualities. As in most epics, they were generalized rather than individual, and there was little development of character, making it difficult for an audience to identify strongly with them. Most successful were the more intimate moments, especially the touching *pas de deux* for Rauni (Tait) and Lemminkainen (Ashmole) when she reveals her pregnancy, and a charming sequence for Rauni and her friends as they danced in the woods. Much of the choregraphy had the feel of folk dance, but without its earthy strength.

As in all Bintley's ballets, there were striking theatrical moments, for which the credit had to be shared with his designer Terry Bartlett, whose sets evoked a credible harsh, legendary land, full of mists and brooding shadows, effectively, if sometimes too dimly lit by Mark Henderson. (A new breed of lighting designers often overlooked the fact that ballet is primarily visual, and audiences liked to see what was going on.) The ballet had a mixed reception, but audiences on tour enjoyed the theatricality of the production, even if the press found the plot confused and the choreography conventional.

Five days later the company added to the repertory Hans van Manen's *5 Tangos*. Since its creation in 1977, it had been danced by companies all over the world, audiences everywhere responding to the hypnotic tango rhythms. As usual, van Manen had deliberately limited himself choreographically, but the inventiveness and variety that he could inject into his ballets was amazing. Led by Highwood and Ashmole, seven couples, dressed in predominantly black costumes, with touches of red, glided, swooped and paraded to the insistent rhythms in choreography that successfully married classical and tango styles. The ballet proved to be the hit of the season, as indeed it had been wherever it had been danced. So popular was it on tour that one critic went so far as to declare that it put *The Dream* and *La Boutique fantasque* firmly in their place.[3]

At the end of September the company set out for an eleven week tour of New Zealand and Australia, calling in at Singapore and Bangkok on the return journey with a small group going on to Rome – the longest overseas tour yet by the Sadler's Wells Royal Ballet. The Australian tour had been under discussion for seven years, and was now possible only because of the considerable financial support of Barclay's Bank International and the British Council. The repertory was limited to *Concerto*, *Prodigal Son*, *Paquita*, and *Elite Syncopations* for New Zealand, with the addition of *The Two Pigeons* and *The Invitation* for Australia; *Swan Lake* was only to be seen in Singapore and Bangkok. It was not a particularly strong nor representative repertory, and *The Two Pigeons* which the Australian impresario insisted upon, had never been popular in Australia when it had been in the repertory of Australian Ballet.

The two week New Zealand tour opened in Wellington on 25 September with *Concerto*, *Prodigal Son* and *Paquita*. The arts in New Zealand were at a low ebb, the national opera company had folded and the New Zealand Ballet was reduced to seventeen dancers. It was rare for New Zealanders to see full scale productions with an orchestra and this leg of the tour was sold on its 'full London productions' and live orchestra, both of which were much appreciated, and audiences were warm and enthusiastic. Local interest was naturally centred upon the

New Zealand members of the company – Kennedy, Gillian Maclaurin and conductor Ashley Lawrence. The highlight of the entertaining was a special Marae, the traditional Maori greeting ceremony, to which the dancers were invited by the Maori Queen, Dame Te Ata-i-rangikaahu.

The company left New Zealand for Australia on 10 October. One of the sponsors for the Australian visit was Benson and Hedges, bringing out in force MOP UP (Movement Opposing the Promotion of Unhealthy Products) and BUGA UP (Billboard Utilising Graffitists Against Unhealthy Promotions) protesters in several cities, providing plenty of extra free publicity for company and sponsor.

Her Majesty's Theatre Brisbane, where the tour opened, had an imposing façade, but conditions were worse than anything now experienced in England. Although there was a light and airy studio at the top of the building, backstage was a mass of featureless winding corridors and rickety wooden staircases, and the rain seeped depressingly into the dressing-rooms. Nobody was really surprised to learn that the theatre was due for demolition once the city's new arts complex was completed.

Where possible, the Australian dancers were given the chance of performing in their home towns, thus Donovan danced leads in Brisbane, Petal Miller in Perth and Reeder in Sydney. Price, however, was prevented by injury from dancing in his native Sydney. He was not the only dancer incapacitated and younger dancers, notably Madgwick, Michael O'Hare and Chenca Williams, were brought into leading roles by a crop of injuries.

On 17 October the company flew to Sydney, where they performed in the vast shabby Regent Theatre, which seated over 3,000 in an auditorium from which the paint was peeling off the walls. It was hardly surprising if the company cast envious eyes at the luxurious Sydney Opera House, where Australian Ballet often appeared. However, performances at the Regent were packed, even though there was only one ticket price and little change of repertory.

The low point of the tour came in Melbourne. They had been booked into the Palais Theatre, in the suburb of St Kilda – another dingy auditorium holding over 3,000. The company could not hope to compete with the next door amusement park. Backstage was cramped and squalid in the extreme. Thankfully they moved on to Adelaide, where the Festival Theatre was in a modern arts complex, with spacious dressing-rooms and the first proper rehearsal room of the tour. Unfortunately the stage floor covering was alarmingly slippery and, as resin damaged the lino, the company had to improvise with Coca-cola. The final date on the tour was His Majesty's Theatre in Perth, a well restored Edwardian theatre, reminiscent of many back home in England.

The tour could hardly be called an unqualified success. The company had been warned of the harshness of Australian critics, but, even so, the violence of their reaction came as a shock, and it was not much comfort to learn that equally stern judgements were often meted out to local companies. In the twenty years since the Touring Company visit conditions had changed drastically. There was great enthusiasm for dance throughout Australia; almost every state now had its own dance company, and Australian Ballet and the contemporary Sydney Dance Company had international reputations. Wright had been badly advised over the repertory, and dissuaded from taking any of the newer works, and many critics felt that, with so few ballets, they could not judge the company properly. Local critics attacked the company, its repertory and standards, although Peter Williams reported back to *Dance and Dancers* that the company was dancing well.

What had been expected was virtuosity dancing, and the repertory gave no chance to dazzle, except in *Paquita*, where the more lyrical charm of the English cast was far from the brilliance and grandeur demanded by the Australian critics. The general feeling was expressed by Neil Jillett in *The Age* – 'Of the dance companies that have come here in the past ten years or so the Sadler's Wells Royal Ballet is probably the one with the dullest repertoire and the least exciting teamwork, although it does have some fine individual dancers.'[4] *Prodigal Son* was the most admired ballet and *Elite Syncopations* was, as always, enjoyed everywhere. Tait ran away with all the good notices, of which Sonia Humphrey's in *The Australian* was typical – 'She enriched everything in which she appeared ... she has a sureness and a command of her body which allows her to use it to convey emotion. She is an actress of no mean dimension and handles humour as well and as subtly as she carried heavy drama.'[5] But on the whole critical reaction was so bad that Wright began to suspect anti-British feeling.

The public, however, received the company warmly, and everywhere there were names from the past to greet them – Jackson and Chatfield in Auckland, van Praagh and Fifield in Perth, Aldous and Strike in Sydney and former Touring Company soloist Hilary Debden in Melbourne. The itinerary, however, meant long flights on what should have been the dancers' free days, and there was insufficient time to settle into each new venue before the opening. There was also little chance of rehearsal with the orchestra, which was composed of a core of thirteen players, augmented in each city. The company was worked hard, with little time for sightseeing, for in Australia they had been joined by notator Deborah Chapman to begin work on the ballets for their forthcoming season in London.

After the burdens of the tour it was perhaps only to be expected that the Sadler's Wells season which opened in December was plagued by injury and illness. The real company strength was shown as senior artists stood in for injured juniors, and juniors eagerly seized their chances, among them Madgwick as a brilliant and joyous Lise and Michael O'Hare as a likeable and natural Young Man in *The Two Pigeons* and Franz. So depleted were the ranks that when former Touring Company and New Group soloist Brian Bertscher looked in to see his old colleagues, he was greeted with relief and sent on as the Poodle in *La Boutique fantasque*. Almost in defiance of the Australian reports, the company was dancing well.

At the end of January 1983 the company set out on a long regional tour that would take them through into the spring. It was in Birmingham on 13 April that they premièred *The Winter Play*, Jonathan Burrows' first full ballet for the company, with a commissioned score by Dudley Simpson and designs by Ian Spurling. As his theme, Burrows took the midwinter fertility rituals, which in England had become crystallized in the Mummers' Play. At the shortest day the leader knows that his power is fading and that he must die for the good of the community. Men disguised to preserve their anonymity ritually put him to death, and his power is transferred by the Doctor to the body of a new leader.

Burrows based his choreography upon the English folk dances – Morris dances, sword dances for the execution sequence, Lancashire clog dances and, as the folk dance traditions on which he drew concentrated on the men, he introduced the somewhat extraneous 'The Walking of the Girls' from the Isle of Man. The finale also drew upon rock and roll and court and period social dances like the galliard and the minuet. The Doctor, tap dancing his magic around the fallen leader, was more akin to Voodoo gods than English myths, and Bintley seized with relish upon the chances that the role gave him.

Ian Spurling's designs cleverly blended contemporary and folklore styles, like the blouson tops which turned inside out to become the traditional ribbon costumes of the Mummers. The mood of the ballet was set by the huge face on the backcloth – the mythical Pan-like Green Man, drawing sustenance from his root-like hair spread about him.

At the end of the tour it was announced that Bintley was to be

Carl Myers as The Leader in *The Winter Play*

appointed Company Choreographer, a title that was later changed to Resident Choreographer. He was reported to be working on three ballets, all with commissioned scores. One of the most encouraging features of Bintley's works was his search for new collaborators, both in music and in the links he was forging with a new generation of designers.

It was in May that London first saw the *Swan Lake* as the Sadler's Wells Royal Ballet came into the Opera House for a short season. The production looked even more magnificent upon the Opera House stage and James Monahan concluded that, 'The tourers have beaten the residents at their own game.'[6] The only problem was that, excellent though the company had become, they lacked a true ballerina to give the ballet focus and intensity. Wright's principals had intelligence, artistry, eloquent movement and lyricism, but they lacked the final authority and breeding that came from the classics forming an integral part of their performing traditions; it was perhaps only now that the true extent of the damage done during the period of the New Group could be seen upon the work of those older principals whose classical careers had been interrupted.

The final new work of the 1982–83 season, premièred on 10 June during the company's visit to Exeter with the Big Top, was *St Anthony Variations* choreographed by Michael Corder around the sunny talents of Kennedy. Corder dedicated the ballet to Ashton, and kept his cast relentlessly on the move performing a great many classical *enchaînements* without any particular shape or purpose, which Jann Parry in the *Observer* aptly described as 'the balletic equivalent of having an opera chorus hum along to the music because no one has supplied a libretto'.[7]

In order to reduce the workload upon the dancers, it was decided to cut the number of performances over the next season. This would reduce the strains upon the dancers, and allow more time for less stressed rehearsal periods and, it was hoped, reduce injury, but it was also partly a financial decision. Overtime was costing more and more. A dancer's working week was now thirty-three hours. As performances counted as three hours and there were eight performances a week, that left only nine hours in which to keep the repertory rehearsed, create new works, revive old ones, rehearse covers and teach and coach roles – so overtime was inevitable.

Costs were escalating, especially as touring allowances had also significantly increased. The demise of theatrical digs left a big gap in touring dancers' lives, and even small hotels were now expensive. In spite of increased allowances and special rates from hotels, it was no easier making ends meet if one was to live decently on tour. When dancing abroad, it was specified that the dancers should be accommodated in the best hotels available, so it was not surprising if they did not want to lower their standards too much back home in England. For those who had been touring for years and had built up their own contacts life on tour could be relatively pleasant, but it was the new young recruits who had the hardest time.

The 1983–84 season got off to a rousing start with a Royal Gala in the presence of Princess Margaret at Sadler's Wells, heralding the launch of a £5½m fund raising drive for the renovation of the stage area. For the occasion, Tait and the company pianist, Stephen Lade, devised *Owed to the Wells*. In a diverting double act, Wright and Sadler's Wells Director, Stephen Remington, demonstrated the alterations needed if the theatre was to be made fit for ballet – ridding it of backstage obstructions, raising the ceiling so that scenery could be hung and lit

David Bintley rehearsing *Choros*.

properly, and widening the proscenium to improve sightlines and extend the stage. The dancers gave entertaining and eloquent expression to the difficulties in an all-singing, all-tapping excerpt from *Swan Lake*, including four bad-tempered cygnets 'hating each other very much' in the overcrowding which frayed nerves to breaking point.

Bintley's new work for the season was *Choros* with a commissioned score by Aubrey Meyer and designs by Terry Bartlett premièred on 20 September. Bintley explained, 'The idea is to show what it feels like to dance – how I feel when I am dancing. Perhaps it looks horrible but it feels wonderful, and I want to show what how it feels *should* look like.'[8] The ballet was made up of six dances with titles derived from ancient Greek, and the costumes artfully hinted at archaic Greece, but both design and choreography were firmly of 1983. Set in a cool, white gym, surrounded by wall bars, the dancers executed a fast moving sequence of dances, bubbling with invention. The score was lively and vivid, and Bintley matched it with a 'rapid array of contortions, contractions, unusual curves and angles and staccato changes in direction and tempi'.[9] There was, indeed, almost too much going on and at times the movement became relentlessly restless, until the audience was almost as breathless as the dancers.

Led by Tait and their newly-acquired principal from the Resident Company, Michael Batchelor, the cast looked athletic and fresh, and Bintley used their individual qualities to advantage, particularly Batchelor, and Price in the ingenious Pyrrhic solo with a mask.

Six weeks that autumn were spent in Canada, where both Royal Ballet companies had appeared, but never outside the major cities. The tour had been mooted in 1967, but had taken sixteen years to come to fruition, and required both state and commercial funding to make it viable. It was not possible to take a wide repertory, but the visits to each centre were short and the chosen ballets, *Swan Lake*, *Raymonda Act III*, *Night Moves* and *The Invitation* gave a good idea of the company's abilities.

The company arrived in Canada as Le Wells Royal Ballet de Sadler, and opened in Kitchener, Ontario, on 29 September. It was to be a very different tour from Australia, shorter, most of the stages in modern arts complexes and with a much lighter schedule, for Canadian unions forbade the dancers to rehearse for more than two hours on the day of a performance – a ruling introduced to protect dancers on one night stands.

Swan Lake on the opening night on 2 October at the Centre in the Square, the huge arts complex in Kitchener, was a triumph. There was a packed house and the company received a standing ovation. From Kitchener they moved on to one of the longer dates, five performances at the National Arts Centre in Ottawa, then on for seven performances in Toronto (with time for the mandatory visit to the Niagara Falls), and seven in Winnipeg, then across to Regina and Saskatoon, Edmonton, Calgary and Vancouver.

In Winnipeg the season coincided with the celebrations surrounding Arnold Spohr's twenty-five years as director of the Royal Winnipeg Ballet, and the companies joined forces for a gala in his honour. Here, also, the Sadler's Wells Royal Ballet gave the hundredth performance of *Swan Lake* and Wright went on as the Italian Ambassador in Act III to mark the occasion. Incredibly, Ann Carol in the Neapolitan, and Morse and Denis Bonner in the Czardas, had danced the same roles in every one of the hundred performances.

The company was praised for the versatility of the repertory and the individuality of the dancers. Although some felt that the magic was missing from *Swan Lake*, *The Invitation* was outdated, and that *Night Moves* fell between abstraction and literalness, the dancers themselves quickly won over audiences with their skill and enthusiasm. *Raymonda Act III*, however, always drew gasps of delight and applause, and the company had a great reception. Of the dancers, Roland Price had a particular success, especially as Benno, evoking rapturous applause for his clear, forceful dancing.

In England it was back to the familiar rounds of the regions before returning to Sadler's Wells at the end of December. The company looked on top form, dancing every role with conviction, and, everyone noted with satisfaction, senior artists appearing in character and cameo parts with enthusiasm and commitment. The season included *Giselle*, marking the fiftieth anniversary of its first performance by the Vic-Wells Ballet, with Markova and Dolin in 1934. At the anniversary performance on 2 January (1 January the actual anniversary being a Sunday) Barbieri danced Giselle for the hundredth time in the production. It was, however, an occasion tinged with sadness, for Kelly's performance as Albrecht was to be his farewell to classical roles. A true *danseur noble*, he had set a magnificent example in style and bearing to the younger dancers. It was good to know that his experience would not be lost, and that, as Ballet Master, he would find as much satisfaction in teaching others as he had found in performing.

Guest artist for the season was Evelyn Hart, from The Royal Winnipeg Ballet, dancing in *Elite Syncopations* and *Giselle* with Ashmole. Technically strong, with a fine-boned, slight physique, she was a spirited village girl in Act I and a delicate spirit in Act II, but it was a performance in which calculation was more obvious than inspiration.

The pleasures of the season included a delightful debut as Swanilda by Donovan and a sparkling Pineapple Poll from Madgwick. The company traditions of demi-caractère performing, enthusiasm and effervescence were in safe hands in a younger generation. If the company would never be that rare thing, a great classically pure company, it was something equally valuable and more versatile, a demi-caractère company of artists who loved performing and communicated that love to their audience.

Chapter XXII

Over the previous year the company and its management had been under scrutiny once more as Clive Priestley of the Cabinet Office Management and Personnel Office investigated the running of the Royal Opera House and the Royal Shakespeare Company for the Minister for the Arts, Lord Gowrie. Covent Garden and the RSC were more in debt than other arts companies and the Minister was anxious to know why. The Priestley report found no basic mismanagement and most departments at the Opera House running as economically as possible, and concluded that the two organisations were in debt simply because they did not get enough money in the first place. The Covent Garden debt, it was considered, could be eliminated if the Sadler's Wells Royal Ballet was abolished, but that was rejected as unacceptable, both politically and artistically. In fact, the company was held up as an example to the others of the most economical procedures and systems to follow. In passing, Priestley also stated what many had suspected – that the Covent Garden Board did not know or care enough about ballet, particularly the Sadler's Wells Royal Ballet, which, disgracefully, only two of them had ever seen out on tour.

The success of the company was its best guarantee of survival. Success continued as they revived in March 1984 one of the legendary works from the Diaghilev Ballet repertory – Michael Fokine's masterpiece *Petrushka*. John Auld, who had retired from the administration of the Sadler's Wells Royal Ballet in 1981 through ill health, mounted the production. He had known the ballet from the Borovansky Ballet in Australia, Borovansky had known it from his days with the De Basil Ballets Russes, and the De Basil company were the heirs of the Diaghilev dancers, so the pedigree was certainly auspicious. The ballet emerged like new, with no trace of a period piece. Benois' sets and costumes were perfectly realised, restoring their reputation as some of the most distinguished ballet designs ever created. 'Everything about the production rings true', wrote Mary Clarke, 'and this revival makes clear why *Petrushka* has its place in ballet history as the perfect collaboration between choreographer, composer and designer.'[1]

With its demi-caractère demands and myriad cameo roles *Petrushka* was a gift for the Sadler's Wells Royal Ballet. Senior artists and staff were pressed into service in key crowd roles, ensuring that the revival had a mellow weight and depth; Plaisted was the Grandfather of the Fair and the Chief Nursemaid was Landa, a lovely study in warm, mature womanhood, while her Coachman companion was Wicks, sturdy and strong. The first night Petrushka was Dubreuil, with a sound, traditional interpretation, if lacking pathos. As the Ballerina, Katrak was the perfect automaton, wide-eyed and vapid, while Kelly and later Myers captured all the Blackamoor's lecherous, slow-witted vanity; Bintley was a cunning and sly Showman.

The revival was, however, primarily a company triumph, and a great success with audiences. It was highly praised by the critics, although some felt that the company really lacked the numbers to bring off the teeming life of the Fair, but the dancers made up in vitality and bustle for their small numbers, and also managed several satisfying cast changes. Graham Lustig was a touching Petrushka, but the highest praise went to Bintley's interpretation – a misshapen, sawdust-filled body, his face expressionless, his arms flailing, through which was glimpsed the frustrated, angry spirit that infused the unyielding body with passion and life.

It was Bintley's year. At the beginning of the spring Sadler's Wells season, on 3 April, Princess Margaret presented him with the *Evening Standard* award for achievement in ballet in 1983. It was a recognition of his amazing progress over a season which had seen the production of his first three act ballet, and also his continuing search for new composers and designers – thus carrying on the traditions established by de Valois in the 1930s and by John Cranko in the days of the Theatre Ballet.

Bintley's work was characterized by its diversity and his willingness to take risks in subjects and collaborators. His next ballet, *Metamorphosis*, on 10 April, was an example, with a first commissioned score from Peter McGowan, a member of the Sadler's Wells Royal Ballet orchestra, and a libretto after Kafka.

Metamorphosis was Kafka's nightmare story of a man transformed into a beetle. Bintley's version was less a study of a personal tragedy than an examination of the effects of that tragedy upon the family. The opening scene was a nightmare perspective city street, brilliantly created by Mike Beckett, with Gregor Samsa an isolated, ineffective figure amid dehumanized crowds. The family home was an equally oppressive room, in which the family gradually tried to come to terms with Gregor's transformation and themselves. In the end, the young sister accepted responsibility for ridding the household of this terror and lifting the burden from the family. The main problem was that the protagonist was off stage, his presence only felt behind the door of his room, and once the basic developments within the family had been established there was nowhere for the ballet to go. Bintley combined natural, and often conventional, gestures and classical choreography with mixed success, but in the end it was the subject itself that defeated him.

The ballet was strongly cast and the dancers rewarded him with performances that disguised some of the longueurs and the thinness of some of the choreography. Leanne Benjamin in her first created role as Gregor's sister, was youthfully touching, and Bintley effectively used her long line to express the character's anguish. As the ineffectual Mr Samsa, who through the tragedy gains a strength and position in his household that he had not known before, Kelly was superb, as was Barbieri in one of her rare mature roles as Mrs Samsa, winning compassion for the woman's life of drab hopelessness.

13 April brought Jennifer Jackson's first ballet for the company. *Common Ground* was set to Lennox Berkeley's *Serenade for Strings*, and had designs by Ella Huhne – white sets and costumes with 'charred' edges. A cheerful and high-spirited work, it used classical steps given unexpected little twists by the angles of feet and hands. It was a ballet that yielded all at first seeing, but among its many pleasures was a stylish performance by a predominantly young cast which included Donovan, Samira Saidi, Michael O'Hare and David Yow.

During the season Ashmole gave his last performances before leaving to join Australian Ballet, and it was a cause of great sadness to his many admirers that his last weeks were dogged by injury. His going created a serious gap at a time when Kelly, Dubreuil and Myers were relinquishing major roles. Their likeliest heir was the young Australian Roland Price, elegant and with a remarkable jump, who had yet some way to go to full maturity, both of personality and of dancing; he could also be an unreliable partner and a somewhat bland interpreter. It was now that

Swan Lake proved its importance in the repertory, in bringing on the younger dancers, and stretching them technically and interpretatively. There were many unexpectedly good performances notably Wicks as an aristocratic and credible Prince Siegfried, proving that intelligence and style can do much to overcome limited classical technique.

Since the 1960s, the number of non-English dancers available to the Royal Ballet had diminished. South African dancers had been officially banned since 1961, but over the years, as Commonwealth countries began to establish their own ballet companies and schools (many founded or staffed by ex-Royal Ballet dancers) the number of dancers from this source also grew less. There were times when it was necessary to bridge the gap between the performing generations as older dancers came to the end of their performing careers and the younger ones grew into leading roles. Wright was never afraid to bring in fresh blood from abroad, which he could do so long as he could prove there was no suitable English dancer available to him.

Thus guest artist for the season and the subsequent regional tour in *Giselle*, *Raymonda Act III*, *Petrushka* and *Les Sylphides* was Ana Botofogo from Rio de Janeiro. Dark and passionate, in *Giselle* she was an exotic growth in the peasant village, but she had none of the expressive acting of the regular principals, most notably Tait and Barbieri.

The 1984–85 season opened in September in Cambridge, with Evelyn Hart and Henny Jurriens from Dutch National Ballet as guests; she was to spend three months with the company dancing the classics, *Giselle*, *Swan Lake* and the forthcoming *The Sleeping Beauty*.

The Cambridge visit included a programme of *Les Rendezvous*, *The Dream* and *Façade* in honour of Frederick Ashton's eightieth birthday, and Judith Cruickshank, reporting on the performance for *The Times*, noted with pleasure that, though the ballets had been constantly in the repertory over many years, there was no sign of weariness or boredom in the performances.[2] The same could have been said of *La Fille mal gardée*, and when he came to Cambridge for a matinée, Ashton must have been particularly pleased with Madgwick and Webb as his young lovers. Webb was making his début as Colas, a lovely clean and engaging performance, while she was a sparkling and quicksilver Lise, with amazing breadth of movement within her small frame.

The touring repertory was limited throughout the summer and early autumn of 1984 for the company was working towards a new staging by Wright of Petipa's *The Sleeping Beauty*. The first night was given on 15 October in Birmingham, the fulfilment of Wright's promise that, as soon as the rebuilding of the Hippodrome had been completed and its stage enlarged, he would mount a production suitable for it. The first night was a big social occasion in the presence of de Valois, and such society notables as Bianca Jagger and actor Rupert Everett.

The Sleeping Beauty had always had a particular place in Royal Ballet history, not only because it was the ultimate classical testpiece, but also because it had been associated with some of the most important occasions in the history of the Resident Company. Nicolai Sergeyev had originally mounted it for the Vic-Wells Ballet in 1939, a defiantly ambitious work for a company not ten years old; it was the ballet with which, as the Sadler's Wells Ballet, they reopened the Royal Opera House after the War in 1946, and with which they had established their international reputation in New York in 1949. The Touring Company had performed a mirror image of the Covent Garden production, which was not ideal for touring, nor were they allowed to dance it in London. Wright wanted to create a special production for the Sadler's Wells Royal Ballet, rejecting all idea of anything akin to that performed at Covent Garden – he was now indeed challenging them on their own ground.

He dedicated the production to de Valois:

> It is entirely because of Dame Ninette de Valois's extraordinary vision in first inviting Nikolay Sergeueyev (sic) to mount *The Sleeping Beauty* for the Sadler's Wells Ballet in 1939 – the forerunner of the various productions that have been performed by The Royal Ballet ever since, including her own beautiful version produced in 1977 – that producers like myself now have the knowledge and background to make their own productions of this masterpiece. We all owe her an immense debt of gratitude and I dedicate this production to her with much affection.[3]

Wright first produced Petipa's masterpiece in Cologne in 1967. There followed a highly imaginative, if not totally successful, fairytale Gothic version for the Royal Ballet at Covent Garden in 1968 and another for Munich in 1976. The Sadler's Wells Royal Ballet production followed his 1981 version, for Dutch National Ballet and he also selected the same designer, Philip Prowse.

Wright preserved most of the choreography from the Sergeyev version. As in the original St Petersburg production, however, the Lilac Fairy became a non-dancing role; Carabosse was a magnificently vengeful character, and their opposing natures were clearly established

Galina Samsova as Carabosse and Margaret Barbieri as the Lilac Fairy in *The Sleeping Beauty*.

visually. Wright created a pleasing new Garland dance, which also provided the setting for the entrances of the four suitor Princes, and, after Aurora fell asleep, he restored the lamentation over her body by her parents before she was laid at the foot of the phallically symbolic obelisk which dominated the set.

Aurora's hundred year sleep was represented by the shortest of pauses, but the time difference was made clear in the panniered hunting costumes of the Prince's entourage. Because of the difficulty of touring a proper panorama, Wright created some somewhat conventional choreography for the nymphs amid which and much dry ice the Lilac Fairy and the Prince wended their way to the castle gates. There was a lowering of tension at this point, although the confrontations with Carabosse before the awakening did help to establish some sense of conflict before the Prince finally awoke Aurora.

The major change in the last act was the use of the Jewel Fairies music as a *pas de quatre*, using one of the Ashton variations from Florestan and his Sisters sequence for one girl's solo, and Petipa for the second; Wright choreographed two of his best ever solos for the men, fluid and bouncy and effective showpieces for a succession of male dancers. As the curtain fell, a dazzling shower of golden rain was released over the whole stage.

It was a handsome and extremely serviceable production. Wright had understood the basic formality and conventions upon which the court scenes were based and which were reflected in the formality of the choreography. While not as consistently original a vision as his *Swan Lake*, Prowse none the less created costumes and sets of great sumptuousness, which made it easy for the dancers to move with correct · dignity. 'The imaginative skill of producer and designer have overcome all the requirements of touring mobility to create a world of grandest opulence and theatrical magic.' wrote Clement Crisp, 'Like Bakst, Mr Prowse has the taste and wit to convey correct historical outline of dress while yet retaining that vital element of theatrical fantasy ... Throughout the staging there is a recognition of the dramatic savour – so strong in the music – that must inform the choreography. .... A masterpiece has been honoured.'[4]

Not unexpectedly, the production stretched the fifty members of the company to their limits. The dancers' sense of confidence and conviction was remarkable, and they attained a sense of pomp and ceremony, that set the atmosphere from the start. Especially good were the human touches brought to the minor roles – and among the many incidental pleasures were the playing of the disdainful suitor princes, the affectionate yet regal King and Queen (Kelly and Landa were the first of a notable dynasty), and a bossy and obsequious Cantalabutte. Samsova was the first Carabosse, commanding in her vengefulness, and later Highwood and Landa were to prove equally effective. Barbieri brought all her gracious sweetness to the Lilac Fairy, while, as Cantalabutte, Morse, in bearing and character, looked set fair to equal Leslie Edwards in his famous interpretation for the Resident Company.

The standard of dancing throughout was encouragingly high,

although there would always be problems in finding an equally matched group of fairies for the Prologue variations and for the last act solos. Missing, however, was a true classical ballerina for Aurora. Tait had never, at any point in her career, considered herself a classical ballerina, and though her intelligence and musicality were never in doubt, she lacked the grand manner. Barbieri was Romantic rather than classical, and Kennedy was bright and sweet, but had probably never seen the ballet with a true ballerina to know just what the role was about. Among the Princes experience told, and it was Dubreuil who provided the correct dignity, romantic presence and reliable partnering. Of the other leading roles, there was a sparklingly promising Bluebird *pas de deux* from Madgwick and Yow.

The production was sponsored by the West Midlands Arts Council and the Friends of Covent Garden and cost over £150,000, but, like *Swan Lake*, it was built to last. It was usual to build rather flimsy sets for touring, because they were easier to set and travel, but Wright firmly believed that solidity was necessary if designs were to wear well over the years and retain their pristine appearance. Hence the sets and costumes were substantially made and the wisdom of the decision became clear in the coming years. *The Sleeping Beauty* began to earn its keep immediately, and was danced no less than thirty-seven times between its première and the end of the tour in December.

On a smaller scale, on 3 January 1985 at Sadler's Wells, the company premièred Jennifer Jackson's *Median*, set to Stephen Montague's *At the White Edge of Phrygia*, designed by Ella Huhne. It took the broken lines of *Common Ground* even further, and the static poses were more notable than choreographic flow. It made good use of the dancers, effectively contrasting Benjamin's flexibility and Tait's more compact line, but there was no sense of emotional involvement and the ballet never achieved any definable statement of emotion or mood.

Schedules were beginning to be much more sensibly organised, with proper breaks before and after tours. Thus there was a month of rehearsals before the company set off to the other side of the world for a return tour to New Zealand and visits to Seoul and Bombay. There was again a good deal of criticism of the repertory, which consisted of *The Sleeping Beauty*, *Giselle* paired with *5 Tangos*, *La Fille mal gardée* and *Swan Lake* – no recent ballets and nothing created specially for the company. *Dance and Dancers* tartly pointed out[5] that de Valois had always made it a condition of foreign tours that there should be works by company choreographers, even if they had no international

Nicola Katrak, Graham Lustig and Michael O'Hare in *Les Rendezvous*.

reputation. Also the company had had to bring in two male guest artists, Lindsay Fischer from Dutch National Ballet and Petter Jacobsson, a Swede who had been working in England with London Festival Ballet.

The New Zealand visit was as successful as that of 1982. The classics were unfamiliar in a country where only small ballet companies operated infrequently, dancing to taped music with basic sets and costumes.

If this was a novelty in New Zealand, it was even more so in Bombay. The Sadler's Wells Royal Ballet was the third company in six months to appear there, following the Bolshoi Ballet and Paris Opera Ballet led by Nureyev. Neither of these groups, however, had presented full productions with live music, and it was these that captured the imaginations of the Indians. The production India really wanted to see was *Swan Lake*, but in the event they settled happily for *Giselle*. The season was a triumph and the dancers were fêted in the streets. 'It's been far more important than we realised when we got here,' said Peter Wright. 'It hasn't been a ripple of response but a tidal wave.'[6] Audience and press alike felt that of all the companies they had seen the Sadler's Wells Royal Ballet was the 'glittering and magnificent crown'.[7] They were praised for their involvement in the drama, for the flawless *corps de ballet* and for the technical perfection of the production. 'Peter Wright must be a proud man indeed to lead such a superbly dedicated team,' wrote Jimmy F. Pochkhanawalla in the *Indian Express*. 'True there were no death defying leaps and grand pirouettes. We went to see a ballet, not a circus. It is a tribute to the excellence of their art that each soloist blended into the whole ballet. No effort was made to show off. The result was a production that is truly a success.'[8] 'It was as if we had all been caught in a pleasant dream, suspended in time with the hours speeding by on swift wings', extolled Vinod Advani in *Mid-Day*.[9]

Events back at Sadler's Wells, however, were assuming nightmare proportions. The principal source of funds for the theatre was the Greater London Council, which was abolished on 1 April 1985, thus leaving the theatre with insufficient money to finance the remainder of the year. The Arts Council could only fund companies, not buildings, and though it eventually agreed to increase grants to the companies who used Sadler's Wells as a London base so that they could pay economic levels of rent, it was not enough to guarantee its future. Questions in the House of Commons brought little result. Fortunately a saviour in the form of the Digital Equipment Company stepped in to ensure its immediate future.

It was not, however, to its home theatre that the Sadler's Wells Royal Ballet came on its return from India, but to the Royal Opera House. The season opened on 30 April with a gala performance of *The Sleeping Beauty* in aid of the Royal Opera House and Sadler's Wells building funds. *Swan Lake* was also in the repertory, as well as a triple bill of *Les Sylphides*, *Petrushka* and *Choros*. It was almost a deliberate flaunting of their recent successes – particularly as the Resident Company had only just performed *The Sleeping Beauty* itself, and the reception of Bintley's ballet was in sharp contrast to a recent run of unsuccessful creations by several choreographers at the Garden.

In the June Birthday Honours List Peter Wright was created CBE, a fitting tribute to his work over the last ten years. Audience and company were delighted. He had taken a failing, disenchanted group of dancers and given them back an identity and a purpose. He had supported them, fought for them, restored their confidence and they had rewarded him with performances of which he could be proud.

Wright had the ability to see his company as an entity and yet as individuals – it was a wide-ranging vision. 'He can encompass an enormous number of things and an enormous number of people at one time,' explained Desmond Kelly. 'That was one of my carps with the (Resident Company), that as far as some of us were concerned, the direction could only see half a dozen dancers in one particular period – its focus was too specific. Whereas Peter bridges the whole company. He can make every member of the company feel terribly important, and that's why the morale of this company is so good.'[10] He also asked, and often got, the impossible, but his dancers, from principals to *corps de ballet*, thought of him not as an all powerful director (although he was that as well), but as an approachable human being to whom they could all relate.

The last new ballet of the season was David Bintley's *Flowers of the Forest*, premièred in Birmingham on 14 June. It grew out of a ballet he had created for dancers from The Royal Ballet, who had paid a working holiday with Lorrayne to Israel in 1979. This short ballet, set to Malcolm Arnold's *Four Scottish Dances* was made the first movement of *The Flowers of the Forest*, and Bintley added Benjamin Britten's *Scottish Ballad*, to make a work that married Scottish and classical dancing. In an effective stylised abstract landscape by Jan Blake, he created a first movement that was an affectionate 'picture postcard' image of Scotland, using the more obvious Scottish dance steps to give national style to the basic classical vocabulary. It was lively and amusing, mixing wit and sentiment, contrasting an effective drunk dance for O'Hare and Lustig, during which their disillusioned girls, Madgwick and Donovan, performed a sword dance using the boys' outstretched legs as the swords, with a gentle *pas de deux* for Barbieri and Dubreuil. After this the curtain descended and the dancers took calls.

The second scene was in more serious mood reflecting Britten's sombre setting of traditional Scottish airs including the *Lament for Flodden* from which the ballet took its name, and evoking the true historic feel of Scotland. The central section was a *pas de deux* for Tait and Price, tender and overwhelmed with sorrow. With the lightening of the mood, the dancers from the first movement returned, and the ballet ended in a display that made much use of fast and brilliant footwork – which used to be such a characteristic of the Royal Ballet style, but had become blurred in recent years. It was a ballet full of lovely dancing, especially suiting the men in the company, with its soft, flowing style, and showing off their high, springy jumps. It was a fitting conclusion to a highly successful performing year, which had seen the company triumph in the classical repertory and prove equally successful in creating new works.

The whole Royal Ballet was in a state of flux. Norman Morrice had not proved the success that had been hoped in revitalizing the Resident Company, and Anthony Dowell had now been appointed to take over at the beginning of the 1986–87 season. The Sadler's Wells Royal Ballet was in a process of assimilation; having lost several dancers besides Ashmole, they were breaking in the new dancers, like Jacobsson, who had now joined them as principal, and bringing on their own soloists like Benjamin, Michael O'Hare, Miyako Yoshida and Mark Welford.

A new ballet by Derek Deane had been scheduled for the autumn Sadler's Wells season, but had to be postponed. To fill the gap the company revived *Twilight*, danced by guest artists Haydée and Cragun, and mounted Balanchine's *Tchaikovsky pas de deux*. This was a highly unsuitable repertory piece, depending on fiendishly difficult virtuosity, which the company could not supply.

During the season, on 4 October, Michael Corder produced his best ballet to date – *The Wand of Youth*. It took its title from the Elgar score, to which Corder added an excerpt from the *Nursery Suite*, creating a gently nostalgic vision of England on the brink of the First World War. The developing relationships between the carefree children were contrasted with the maturer love of their parents, and then was revealed the tragedy to come in a vision of the blighted landscape of war torn France and the dead men as ghostly witnesses of their women's grief.

Corder's influences were obvious – Ashton's *Enigma Variations* in the nostalgia, and MacMillan's *The Invitation* in the children's dances and *Gloria* in the war episodes – but he nevertheless presented a personal statement of his theme in choreography that was now perfectly subjected to the characters and emotion. As the parents, Barbieri with Dubreuil and Samira Saidi with Nicholas Millington presented credible adult relationships, while Benjamin and Michael O'Hare were perfect as their children, blithe and innocent, growing up in the golden glow that symbolized the era before the War. Charles Maude designed a set evocative of an Edwardian country house, which allowed the action to take place both in and out of doors, and through which at the end the blasted landscape of dead trees and trenches was revealed. The ballet looked exceptionally handsome, and was Corder's most promising work to date.

Promising, too, was Madgwick, who made her debut as Princess Aurora on the subsequent tour. It was a delightful performance, confident and sparkling, with a sensitive feeling for the development of the character through the choreography. Small and finely made, she had time to pace her movements through the music to give the choreography clarity and flowing space, punctuated with poses of sweet authority.

New ballets by two soloists, Susan Crow and Graham Lustig, were in preparation. They were set strict limits within which to work – each ballet had to be short, for a small group of dancers with no individual predominating and music scored for only a small ensemble. Money was tight and they had to work within very restricted budgets so there would be little chance of hiding poor choreography under visual splendour. The results, seen in Eastbourne on 13 December at the end of the autumn tour, proved what had sometimes been forgotten – that discipline and economy were no bar to imaginative creation.

Crow's ballet *Track and Field* used David Diamond's *Rounds for String Orchestra*, and took its theme from Degas' painting of the Young Spartans. She fused images from both ancient and modern athletics, though owing more to the classical tradition than the modern, and showed a promising fluency, intelligence and confidence in the expressive potential of dance. The action was set against an ingenious backcloth by Tim Shortall, dominated by a figure that was half an ancient Greek and half a modern athlete, bisected by a scientific graph line.

Lustig chose as his score Walter Leigh's Concertino for Harpsichord and String Orchestra, which evoked in his mind a garden maze, filled with living statues. *Caught in Time* was less notable for its originality of movement than for a welcome sense of grouping and use of the ensemble, particularly in the way that movement passed from dancer to dancer and frieze melted into frieze. Like *Track and Field* it was unpretentious and extremely enjoyable.

Both ballets were on show in London in January 1986. The Sadler's Wells season was short, for the company was preparing for a tour to North and South America. Compared with past Royal Ballet tours of the continent and that of the Sadler's Wells Theatre Ballet in 1951, this would be small beer indeed, lasting just two months, but even so covering an area from Boston to Miami and then taking in Mexico City,

Sandra Madgwick as Princess Aurora and Michael O'Hare as Prince Florimund
in *The Sleeping Beauty*.

Photograph by Leslie E. Spatt.

Caracas and ending in Rio de Janeiro. Since the 1960s America had seen little of The Royal Ballet, and the last visit by the Covent Garden company in 1981 had not been a great success. New York was now regarded as the dance capital of the world, and the supremacy in the classics, on which the Royal Ballet reputation in America had rested, had long since been challenged by other companies. New York had never cared for The Royal Ballet's new choreography, living as it did in a ferment of new and experimental work. The last two decades had also seen the setting up of many local companies throughout North America. It was all very different from 1951, when even major cities had only the occasional visit from a touring company. Now every town had regular access to ballet if only on television.

The repertory for the tour was limited to *The Sleeping Beauty*, *Paquita*, *Flowers of the Forest*, *Petrushka*, *Choros* and *Elite Syncopations*, with *Coppélia* for Mexico City and *Prodigal Son* for Central and South America. *Swan Lake* might have been a wiser choice, but *The Sleeping Beauty* was rarely seen in America, while almost everyone had a *Swan Lake* of sorts. But it would inevitably revive memories of and invite comparisons with the successful Messel-designed production on which Royal Ballet prestige in America had been built.

On loan from the Resident Company for the tour was Derek Deane, who had been dancing the classics with the company on tour, and nine extra dancers were borrowed from the School. Thus augmented, the Sadler's Wells Royal Ballet left London on 27 January and headed for Boston where they opened in the Wang Centre on 30 January with *The Sleeping Beauty*.

The reception in Boston set the tone for the tour. While the pagentry and spectacle were enjoyed and the dancers' sense of style and bearing in wearing period dress were praised, the actual dancing was not. To America, the quieter classical style of the British seemed miniature, genteel and tame compared with their own dancers' expansive energy and the sense of danger. What was seen as assertiveness and panache in England, here seemed lacking in dynamism and pace. But even more distressing to most of the reviewers was the decline in technical standards from what they expected from The Royal Ballet.

Undoubtedly standards in Boston were affected by no less than fourteen of the dancers suffering from gastro-enteritis, and five were still incapacitated on the eve of the New York opening. 'I have never known anything like it in all my career,' reported Wright. 'I have rearranged the cast so often, even I have lost track of who might come on next.'[11]

Performances in New York were at the Brooklyn Academy of Music. Kennedy, who was to dance the opening Aurora, was suffering from bronchitis, and it was not surprising if her performance was somewhat muted. The general public enjoyed the company, and although the daily press was favourable, both productions and dancers were savagely attacked by the weekly and monthly dance critics. Thus Clive Barnes in the *New York Post* found Wright 'a wonderfully adroit director, (who) understands this old Imperial Russian ballet with a fidelity you would search for in vain in the Soviet Union. It is a production above all imbued with reverence and authority – and a sense among the dancers of almost autocratic rightness',[12] although he found the dancers small scale and lacking in personality. Anna Kisselgoff in the *New York Times* called it 'one of the best ... to be seen today', and found in it a unity of conception 'that is both theatrically and philosophically effective ... the British view is the one we learned to love over the decades with the Covent Garden company and the smaller Sadler's Wells Royal Ballet does very well in the same tradition'.[13]

Arlene Croce, however, one of the most respected of American dance critics, went so far in her attack on *The Sleeping Beauty* as to descend to the cheap jibe of referring to Wright as 'Mr Wrong' in his approach to the classics. She recognised the gifts and talents of the individual dancers 'but their shabby schooling denies them range and force of expression' and though they possessed stylistic unity, that merely meant that 'everyone was bad in the same way'.[14] On the other hand, Jack Anderson in the *New York Times* saw that 'though charismatic soloists can be wonderful, the lack of them need not be disastrous, for good teamwork never fails to make a performance a satisfactory whole'.[15] He denied that softness automatically meant weakness, but did admit that he longed for an occasional glint of diamantine brilliance.

On the whole the dancers were judged to be decorous, genteel, restrained and untheatrical. The best reviews went to the mature dancers, Samsova and Barbieri, Kelly, Landa and Morse, who were filling out the mime roles with an authority and grace unknown in America.

One programme was devoted to Bintley, as choreographer and performer – *Choros*, *The Flowers of the Forest* and *Petrushka*, with Bintley in the title role. The New York press recognised him as a choreographer of skill and talent, but he was also thought to be uneven, and lacking in invention in a city where experiment and innovation were highly prized. He was judged to be most successful in the choreography for the men in *Flowers of the Forest*, and it was noted with satisfaction that the company was developing male dancers with soft, high jumps. As Petrushka, he was judged to be emotionally hollow, and again most praise went to the dancers playing the character roles. In both choreography and interpretation, it was felt that Bintley offered intellect as a substitute for emotion.

It was, however, impossible for New York to get to know the company and its quieter pleasures in a week, and perhaps expectations had been pitched too high. The company was judged against the best that the Resident Company had had to offer in the heady days of the 1950s and 1960s. However, while no single dancer captured the New Yorkers' imagination, the company as an ensemble was recognised.

From New York the company moved on to Cleveland, then to Miami. Here it had been hoped that Prince Charles, then visiting Texas, could be persuaded to come to the opening gala, and when this proved impossible Peter Wright had the idea of inviting Margot Fonteyn, now in retirement in Panama, to make a guest appearance as the Queen in *The Sleeping Beauty*. Her performances were not surprisingly highly publicized and her radiant unexaggerated characterization won many hearts. It was the first time that many of the younger dancers had ever seen her and it was sad to realize that she was already a stranger to a new generation. It was in Miami that the company gave the one hundredth performance of *The Sleeping Beauty*, a total reached in under eighteen months, an indication of the hold that the classics were once again establishing on the repertory.

From Miami they moved on to Sarasota and Clearwater, and then Mexico City. Here tickets were expensive – 10,000 pesos, which was enough for a peasant to live on for a month. Not surprisingly society figured large in the audience; they didn't applaud much and hurried away immediately the curtain fell. But enthusiasm grew throughout the visit, culminating in the televized performance of *Coppélia*, the fees for which the company had agreed should go towards the funds to help victims of the recent earthquake. This performance was attended by a younger and less exclusive audience, which inspired the company to give one of its best performances. At the end the house lights went up to reveal the entire audience on its feet applauding as the orchestra played *Las Golondrinas*, the traditional Mexican song of farewell.

Wright was anxious that on tours abroad dancers should, if possible, have time to see new cultures, especially in countries like Mexico, with their entirely different unwesternized way of life and time was made in the busy schedules for sightseeing.

The stage staff on foreign tours rarely found much difficulty in communicating with local crews. As John Hart, their Master Carpenter put it, 'To theatre people anywhere in the world, a piece of scenery is a piece of scenery is a piece of scenery. We understand one another.'[16] Scenery might have been scenery, but technology was a different matter when in the high-tech theatre of the Fundación Teresa Carreno in Caracas a power cut upset the computerized flying system for the scenery. This had been installed by a firm in San Francisco and was so advanced that no one on the spot could unravel its complexities, and even though the manual override was discovered, only half the scenery could be used.

The tour ended in Rio de Janeiro, where the company was greeted by a letter from the British Council accompanied by a list of do's and don'ts in that most violent of cities. Already unsettled nerves were not helped when a man was shot outside the stage door during the opening performance of *The Sleeping Beauty*. The company opened the Festival Internacional de Danza, and the high seat prices meant small audiences. There was not much publicity surrounding the visit and what there was concentrated on the special gala attended by Princess Anne, which rose to hysterical proportions in Rio and England when it was revealed that threats had been made to kidnap her. All Rio society attended the gala, and the company danced to a couture dressed audience, glittering with jewels, far grander than anything to be seen in London over the past few years.

The tour ended on 26 March, after which the company had a short break before returning to England to put the final touches to a new Bintley ballet. It was now recognized that the punishing schedules of previous years had greatly contributed to the stress and injuries that seemed inevitably to follow a foreign tour, and the management was taking a much more enlightened view of planning. The gruelling long tours in England and abroad were a thing of the past and, although with their eight performances a week the Sadler's Wells Royal Ballet worked harder in concentrated bursts than the Covent Garden company, the gap between the total number of performances a year between the companies was not nearly as great as it had been.

It was difficult, now that the company had increased to cope with the classics, to keep all the dancers involved all of the time. Wright had to keep a delicate balance between overworking and underworking the dancers, especially those in the *corps de ballet*. It was also hard to keep the boys interested, as the classics were not as rewarding for them as for the girls – though Wright's productions were notable for giving them more chances than those of the 1960s.

This was doubtless one reason behind Bintley's drive to create large works drawing on the whole company, and during the American tour he had been working on his second full-length ballet, again with Terry Bartlett as his designer. *The Snow Queen* took as its starting point the eponymous Hans Christian Andersen fairy tale, but reduced to the basic story of the magic mirror, which pierces the hearts of men, blinding them to human emotion and making them see only evil and ugliness; thus they are bound to the cold Snow Queen. He changed Andersen's happy ending where the hero, Kay, is redeemed by the love of Gerda, and in his version Kay becomes aware again of human love, but too late, and is doomed to follow the Snow Queen for ever. Over and above this Bintley wove into the scenario elements of European folk traditions surrounding winter and summer rites and the solstice festivals. He had always been much attracted by the myth element in fairy tales, and he tried to find in them a relevance for the modern world.

Bintley conceived each act in a different style; the first was based on folk dance, the second mixed character and classical, while the third was pure classical. The music, based on themes by Mussorgsky, orchestrated and amplified by the company's principal conductor, Bramwell Tovey, was full of vivid rhythms and atmosphere. The story seemed thinly stretched in a work lasting over three hours, the choreography was full of padding and the Prologue and Act III were spun out far beyond their thematic potential. Bintley had problems in creating expressive choreography for his supernatural characters that would establish them as elemental forces; Kay and Gerda were not sufficiently characterized to make them sympathetic protagonists, and the Snow Queen was a one-dimensional character. What the ballet most lacked was simple humanity, and it might have been asked if Bintley was wise to concentrate on such vast, mythical and inhuman subjects.

The dancers provided the roles with some of the personality and individuality lacking in the choreography. Most of the best dancing went to subsidiary characters and Lustig had a fine bold solo as the Snow Queen's White Dwarf and Michael O'Hare took most of the other honours with his bottle dance at the betrothal celebrations. Benjamin was a gentle Gerda, but Price was not a strong enough actor to make much of Kay, although the choreography showed to advantage his bold, sweeping movement. Saidi and later Laura Hussey, did what they could to establish the Queen as a dominating supernatural force.

The Snow Queen. Laura Hussey as the Snow Queen and Andrew Bromiley as Kay as a boy.

The gala première in Birmingham on 28 April 1986, in aid of the NSPCC, was graced by the presence of Princess Margaret. All the performances that week were sold out, and the ballet was to prove more successful with the general public than with the critics. How much of its success was due to the fact that full-length ballets were automatically more popular on tour than triple bills was difficult to determine; the public still felt that a spectacular three-act ballet gave them better value for money than three short works, however distinguished.

During the ensuing weeks, the company was much concerned with their forthcoming visit to Israel as part of the Israel Festival. In the wake of Britain's involvement in the United States' bombing of Libya, they feared they would be prime targets for terrorist attacks, and even Mrs Thatcher's recent safe visit to Israel failed to quell their fears, as they felt they would hardly warrant the same level of protection. Victor Hochhauser, promoter of the tour with the British Council, was afraid that, if the tour did not go ahead, relations between Israel and Britain might be harmed. The press was highly critical of the company's fears, feeling that the cancellation of the tour would be a triumph for terrorism.

Eventually a group of dancers and administrators, including Barbieri, Jennifer Jackson and Paul Findlay from the Royal Opera House, went out to assess the situation for themselves. Having seen how much security was built into everyday life in Israel they were reassured, and even more so when they learned that their security firm would be the same as for Mrs Thatcher's visit. On their return the company voted to go ahead with the tour. Ironically, in view of their previous fears, once in Israel they were a constant worry to their guards, as they kept giving them the slip and disappearing on unescorted sightseeing trips.

The ballet for the visit was *Swan Lake*, which had never been seen in its entirety in Israel. They performed in Caesarea, in the beautiful amphitheatre built by Herod, with the sea as a backdrop and the night sky above, which made up for the fact that the scenery could not be used. The dressing-rooms for the principals were below stage, in the catacombs, hewn out of the solid rock. In Jerusalem they danced at Sultan's Pool, below the old city wall, with 8,000 seated on the grassy slopes around the vast hollow. Audiences were enthusiastic and appreciative, especially of the live orchestra (the Israel Sinfonietta), as most dance companies in Israel used taped music.

David Ashmole was a welcome guest in Cambridge at the beginning of the 1986–87 season and subsequently at the Royal Opera House. At the end of the London season the company lost one of its most stalwart performers, Carl Myers, whose place was filled by Joseph Cipolla, former dancer with Dance Theatre of Harlem. As he could not find the talent he needed in the school, and as time would be needed to develop principals from within the company, Wright was now sometimes forced to look outside the Royal Ballet for his dancers. He believed, however, that new blood was good for the company, and stopped it from becoming too parochial. He also brought in as guest artist Stephen Heathcote, from the Australian Ballet, while Price went out to dance in Australia in his place.

It was on the autumn tour of 1986 that Miyako Yoshida made her debut as Odette-Odile. Tiny and irreproachably correct, she had all the technical control and neat precision of movement that characterized Japanese dancers, allied to a sweetness of personality that boded well for her future. It was an enchanting mixture of Oriental control and more assertive personality than was usual with meticulously trained but often mechanical Japanese dancers. Her dancing was gently circumscribed, deliciously miniature without being underprojected or cramped. She needed time to grow into the expressive potential of the classics, but it was a talent bright with promise.

The tour was dominated by the full length ballets *Swan Lake* and *The Snow Queen*. The only work new to the repertory was a short-lived revival of Frank Staff's charming miniature *Peter and the Wolf*, created in 1940 for Ballet Rambert. It made amusing use of everyday prosaic objects like stepladders and mops to create a sophisticated adult view of a child's world in which the story was played out.

If the present and the future of the company looked bright, however, thoughts were turning to the past as the company embarked upon its winter season at Sadler's Wells. The season was the company's first chance to commemorate the foundation forty years before of the Sadler's Wells Theatre Ballet and typically the company chose to celebrate by looking both forward, with new ballets by Jackson and Bintley, and back, with revivals of Ashton's *Capriol Suite* and *Valses Nobles and Sentimentales*. The repertory reflected a judicious balance between the old and the new, celebrating Ashton and de Valois (*Checkmate*), Cranko (*Pineapple Poll*), and MacMillan (*Solitaire*) as well as Bintley (*The Snow Queen*) and *Coppélia*.

The highlight of the season for both the older audience and the new was the revival of *Valses Nobles et Sentimentales*, which formed part of the 'anniversary' programme on 9 January 1987. It was Wright who originally had the idea of putting the ballet back together again, drawing upon the memories of those who had appeared in it; once the basic framework was set, Ashton undertook the revision and polishing. It emerged as fresh and inventive as ever, a supreme example of a ballet of subtle implication and mood rather than narrative. It also brought home to a modern audience, ready to equate time with progress and progress with improvement, just how good those original fifteen- and sixteen-year-old Theatre Ballet dancers had been. The ballet now had an older cast, led by Tait in Heaton's original role, with Millington and Wicks as her attendant males. As with the company itself, a more professional and mature charm had replaced the innocence and sense of extreme youthful potential that had characterized the original.

Also coming up as fresh as ever was the wit and style of *Capriol Suite* and the delicate sentimentality of *Solitaire*, to which, to everyone's relief, the Desmond Heeley designs had been restored. *Pineapple Poll* completed the programme, with Donovan giving her now masterly performance as Poll, full of bubbling fun and feminine warmth, while Dubreuil was an elegant and witty Belaye.

Everyone might have been forgiven for seeing it as a night for sentimental reflection – especially as the audience included Nerina, Lane, Heaton, Page, Poole, Trecu and Kersley. Most would have been at the best only names to the young dancers who were their successors. The audience was also delighted to welcome back Gable, this time as the Narrator in *Peter and the Wolf*.

The programme on 15 January had its eyes fixed firmly on the future, a salutory reminder in *Checkmate* of what young choreographers had to aim for. Jackson's *One by Nine* was a series of encounters for one man (Cipolla) and nine women, which she described in the programme as 'Action and reaction between representations of the nine Muses and the Artist'. It mixed classical and jazzy steps, and showed Jackson's usual craftsmanship, but remained ultimately unsatisfying.

Bintley's new work, *Allegri Diversi*, proved one of his best. He used little-known works by Rossini, full of sparkling melody and speed, qualities which he reflected in his choreography, which was full of allegro brilliance, and dazzlingly fast footwork. Terry Bartlett's setting of a formal Italian garden in 'cubist' style admirably reflected the style and form of the choreography. It was, for Bintley, refreshingly simple and made use of a relatively restricted vocabulary, which showed off his dancers to advantage, but it was a killer to perform. They showed how much hope the company contained for the future, for most still had their maturity before them – Donovan, Madgwick and the even younger Anne Little, Webb, Michael O'Hare and Jacobsson.

The season was not just a nostalgic look back but showed the strengths of the past translated into hope for the future in performances by a young company, judiciously sprinkled with maturity and experience. It was a balance Wright had astutely contrived. To many it seemed as though the company had come full circle, but this was deceptive. It was rather a spiral, moving upwards and expanding outwards, but never losing touch with its roots. It had taken the best of what the past had to offer, but never at the expense of a forward-looking constructive policy on which the future could build towards something new. Thus it had kept faith with de Valois' original aims.

Part 4

Towards Birmingham

Chapter XXIII

From the triumphs of the anniversary season, the company set out on the 1987 winter tour. They had no time to rest upon their laurels for they were hard at work upon three new ballets, choreographed by Lustig, Crow and Derek Deane. All would be premièred in Birmingham, a sign of the growing links between the company and the city which had already seen the first performances of *The Sleeping Beauty*, *The Snow Queen*, *The Winter Play* and *Flowers of the Forest*. But the Birmingham visit was to prove momentous for another reason.

It was during the season that Richard Johnston, director of the Birmingham Hippodrome, met with Wright and General Manager Christopher Nourse. On behalf of the City Council, he laid before them the proposal to move the Sadler's Wells Royal Ballet to Birmingham, with local funding and a theatre transformed to give them facilities equal to those of the Resident Company. Wright and Nourse were 'stunned by the enormity of Birmingham's proposal, excited by the opportunities which on the face of it would be the Company's, fearful of the problems which might arise'.[1] Initial approaches had already been made to the Royal Opera House and the Arts Council, and, while the company continued its tour, preliminary discussions began.

Lustig's *Paramour*, Crow's *Private City* and Deane's *The Picture of Dorian Gray* were premièred on 19 March. Most successful was *Paramour*, which revealed not only Lustig's facility for creating steps, but also the ability to structure a work, to use a small *corps de ballet* with confidence and blend choreography, Poulenc's music and Nadine Baylis' economical but evocative design into a homogeneous ballet of fleeting emotions. 'Tait' flirted with 'Samsova's' escort as well as her own until, in a delicately ironic ending, the two women confronted each other, and it was left in doubt who was having an affair with whom.

A highly successful season at the Opera House followed the tour, during which the company celebrated the fiftieth birthday of *Checkmate*. They then embarked upon a tour of Eastern Europe before ending the 1986–87 season with their first visit to the Isle of Wight with the Big Top. 1987–88 would be an exciting year, for it included a six week tour of the Far East during which company would make its début in China, and return visits to Japan.

Meanwhile, discussions continued between the Royal Opera House and Birmingham. In November 1987 the Royal Opera House Ballet Board commissioned an independent study of the scheme from David Allen, who knew the company well, having worked on the Priestley report in 1983. His brief was to investigate the relocation plan, 'taking full account of the facilities potentially available at Sadler's Wells Theatre itself and other London venues. To assess the financial implications of these options while having principally in mind the need to enable the Company, without severing its links with the Royal Opera House or the Royal Ballet School, to develop its role of performing classical ballet throughout the United Kingdom.'[2] Allen consulted the company management, Jeremy Isaacs, who had succeeded John Tooley as General Director of the Royal Opera House, Anthony Dowell, Merle Park, Director of the Royal Ballet School, all the technical departments of the Opera House and every member of the Sadler's Wells Royal Ballet – dancers, orchestra and staff.

Wright was also asked for a development plan, '"putting to one side the present financial constraints of the ROH and assuming an ideal world, whilst avoiding profligacy". He and (Nourse) sat for hours discussing the endless possibilities, musing over various ideas. These meetings occurred everywhere; on trains, in taxis, at the Empire Theatre in Sunderland, in East Berlin, in Tokyo's New Takanawa Prince Hotel – wherever we had the time and space.'[3]

In November 1988 the Main Board of the Royal Opera House agreed unanimously that 'the House should in principle accept the City of Birmingham's invitation to provide a new headquarters for SWRB in Birmingham from the autumn of 1990, subject to confirmation that the Arts Council would provide the necessary funding, that the finances of the Royal Opera and Royal Ballet would not be adversely affected and that the other necessary financial arrangements would be satisfactorily concluded and confirmed'.[4]

Marion Tait, Galina Samsova and Petter Jacobsson in *Paramour*.

The relocation was announced at a press conference on 12 January 1989. Isaacs had no doubt about the benefits of the move: 'It is clear that the Sadler's Wells Royal Ballet's future artistic development will best be secured by basing the Company in Birmingham. The facilities to be built and the new money to be made available add up to an offer we cannot refuse.'[5] Birmingham City Council would provide £1 million for three years after the relocation at the Hippodrome, a sum to be matched by the Arts Council; there would be £1 million available in relocation costs and £4.1 million for an extension to the Hippodrome, consisting of three large studios, a practice room, physiotherapy unit, gym, green room, changing rooms, video rooms, wardrobe storage and offices. It was a far cry from the cramped conditions at Sadler's Wells. They would still be part of the Royal Ballet organisation, drawing dancers from the school, and managed by the Royal Opera House which would continue to provide technical and production back-up.

The company would appear in Birmingham for five weeks a year besides increasing performances throughout Britain, but Wright was insistent on maintaining the number of performances in London, with seasons at both Sadler's Wells and the Royal Opera House. Besides ambitious plans for the repertory, he wanted to bring in distinguished choreographers and increase the time spent by guest teachers with the company.[6] There were also plans to extend education links with schools, helping build a knowledgeable local audience outside London. Once the company had become the West Midlands 'own', it would be possible to build audiences for all programmes, including more adventurous triple bills.

At the press conference, Wright paid tribute to the support and facilities that Sadler's Wells had offered over the years, but the special relationship between company and theatre, which had existed for more than half a century, was now over. For years Sadler's Wells had lurched from crisis to crisis, and, for the last year, the management had been trying desperately to raise funds to make the improvements which might induce the company to stay; at the same time they had been building a small studio theatre which could not but be financially unviable. But they could not compete with the resources offered by Birmingham.

Wright had been in constant touch with de Valois. Typically, she spent no time dwelling on the past, but looked to the future, and was enthusiastic about the advantages of the move. In fact, Birmingham might have been the original home of the Royal Ballet. In the 1920s she was looking for a repertory theatre in which to found a British ballet

Miyako Yoshida and Petter Jacobsson in *Theme and Variations*.

Photograph by Leslie E. Spatt.

company, and so approached Lilian Baylis at the Old Vic, and Barry Jackson at the Birmingham Repertory Theatre, who was also producing plays and operas in London. Jackson turned her down with the crushing remark that he was losing enough money without starting a ballet company and for such a venture he wouldn't choose de Valois anyway, but Bronislava Nijinska, the brilliant choreographer sister of Vaslav Nijinsky – a statement which de Valois regarded as a serious error of judgement.

During the relocation discussions, the company had not been idle, although Michael Corder's pseudo-Elizabethan *Gloriana*, produced on 13 November 1987, Graham Lustig's conventional *The Edge of Silence*, which followed on 14 January 1988, and Lynn Seymour's pseudo-Egyptian *Bastet*, first seen on 24 June 1988, did nothing to enhance their reputations. There was, however, an excellently danced staging of Balanchine's *Theme and Variations*, the dancers amazing their teacher, Patricia Neary, by the speed with which they picked up the difficult choreography.

In many ways the company had never been stronger. The varied and wide-ranging repertory meant plenty of opportunities for all, and a new generation of principals and soloists grasped every opportunity they were offered. Madgwick, Yoshida and Donovan, Yow and Michael O'Hare were steadily growing as artists. Behind the scenes, a succession of fine teachers were brought in to work with the company – including Hans Brenaa, Christine Anthony, Alan Beale and Eileen Ward – and the notable all-round improvement among the boys could be traced to Desmond Kelly's influence. Kelly's vital work with the company was recognised by his appointment as Assistant to the Director and Ballet Master.

On the choreographic front it was left to David Bintley to produce a hit – *Hobson's Choice*, premièred at the Royal Opera House on 13 February, 1989. Dedicated to de Valois, it was based on the eponymous Harold Brighouse comedy, tracing the decline of the tyrannical drunken bootmaker, Henry Hobson and the rise of his daughter, Maggie, who marries his chief bootmaker, Will Mossop, and eventually takes over the business. It was overlong, but the choreography was buoyant, and some of the most strongly characterized that Bintley had yet created and it was good to see him dealing with fully rounded characters rather than epic heroes or fairy-tale beings. There were marvellous roles for everybody, especially Donovan as a sternly practical Maggie, Michael O'Hare as Will Mossop, developing from downtrodden to manfully

Hobson's Choice. Karen Donovan as Maggie Hobson, Michael O'Hare as Will Mossop, Sandra Madgwick as Vickey Hobson and Cenca Williams as Alice Hobson.

confident, Kelly as a blustering Hobson, and well-rounded characters for Chenca Williams and Madgwick as Maggie's sisters, and Wicks and Cipolla as their beaus. Thus the announcement of the Birmingham move found the company performing as zestfully as ever, seemingly with no doubts in the world about their future. It was a tribute to the confidence that they had in their Director and his plans.

Others were waiting in the wings. Michael O'Hare's younger brother, Kevin, was beginning to assume increasingly important roles, as was American-born Bonnie Moore. June 1989 saw the choreographic debuts with the company by two more of its own dancers, Vincent Redmon with *Auras* and William Tuckett with *Those Unheard*. In the same month Dame Ninette laid at the Birmingham Hippodrome the foundation stone for the new studios and company facilities.

One final detail remained – the new name for the company. Few were surprised, however, when it was announced that in September 1990 the company would become The Birmingham Royal Ballet – the seventh name change the company had undergone since 1946.[7] Peter Wright's plans for the move reflected the company's position as the regional arm of The Royal Ballet, a classically based company built not only on a foundation of the great classics, and 'a heritage repertory' drawing upon important ballets from all sources, but a major creative force in presenting new works by established and young choreographers.

The importance of the relocation cannot be minimized. The Sadler's Wells Ballet had grown to a point where it rivalled the achievements of the Resident Company itself, and two such companies based in London was no longer feasible. The regions had become increasingly important; Glasgow had Scottish Ballet, Manchester Northern Dance Theatre and small modern dance groups flourished in other cities. Now the Midlands would have its own company. Not for the first time in its existence, the 'other' Royal Ballet stood on the brink of a new era.

Dame Ninette de Valois laying the foundation stone of the new studios at the Birmingham Hippodrome.

Photograph by Alan Wood.

Part 5

The Company

Chapter XXIV

The 'second' Royal Ballet has often been referred to as the 'sister' of the Covent Garden company. A family analogy is not out of place in the close knit world of ballet, especially in the great national companies where the dancers grow from a single school together from childhood or at least mid-teens, sometimes until retirement. The Royal Ballet is heir to a great tradition, and, like most inheritances, that brings obligations and expectations. For the eldest child who is the inheritor that implies responsibilities and duties, while the younger can be more wayward, more daring, allowed the freedom to develop untrammelled by expectations and the demands of tradition. The older child sets an example and more is asked of him, while the younger is often regarded with indulgent affection, allowed to experiment in a way that is often denied to the elder. So it has been with the 'other' Royal Ballet.

The Royal Ballet is one of the few companies in ballet history to have two separate branches, self contained, but from the same roots, each with its own role to play. The particular personality of each stems from those different roles, the conditions under which they perform and the different audiences to which they play. That the 'second' company has survived the traumas of change of management, change of policies, changes of director and fluctuations of public taste is a tribute to its solid foundations and the determination of its successive Directors to follow de Valois' aims. Her mixture of vision and practical organisational skill gave her companies the roots and structures from which to flourish by founding a school, then companies within existing theatre organisations, then assuring, through the Royal Charter, their independent existence from those theatres.

313

So the company could develop and change without destroying the foundations. The times of crisis, as when the Theatre Ballet left the Wells, or the 1970 reorganisation, were periods of rebuilding, and ensured that the company never declined into apathy and atrophy. Indeed, it emerged even stronger, drawing upon the past to feed the future – the Touring Company expanding to take in the great classics, the New Group returning to the Theatre Ballet principles of building a new repertory. The Birmingham Royal Ballet draws upon the best of its predecessors' achievements – the creativity and development of young talent of the Theatre Ballet and the classical achievements of the Touring Company.

As the first generation of Theatre Ballet dancers came to maturity, it became increasingly difficult to see the company as a group of graduate students *en route* for Covent Garden. After a decade change was inevitable. Under Field, a company evolved within which dancers could grow to maturity and, given the classics, have the same chances as the dancers at Covent Garden. It was the Royal Ballet's showcase in the provinces and abroad, while the Resident Company was the London and American showcase. This new policy was, however, at the expense of creativity and a home base; by the end of the 1960s the company was exhausted. So the management opted for a small group and experiment – an extraordinary misjudging of the spirit of the times – and it was left to Wright to find the balance between the classics, the established repertory and the acceptable face of the new that gives the present company its particular character. The re-establishment of the company at Sadler's Wells meant that the dancers could rest, recharge and work in a way that had never been possible in the gypsy life of the Touring Company but which had been the norm for the Theatre Ballet.

Rest periods are vital, for life on the road exacts its own toll. As Last put it, 'Nobody who's been in the touring company has ever been a frustrated dancer, but they have racked their bodies a lot, and the world of touring is very hard. And you have to be on your mettle every day because you're in a new town and the stage is different. You're never on automatic pilot. That really wrecks you. That has never changed.'[1] Also, 'You learn stagecraft, how to scale a performance to the size of the theatre, how to handle an audience. You learn from your mistakes more quickly because you dance a role more often. So you don't get in a tizzy worrying.'[2] For a Resident Company dancer like Sibley, three or four performances a week might be physically 'exhausting, but nevertheless you had the rhythm of being on all the time and not being *pounced* upon, by all the critics, by everybody. The relief when one was away and could try things out a bit and experiment, knowing you had two or three of them coming up . . .'[3]

Many opt for a life on the road because of the greater opportunities and their enthusiasm communicates itself to the audience; it is a shared experience, far from the sometimes rarefied performances at the Opera House where dancers can give the impression that audiences are privileged observers of a private rite. 'Audiences on tour are so genuine', explained Marion Tait. 'They come because they've saved up for their one night at the ballet and, I'm not being condescending, they come to be entertained. That's our job – we're entertainers. There's no great highbrow thing and I think they forget that at the Garden. The audiences do and I'm sure the dancers do.'[4] Thus touring has bred a particular type of dancer.

Like the Resident Company, the 'second' company style is a reflection of the works of the Royal Ballet's first great choreographers – the lyrical understatement of Ashton allied to the theatricality and characterization of de Valois. It is a style of quiet pleasures, stylish, gracious, and neat, though at their worst these qualities can fade into gentility, meekness and 'good taste', which the 'other' Royal Ballet has always guarded against by a good helping of liveliness and vigour, which compensates for any lack of finesse. Ashton always felt it extremely valuable that the Royal Ballet had two companies, one pre-eminent in classicism, the other with demi-caractère liveliness. De Valois pinpointed 'sentimentality' as 'the tragedy of the English dancer . . . beyond toleration because of its negative refinement'.[5] She suggested as an antidote to this tendency encouraging characterization, and this is what the 'second' company has drawn upon throughout the vicissitudes of its existence and may help to explain why it sometimes seems adrift in the realms of pure classical ballet. If it has at times lacked a great classical ballerina, it should be remembered how rare such a creature is and often how limited. The 'second' company has rather demanded versatility of its dancers, for flexibility and adaptability are integral ingredients in its character. The company has never rigidly looked for a dancer of a certain physical type, and it is to be hoped that there will always be a place for the dancer of exceptional talent who may not fit into the fashionable ideal. It has never been a closed shop, and dancers from many backgrounds and schools have enriched its performances.

The present dancers retain the typical 'second' company vigour and individualism, combined with a greater sophistication born of a less rigid company structure and less concentrated touring. They have travelled the world and the management has tried to ensure that they had some time to absorb the different cultures. Less hectic scheduling and better planned tours have left the dancers freer to develop as individuals outside the company.

In what is a profession for the young, the company has always stood for youth, but now it is judiciously sprinkled with maturity and wisdom. Wright ensures, as de Valois did, that experience is not lost to the company, but is used for the benefit of the younger dancers. The original Theatre Ballet was primarily a group of very young dancers with a sturdy individualism on the brink of maturity; the Touring Company developed more mature dancers, with their own gritty professionalism, learnt from the rigours of constant touring. Ballet companies were still relatively inward looking, a problem exacerbated by being almost permanently on the road, and this could inhibit the development of young artists. Touring abroad was, for them, a change from the unrelenting provincial grind at a time when most towns outside London were not particularly stimulating.

The company has won countless admirers, especially among the regular balletgoers, who often prefer the 'second' company to the 'first'. To less knowledgeable audiences, it has given good value entertainment – which is not to be patronizing, but practical; if they can so attract audiences, there is the chance of them coming back for the less familiar works. The problems of devising a touring repertory have never changed – the difficulty of balancing ballet against ballet and programme against programme, of playing the familiar against the unfamiliar, and of establishing new ballets. With only one visit a year to most towns it can be difficult to popularize new works, and the instant universal hit like *Pineapple Poll* is very rare.

At each stage of its development, the company has bred directors according to its needs. Moreton was the link to de Valois, with the experience to guide young dancers, while van Praagh mothered and encouraged the youthful potential. Field bullied and cajoled the company to maturity and gave it focus and a new identity. Wright had the vision and determination to bring the company back from a period of decline and restore its self-confidence. All of them without directorial experience when they were appointed, none has disappointed. A company might count itself lucky to have one such director in its history.

The company also developed that rarest of beings – the choreographer. The Royal Ballet has never been the expression of one creative mind, rather it has aimed to draw upon a wide range of subjects and styles grafted onto a distinctive English character of its own. The ballets from the past, especially those of Ashton and de Valois, ensured a repertory for the Theatre Ballet and were examples for young choreographers like Cranko and MacMillan. Most companies would have built a history on the works of one such choreographer. The later addition of the classics was inevitable for the development of the dancers and the continuation of the company.

Whatever damage may have been done by the changes of 1970, it certainly ensured that the company never settled into insularity, as it opened itself to choreographers from abroad in greater variety and quantity than ever before. It was a sign of growing internationalism in dance. That the Sadler's Wells Royal Ballet nevertheless maintained its individuality was another tribute to the strength of its roots. But once stable conditions were re-established, it was not long before David Bintley emerged from its own ranks.

Periods of stagnation are inevitable. It is impossible to be always on a creative peak, nor is it feasible, with eight performances a week, for the company to reach the heights every night. What they have achieved is a high standard of professionalism, which they can rise above to give performances that rank with the best anywhere. For their current Régisseur, Ronald Plaisted, 'They are marvellous. They always surprise you. You shout at them, get annoyed with them, and suddenly they will do something that makes you very proud to be part of the same company.'[6] In the past, the company had to stand by and watch many of its best dancers reach their fullest potential elsewhere, and it is a tribute to Wright that he has established an organisation within which dancers can find fulfilment for their whole careers.

The company has played an important part in raising public consciousness in dance throughout Britain and its influence can only increase with the move to Birmingham. But that influence has extended far beyond Britain – between 1977 and 1989 it appeared in over sixty-two cities in twenty-eight countries, ranging from dance saturated New York to Bombay which had never seen a full classical company. And in many countries they found former company dancers implementing precepts and policies they learnt in their touring days.

The 'other' Royal Ballet has been, for most of its existence, a happy company, mainly because they are constantly occupied and interested in their work. As several dancers and members of the staff observed drily, busy people don't have time to complain, and dissatisfaction usually stems from boredom. The family feeling, affection and intense loyalty of the dancers for their company has never changed. Whatever their individual differences, however much they might complain among themselves, any breath of criticism by an outsider and they all closed ranks. It was never a blind faith – dancers see quite clearly what is wrong as much as what is right – nor was every dancer happy all of the time, but none would trade the experience of belonging to the 'other' Royal Ballet. The work and discipline stood them in good stead when they left. After all, as Last said, 'If you've been a dancer and been a dancer on tour, anything else in your life is going to be easy'[7] – even when 'anything else' meant for many, including herself, directing companies of their own.

Over the years the strong links that bind the two Royal Ballets have diminished. They are still recognisably of the same family, but in the way of families, often do not see much of each other – each leading its own life and coming together only occasionally for family celebrations. The 'other' Royal Ballet has existed as both a prop and a goad to the senior company – the livelier and less inhibited youngster, which has grown to its own independent maturity.

Notes

PART 1

Chapter 1

1 *Dancing Times*, November 1945, p. 50.

2 Arnold Haskell, 'British Ballet Since the War', *Radio Times*, 14.3.1947.

3 Maryon Lane, conversation.

4 Ninette de Valois, *Come Dance With Me*, Hamish Hamilton, 1957, p. 179.

5 Maryon Lane, conversation.

6 *Evening News*, 16.10.1946.

7 Eveleigh Leith, 'Its Own Mechanism', *Ballet Annual 1*, A. & C. Black, London, 1947, p. 151.

8 Peggy van Praagh, *How I Became a Ballet Dancer*. Thomas Nelson and Sons, ed. 1959., p. 43.

9 Ibid., p. 45.

10 Anne Heaton, conversation.

11 *The Times*, 27.12.1945.

12 'The New Company at Sadler's Wells', *Ballet Annual 1*, A. & C. Black, London, 1947, p. 11.

13 Mary Clarke, *Ballet Today*, March–April 1946, p. 17.

14 Scott Goddard, *News Chronicle*, 9.4.1946.

15 Celia Franca, The Sitter Out, *Dancing Times*, May 1946, p. 390.

16 *Ballet Annual 1*, A. & C. Black, London, 1947, p. 12.

17 H.H.H., *Cambridge Daily News*, 23.7.1946.

Chapter II

1 Caryl Brahms, *Evening Standard*, 22.10.1946.

2 The Sitter Out, *Dancing Times*, December 1946, pp. 116–17.

3 *Sussex Daily News*, undated cutting, Royal Opera House Archives.

4 Unidentified Norwich newspaper, Royal Opera House Archives.

5 Stevenson did, in fact, design a handsome set for the ballet, but as the work never got nearer London than Finsbury Park, it was never used.

6 *The Stage*, 3.7.1947.

7 Pirmin Trecu, conversation.

8 Richard Buckle, *Ballet*, November 1947, pp. 5–8.

9 Letter to Richard Buckle, quoted in *In the Wake of Diaghilev*, Richard Buckle, Collins, 1982, p. 105.

10 Mary Clarke, *Ballet Today*, December 1947, p. 22.

11 Peter Brook, *Observer*, 5.10.1947.

12 Richard Buckle, *Ballet*, November 1947, p. 24.

13 P.W. Manchester, *Ballet Today*, March–April 1948, p. 6.

14 P.W. Manchester, *Ballet Today*, May–June 1948, p. 29.

15 The RAD Production Club had been set up to give students some performing experience, and to give young choreographers a chance to learn their craft and production techniques before a knowledgeable and sympathetic club audience. Ursula Moreton was Chairman and de Valois Technical Advisor.

16 The ballet had originally been designed by Hanns Ebensten, a friend and collaborator of Cranko's from their earliest days in South Africa.

17 *Northern Whig*, 3.6.1948.

18 Pirmin Trecu, conversation.

19 John Cranko, 'Choreographer and Company', *Ballet Annual 7*, A. & C. Black, London, 1952, p. 86.

Chapter III

1 P.W. Manchester, *Ballet Today*, November–December 1948, pp. 20–1.

2 Ibid.

3 Later editor of *Dance and Dancers*.

4 Caryl Brahms, *Evening Standard*, 17.11.1948.

5 A.V. Coton, *Sunday Times*, 20.3.1949.

6 CED, *Evening Sentinel*, 31.5.1949.

7 *The Times*, 3.6.1949.

8 The result was the 'stripy' *Rendezvous*.

9 *Manchester Guardian*, 10.6.1949 and other papers.

10 Barbara Fewster, conversation.

11 The Sitter Out, *Dancing Times*, November 1949, pp. 66–8.

12 Barbara Fewster, conversation.

13 Ninette de Valois, *Step by Step*, W.H. Allen, 1977, p. 98.

14 Richard Buckle, *Observer*, 13.11.1949.

15 'Three Matinées at the "Wells"', Anton Dolin, *Ballet*, January 1950, p. 18.

16 Ibid., p. 19.

17 Ibid.

18 John Richardson, *New Statesman and Nation*, 3.12.1949.

19 Anon, *Dance and Dancers*, February 1950, p. 21.

20 John Percival, *Theatre In My Blood*, Herbert, London 1983, p. 76.

Chapter IV

1 Peter Williams, *Dance and Dancers*, May 1950, p. 13.

2 *Peterborough Advertiser*, 9.6.1950.

3 Richard Buckle, *Observer*, 24.9.1970.

4 P.W. Manchester, *Ballet Today*, February–March 1951, p. 4.

5 Arnold Haskell, 'The Prospect Before Us', *Ballet Annual 6*, A. & C. Black, London, 1952, p. 18.

6 The Sitter Out, *Dancing Times*, March 1951, p. 324.

7 Cyril Beaumont, 'Pineapple Poll', *Ballet*, June 1951, p. 21.

8 Ibid., p. 22.

9 Philip Hope-Wallace, *Time and Tide*, 24.3.1951.

10 Arnold Haskell, *Foyer*, Autumn 1951.

11 Peter Williams, *Daily Mail*, 14.3.1951.

12 Cyril Beaumont, *Sunday Times*, 18.3.1951.

13 He performed the role over 300 times, which stands as a record for the most performances in a major role by a dancer in the Royal Ballet organisation.

14 Richard Arnell, 'Harlequin in April' in *The Decca Book of Ballet*, ed. David Drew Muller, 1958, p. 42.

15 Cranko later denied that there was any truth in this ('Harlequin in April', Clive Barnes, *Dance and Dancers*, February 1959), but the association was made by the original press release in April 1951, and, indeed, it would seem otherwise a very unlikely coincidence.

16 Quoted in Clive Barnes, 'Harlequin in April', *Dance and Dancers*, February 1959, pp. 19–21.

17 Arnold Haskell, 'Harlequin in April', *Ballet Annual 6*, A. & C. Black, London, 1952, p. 28.

18 Peter Williams, *Dance and Dancers*, April–July, 1951, p. 15.

19 Pirmin Trecu, conversation.

20 Clive Barnes, 'Harlequin in April', *Dance and Dancers*, February 1959, pp. 19–21.

Chapter V

1 Richard Buckle, *Observer*, 10.9.1951.

2 John Barber, *Daily Express*, 5.9.1951.

3 Clive Barnes, 'Coppélia', *Dance and Dancers*, October, 1951, pp. 14–15.

4 Lionel Bradley, unpublished diaries, Theatre Museum, London.

5 John Barber, *Daily Express*, 12.9.1951.

6 Peter Williams, *Dance and Dancers*, November 1951, p. 12.

7 Richard Buckle, *Observer*, 16.9.1951.

8 Sol Hurok, *S. Hurok Presents*, Hermitage House, New York, 1953, p. 304.

9 David Poole, 'The Sadler's Wells Ballet in North America', *Dancing Times*, December 1951, p. 135.

10 Donald Britton, letter to parents published *Dance and Dancers*, January 1952, p. 8.

11 All quoted in undated cutting from *The Stage*, press cutting books, Archives, Royal Opera House.

12 'Via the Grapevine', *Dance Magazine*, December 1951.

13 David Blair, letter to Lional Bradley postmarked 13 November 1952. Theatre Museum, London.

14 Unidentified newspaper, quoted by David Poole, in 'The Sadler's Wells Theatre Ballet in U.S.A.', *Dancing Times*, January 1952, p. 206.

15 Alfred Frankenstein, quoted in David Poole, 'Down the West Coast', *Dancing Times*, February 1952, pp. 273–4.

16 *The Stage*, 24.1.1952.

17 *Variety*, quoted by Mary Clarke, *Ballet Today*, February 1952.

18 David Poole, 'One Night Stands', *Dancing Times*, March 1952, pp. 333–4.

19 Mrs Doris Thellusson, conversation.

20 Ann Barzel, 'Chicago sees the Sadler's Wells Theatre Ballet', *Dance Magazine*, March 1952, pp. 46–8.

21 *Washington Post*, date unknown.

22 *Sunday Graphic*, 2.3.1952.

23 Anatole Chujoy, 'The Sadler's Wells Theatre Ballet', *Ballet Annual 7*, A. & C. Black, London 1952, p. 84.

24 Doris Hering, 'Sadlers (sic) Wells Theatre Ballet in New York: 1952', *Dance Magazine*, May 1952.

25 Francis Mason Jr, 'Another Letter about the SWTB', *Ballet*, June 1952.

26 John Martin, *New York Times*, 13.4.1952.

27 Lillian Moore, '"Wells" Theatre Ballet in New York', *Dancing Times*, May 1952.

28 David Poole, 'The Sadler's Wells Ballet in North America', *Dancing Times*, December 1951.

29 Anon, *Dance and Dancers*, August 1952.

Chapter VI

1 Mary Clarke, '*Reflection*', *Ballet Annual 8*, A. & C. Black, London, 1953, p. 12.

2 The Sitter Out, *Dancing Times*, October 1952, p. 8.

3 Ninette de Valois, 'The Sadler's Wells Organisation', *Dancing Times*, August 1952, p. 656.

4 Ernest Bradbury, *Yorkshire Post*, 29.10.1952.

5 Lillian Browse, *Spectator*, 30.1.1953.

6 David Poole, conversation. Later, when more money was needed, de Valois suggested that she find another accommodating cigarette firm to advertise. She thought it most unreasonable when it was pointed out to her that she couldn't smoke two brands 'exclusively'.

7 'Hilarion', *Dance and Dancers*, March 1953, p. 7.

8 *Abendzeitung*, undated press cutting, Archives, Royal Opera House.

9 Lionel Bradley, unpublished diaries. Theatre Museum, London.

10 The Sitter Out, *Dancing Times*, July 1953, p. 599.

11 Anon, *Chronicle*, 17.7.1953.

12 JNF, *Chronicle*, 10.7.1953.

13 Anon, *The Star*, 9.7.1953.

14 Quoted in Christopher Sexton, *Peggy van Praagh*, Macmillian, Melbourne, 1985, p. 92.

Chapter VII

1 *Scotsman*, 9.9.1953.

2 Anon, *Aberdeen Press and Journal*, 11.9.1953.

3 Richard Buckle, *Observer*, 11.10.1953.

4 Eileen Anstey, *Nottingham Guardian*, 9.11.1953.

5 Patricia Strauss, letter to *New Statesman*, 11.9.1954.

6 Arnold Haskell, 'The Value of a Dancer', *Dancing Times*, October 1954, p. 16.

7 Clive Barnes, 'What's to be done with Junior?', *Dance and Dancers*, November 1954.

8 Like the 'second' company, London Festival Ballet has undergone periodic renaming in the course of its history. Starting as Festival Ballet in 1950 it then became London's Festival Ballet before settling on London Festival Ballet. In 1988 it became English National Ballet.

9 Harold Rosenthal, *Musical Opinion*, January 1955.

10 Kenneth MacMillan, *Covent Garden Book 15*, p. 24–5.

11 Mary Clarke, 'Danse Concertantes', *Dancing Times*, February 1955, p. 283.

12 Clive Barnes, 'Danses Concertantes', *Dance and Dancers*, March 1955, p. 16.

Chapter VIII

1 Clive Barnes, *Dance and Dancers*, July 1955, p. 14.

2 Lynn Seymour, *Lynn*, Granada, London, 1984, p. 50.

PART 2

Chapter IX

1 John Field, conversation.
2 Ibid.
3 Jim Webber, *Stratford-upon-Avon Herald*, 20.1.1956.
4 John Field, conversation.
5 The company had taken part in a special performance to mark the twenty-fifth anniversary of the reopening of Sadler's Wells Theatre on 6 January, with Fonteyn and Somes as guest artists.
6 Kenneth MacMillan, 'Solitaire', *Sadler's Wells Theatre Ballet no. 1*, Sadler's Wells Foundation, undated.
7 Ibid.
8 Lynn Seymour, *Lynn*, Granada, London, 1984, pp. 58–9.
9 Unlike the Covent Garden company in recent years, the second company has always given another ballet with *Giselle* when on tour. Provincial audiences would have thought themselves very shortchanged otherwise.
10 Ninette de Valois, 'The Royal Charter: A Memorandum submitted by Ninette de Valois 1954', published in *Step by Step*, W. H. Allen, London, 1977, pp. 77–8.
11 Ibid., p. 80.
12 A.V. Coton, *Spectator*, 29.3.1957.
13 Clive Barnes, 'What became of "Junior"', *Dance and Dancers*, March 1957, p. 24.
14 'Curtain Up', *Dance and Dancers*, September 1957.
15 Copy letter quoted in CGC (Covent Garden Committee) (56) 10th meeting 16 October 1956.
16 Minutes Royal Opera House Board of Directors, 14 March 1957.
17 Minutes Royal Opera House Board of Directors, 16 April 1957.

18 *Royal Opera House Annual Report*, 1957–8.
19 Ninette de Valois, 'A statement of Royal Ballet Policy', *Dancing Times*, January 1958, pp. 170, 177.
20 The amount of work to be toured was calculated in 'acts'. Thus each short ballet was one 'act' and *Giselle* and *Coppélia* were calculated as two acts and three acts respectively.
21 Ninette de Valois, quoted *Yorkshire Evening Post*, 22.11.1957.

Chapter X

1 Arnold Haskell, programme note.
2 Peter Williams, 'The Burrow', Dance and Dancers, March 1958, p. 14–15.
3 Clive Barnes, *Daily Express*, 3.1.1958.
4 Andrew Porter, *Financial Times*, 3.1.1958.
5 Lynn Seymour, *Lynn*, Granada, London, 1984, p. 57.
6 Stage Management Report. Royal Opera House Archives.
7 Ibid.
8 Mary Clarke, 'Royal Ballet II', *Dancing Times*, August 1958, p. 500.
9 Anon, *Times Educational Supplement*, 4.7.1958.
10 Ninette de Valois quoted in *Auckland Star*, 16.10.1958.
11 Lynn Seymour, *Lynn*, Granada, London 1984, p. 113.
12 Harold Tidemann, *Adelaide Advertiser*, 16.1.1959.
13 *Adelaide Advertiser*, 30.1.1959.
14 *Sydney Morning Herald*, 27.2.1959.
15 SD, *Otago Daily Times*, 5.3.1959.
16 CES, *Christchurch Press*, 20.3.1959.
17 *Christchurch Star*, 20.3.1959.
18 JJC, *Wellington Evening Post*, 2.4.1959.

19 *Auckland Star*, 11.4.1959.
20 *New Zealand Herald*, 20.4.1959.
21 Clive Barnes, *Dance and Dancers*, December 1959.
22 John Field, conversation.
23 De Valois in conversation with Clement Crisp, *Ballet, Covent Garden Book 15*, p. 16.
24 Patricia Ruanne to Gordon Gow, 'Recruits to Festival', *Dancing Times*, November 1974, pp. 76–7.
25 EAGN, *Liverpool Echo*, 10.10.1959.
26 Alexander Bland, *Observer*, 13.12.1959.

7 'Peter Wright talks about his ballets', *About the House*, Vol. 1, no. 8, p. 15.
8 Clive Barnes, *Dance and Dancers*, April 1964.
9 Alexander Bland, *Observer*, 1.11.1964.
10 Undated letter to *Yorkshire Post*.
11 'The Other Half of the Apple', John Field talking to *Dance and Dancers*, December 1966, pp. 12–15, 46.
12 *Royal Opera House Annual Report*, 1965–66.

Chapter XI

1 Times Special Correspondent, 'A Choreographer's Progress', *Times*, 29.12.1960.
2 Frederick Ashton, quoted in 'Choreographer with a Mind of his Own', *Times*, 22.5.1961.
3 John Field, quoted *Liverpool Post*, 21.2.1970.
4 George Milford-Cottam, 'A Saga of the Provinces', *Dancing Times*, February 1962, pp. 170–174.
5 Meryl Chapell, conversation.

Chapter XII

1 Frederick Ashton, 'My Conception of "La Fille mal Gardée"', *La Fille Mal Gardée*, ed. Ivor Guest. Dancing Times Ltd., London, 1960, p. 9.
2 Meryl Chapell, conversation.
3 Ibid.
4 Marion Tait, conversation.
5 Meryl Chapell, conversation.
6 David Wall, 'A Star by Encouragement', *Dance and Dancers*, November 1976, pp. 20–3.

Chapter XIII

1 Gerald Larner, *Guardian*, 2.11.1965.
2 Clement Crisp, *New Statesman*, undated.
3 John Percival, 'Small-town Revels', *Dance and Dancers*, March 1966, p. 44.
4 Brenda Last, quoted *Bristol Evening Post*, 11.3.1966.
5 Gail Thomas, 'Letter to a Young Dancer', *Dancing Times*, November 1974, pp. 82–3.
6 David Wall quoted in 'Spotlight on David Wall', Malcolm Stewart, *Vogue*, October 1967.
7 Anon, *The Times*, 16.1.1967.

Chapter XIV

1 Paul H. Foster, *Glasgow Evening Times*, 27.9.1967.
2 John Percival, *The Times*, 2.2.1968.
3 Letter by Leonide Massine, published in *Royal Opera House Annual Report*, 1968–69, p. 15.
4 Peter Wright, *Masterclass*, BBC Television, April 1988.
5 Stephen Jefferies, conversation.

6 Royal Opera House Board of Directors, Minutes 28 November 1967.

7 Henry Legerton, conversation.

Chapter XV

1 Peter Williams, 'Moving into the 'Seventies', *Dance and Dancers*, January 1970, p. 18.

2 Gordon Gow, 'Geoffrey Cauley – Emergent Choreographer', *Dancing Times*, May 1970.

3 Mary Clarke, 'Royal Summer', *Dancing Times*, August 1969.

4 Gordon Gow, 'Geoffrey Cauley – Emergent Choreographer', *Dancing Times*, May 1970, pp. 412–13.

5 The towns quoted as those with theatres big enough for the Covent Garden company were Glasgow, Edinburgh, Liverpool, Manchester, Leeds, Newcastle, Oxford, Bristol, Eastbourne, Southampton and Bournemouth.

6 Press statement, Royal Opera House, 9 January 1970.

7 John Field quoted in 'Transformation Scene', *Dance and Dancers*, February 1970, pp. 38–9.

8 'John North Column', *Northern Echo*, 16.1.1970.

9 John Percival, *Dance and Dancers*, March 1970, pp. 30–2.

10 Noël Goodwin, *Dance and Dancers*, June 1970, p. 35.

11 James Kennedy, *Guardian*, 27.7.1970.

12 Clement Crisp, *Financial Times*, 28.7.1970.

13 Henry Legerton, conversation.

PART 3

Chapter XVI

1 John Field in interview with Richard Buckle, *About the House*, Vol. 3, no. 7, pp. 13–15.

2 John Field, conversation.

3 Edward Thorpe, *Kenneth MacMillan, The Man and the Ballets*, Hamish Hamilton, London 1985, p. 94.

4 Desmond Kelly, conversation.

5 John Field, conversation.

6 Joe Layton, 'A Talent to Entertain', *Dance and Dancers*, March 1971, pp. 17–19.

7 Stephen Jefferies, conversation.

Chapter XVII

1 Bill Harpe, *Guardian*, 3.4.1972.

2 David Morse, conversation.

3 John Percival, *Dance and Dancers*, September 1972, p. 18.

4 Gerry Mahon, *Spectator*, 29.7.1972.

5 James Monahan, *Dancing Times*, November 1972, pp. 72–3.

6 *Royal Opera House Annual Report*, 1971–2.

7 Merete Bates, *Guardian*, 27.3.1973.

8 Quoted by Les Freeman, 'Royal Ballet in Israel', *Dancing Times*, October 1973, pp. 22–4.

9 Patricia Ruanne to Gordon Gow, 'Recruits to Festival', *Dancing Times*, November 1974, pp. 76–7.

Chapter XVIII

1 Quoted in *Bournemouth Evening Echo*, 21.10.1974.

2 Clement Crisp, *Financial Times*, 17.2.1975.

3 James Kennedy, *Guardian*, 16.4.1975.
4 Ibid.
5 Kathrine Sorley Walker, *Daily Telegraph*, 17.5.1975.
6 Minutes of an exploratory meeting preparatory to setting up a working party to examine the feasibility of a merger between the Royal Ballet Touring Company and Northern Dance Theatre, 7.1.1976.
7 Clement Crisp, *Financial Times*, 9.10.1975.

Chapter XIX

1 Leonide Massine quoted in 'Massine recalls 60 years of choreography', *Classical Music Weekly*, 16.2.1978.
2 Leonide Massine to Tom Quirke, *Birmingham Post*, 6.2.1978.
3 Kenneth MacMillan to Rodney Milnes, *Harpers & Queen*, October 1978.
4 Programme note.
5 David Morse, conversation.
6 John Percival, 'Torrent of Ideas', *Dance and Dancers*, June 1979, pp. 19–21, 37.

Chapter XX

1 Clement Crisp, *Financial Times*, 23.8.1979.
2 Ibid., 18.8.1979.
3 Mary Clarke, *Dancing Times*, July 1981, p. 683.
4 Bill Harpe, 'Swanning Along', *Guardian*, 28.11.1981.
5 Noël Goodwin, *New York Herald Tribune*, 3.12.1981.
6 Mary Clarke, 'The Sadler's Wells Ballet Swan Lake', *Dancing Times*, January 1982, pp. 248–50.

7 Clement Crisp, *Financial Times*, 30.11.1981.
8 Nicholas Dromgoole, *Sunday Telegraph*, 8.5.1981.
9 JS *Bournemouth Evening Echo*, 13.4.1982.

Chapter XXI

1 David Bintley, programme note.
2 David Bintley to Alan Hulme, *Manchester Evening News*, 22.1.1983.
3 KL, *Strathclyde Telegraph*, 21.2.1983.
4 Neil Jillett, *The Age*, 8.11.1982.
5 Sonia Humphrey, *The Australian*, 2.11.1982.
6 James Monahan, *Country Life*, 2.6.1983.
7 Jann Parry, *Observer*, 18.9.1983.
8 David Bintley to John Percival, *Times*, 4.5.1983.
9 Kathrine Sorley Walker, *Daily Telegraph*, 22.9.1983.

Chapter XXII

1 Mary Clarke, 'Sadler's Wells Royal Ballet's 'Petrushka', *Dancing Times*, April 1984, pp. 576–7.
2 Judith Cruickshank, *Times*, 19.9.1984.
3 Peter Wright, programme note.
4 Clement Crisp, *Financial Times*, 17.10.1984.
5 Commentary, *Dance and Dancers*, April 1985, p. 2.
6 Peter Wright, quoted by Michael Owen in 'The Day the Ballet Hit Bombay', *Evening Standard*, 12.4.1985.
7 Farrah Rustom, *The Daily*, 4.4.1985.
8 Jimmy F. Pochkhanawalla, *Indian Express*, 3.4.1985.

9 Vinod Advani, *Mid–Day*, 3.4.1985.

10 Desmond Kelly, conversation.

11 Peter Wright to Michael Owen, quoted *London Standard*, 6.2.1986.

12 Clive Barnes, *New York Post*, 2.6.1986.

13 Anna Kisselgoff, *New York Times*, 6.2.1986.

14 Arlene Croce, 'The Dreamer of the Dream', *New Yorker*, 24.2.1986.

15 Jack Anderson, *New York Times*, 7.2.1986.

16 John Hart to Jenny Rees, quoted in 'Dancing Down to Rio', *Today*, 4.4.1986.

PART 4

Chapter XXIII

1 Christopher Nourse, 'Sadler's Wells Royal Ballet', *About the House*, Vol. 8, no. 2, Spring 1989, p. 10.

2 'A History of the Proposal to Relocate Sadler's Wells Royal Ballet to Birmingham', issued by Royal Opera House, 12.1.1989.

3 Christopher Nourse, 'Sadler's Wells Royal Ballet', *About the House*, Vol. 8, no.2, Spring 1989, p. 11.

4 'A History of the Proposal to Relocate Sadler's Wells Royal Ballet to Birmingham', issued by Royal Opera House, 12.1.1989.

5 Royal Opera House Press Release, 12.1.1989.

6 Over the last few years, guest teachers with the company have included Sulamith Messerer, Alan Beale, Hans Brenaa, Christine Anthony and Nancy Kilgour.

7 Sadler's Wells Opera Ballet, Sadler's Wells Theatre Ballet, The Royal Ballet Touring Company, the New Group, the Royal Ballet on Tour, the Sadler's Wells Royal Ballet and the Birmingham Royal Ballet. This does not count two periods when the company was just called The Royal Ballet.

PART 5

Chapter XXIV

1 Brenda Last, conversation.

2 Brenda Last, quoted in Godfrey Blakeley, 'Ballet With Swans', *Sunday Telegraph* colour supplement, 16.2.1973.

3 Antoinette Sibley, quoted in Barbara Newman, *Antoinette Sibley, Reflections of a Ballerina*, Hutchinson, London, 1986, p. 102.

4 Marion Tait, conversation.

5 Ninette de Valois, *Invitation to the Ballet*, The Bodley Head, London 1937, p. 206.

6 Ronald Plaisted, conversation.

7 Brenda Last, conversation.

Bibliography

The history of the Company lies buried in the minutes of the Royal Opera House Board of Directors and the Ballet Sub Committee, in the nightly programmes held in the Royal Opera House Archives and at the Theatre Museum, in the press cutting books at the Royal Opera House Archives and in the pages of the specialist dance publications.

PERIODICALS

About The House 1962–1990.
Arts Bulletin – Provincial Touring, No 2, Autumn 1970, Arts Council of Great Britain, London, 1970.
Ballet 1946–1952.
Ballet Today 1946–1953.
Dance and Dancers 1950–1990.
Dancing Times 1946–1990.
Dance Magazine 1951–1952.
Dance News 1951–1952.
Foyer 1951–1952.
Royal Opera House Annual Reports, 1956–1989.
Sadler's Wells Theatre Ballet, No 1, Sadler's Wells Foundation, 1956.

BOOKS

Ballet, Covent Garden Book 15, A. & C. Black, London, 1964.
Ballet Annual 1–18, A. & C. Black, London, 1947–1963.
Beaumont, Cyril, *Ballets of Today*, Putnam, London, 1954.
Bland, Alexander, *The Royal Ballet. The First Fifty Years*, Threshold Books, London, 1981.
Braunsweg, Julian, *Braunsweg's Ballet Scandals*, George Allen & Unwin, London, 1974.
Buckle, Richard, *In the Wake of Diaghilev*, Collins, London, 1982.

Bibliography

Clarke, Mary, *The Sadler's Wells Ballet: A History and Appreciation*, A. & C. Black, London, 1955.

de Valois, Ninette, *Come Dance With Me*, Hamish Hamilton, London, 1957.

de Valois, Ninette, *Step by Step*, W. H. Allen, London, 1977.

Drew, David, ed., *The Decca Book of Ballet*, Frederick Muller, London, 1958.

Fifield, Elaine, *In My Shoes*, W. H. Allen, London, 1967.

Fisher, Hugh, *The Sadler's Wells Theatre Ballet*, A. & C. Black, London, 1956.

Hurok, Sol, *S Hurok Presents*, Hermitage House, New York, 1953.

Koegler, Horst, ed., *Concise Oxford Dictionary of Ballet*, Oxford University Press, London, 1977.

Lester, Susan, ed., *Ballet Here and Now*, Dennis Dobson, London, 1961.

Money, Keith, *The Royal Ballet seen by Keith Money*, Harrap, London, 1964.

Newman, Barbara, *Antoinette Sibley, Reflections of a Ballerina*, Hutchinson, London, 1986.

Newman, Barbara and Spatt, Leslie, *Sadler's Wells Royal Ballet Swan Lake*, Dance Books, London, 1983.

Percival, John, *Nureyev*, Faber & Faber, London, 1975.

- - *Theatre In My Blood. A biography of John Cranko*, Herbert, London, 1983.

- - *The Facts about a Ballet Company. Featuring the Sadler's Wells Royal Ballet*, G. Whizzard/André Deutsch, London, 1979.

Report on Opera and Ballet in the United Kingdom, 1966–1969, Arts Council of Great Britain, London, 1969.

Sexton, Christopher, *Peggy van Praagh. A Life of Dance*. MacMillan, Melbourne, 1985.

Seymour, Lynn, *Lynn, An Autobiography*, Granada, London, 1984.

Sorley Walker, Kathrine and Woodcock, Sarah C., *The Royal Ballet. A Picture History*, Threshold Books, 1981. 2nd edition revised, 1986.

Thorpe, Edward, *Kenneth MacMillan. The Man and the Ballets*. Hamish Hamilton, London, 1985.

van Praagh, Peggy, *How I Became a Ballet Dancer*, Thomas Nelson & Sons, London, ed. 1959.

Vaughan, David, *Frederick Ashton and His Ballets*, A. & C. Black, London, 1977.

Wilson, G. B. L., *A Dictionary of Ballet*, Penguin Books, London, 1957.

Wood, Roger, *The Theatre Ballet of Sadler's Wells*, Phoenix House, London, 1952.

Index

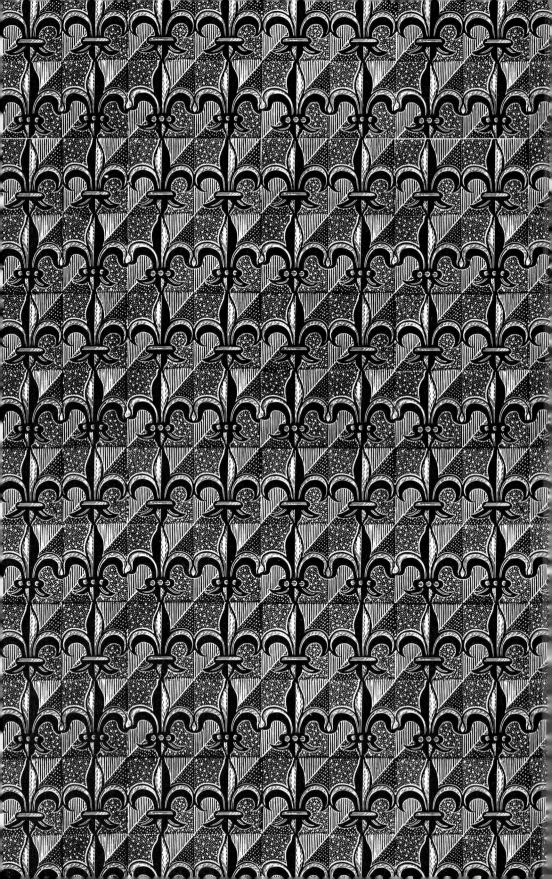